KU-289-531

DIFFICULT WOMEN

DIFFICULT WOMEN

A History of Feminism in 11 Fights

HELEN LEWIS

JONATHAN CAPE
LONDON

5 7 9 10 8 6 4

Jonathan Cape, an imprint of Vintage,
20 Vauxhall Bridge Road,
London SW1V 2SA

Jonathan Cape is part of the Penguin Random House group of companies
whose addresses can be found at global.penguinrandomhouse.com.

Penguin
Random House
UK

Copyright © Helen Lewis 2020

Helen Lewis has asserted her right to be identified as the author of this Work
in accordance with the Copyright, Designs and Patents Act 1988

First published by Jonathan Cape in 2020

penguin.co.uk/vintage

A CIP catalogue record for this book is available from the British Library

ISBN 9781787331280 (hardback)
ISBN 9781787331297 (trade paperback)

Typeset in 10.75/15.75pt Mercury Text G1 Jouve (UK), Milton Keynes
Printed and bound in Great Britain by Clays Ltd, Elcograf S.p.A.

Penguin Random House is committed to a sustainable future for
our business, our readers and our planet. This book is made
from Forest Stewardship Council® certified paper.

For all the difficult women,
and Jonathan – who lives with one.

CONTENTS

Introduction: An Imperfect History   1

1   Divorce   11
2   The Vote   39
3   Sex   69
4   Play   99
5   Work   127
6   Safety   157
7   Love   191
8   Education   221
9   Time   249
10   Abortion   277
11   The Right to be Difficult   303

Epilogue: A Manifesto for the
     Difficult Woman   327
Acknowledgements   331
Sources and Further Reading   335
Index   339

The reasonable man adapts himself to the world: the unreasonable one persists in trying to adapt the world to himself. Therefore all progress depends on the unreasonable man.

George Bernard Shaw, 1903

Or woman.

Helen Lewis, 2020

INTRODUCTION:
AN IMPERFECT HISTORY

What does it mean to be a difficult woman? I'm not talking about being rude, thoughtless, obnoxious or a diva. First of all, difficult means complicated, and this book contains a host of complicated women. A thumbs-up, thumbs-down approach to historical figures is boring and reductive. Most of us are more than one thing; everyone is 'problematic'. In this book, you will meet women with views which are unpalatable to modern feminists. You will meet women with views which were unpalatable to their *contemporaries*. A history of feminism should not try to sand off the sharp corners of the movement's pioneers – or write them out of the story entirely, if their sins are deemed too great. It must allow them to be just as flawed – just as human – as men. 'Why are girls to be told that they resemble angels,' wrote Mary Wollstonecraft, 'but to sink them below women?' We don't have to be perfect to deserve equal rights.

The idea of role models is not necessarily a bad one, but the way they are used in feminism can dilute a radical political movement into feel-good inspiration porn. Holding up a few exceptions is no substitute for questioning the rules themselves, and in our rush to champion historical women, we are distorting the past. Take the wildly successful children's book *Goodnight Stories for Rebel Girls*, which has sold more than a million copies. It tells a hundred 'empowering, moving and inspirational' stories, promising that 'these are true fairy tales for heroines who definitely don't need rescuing'. Its entry for the fashion designer Coco Chanel mentions that she wanted to start a business, and a 'wealthy friend of hers lent her enough money to make her dream come true'. It does not mention that Chanel was the lover of a Nazi officer and very probably a spy for Hitler's Germany. In the 1930s, she tried to remove that 'wealthy friend' from the company under racist laws which forbade Jews to own businesses. In the name of inspiring little girls living in a male-dominated world, the book doesn't so much airbrush Coco Chanel's story as sandblast it with a high-pressure hose. Do you find Chanel's wartime collaboration with the Nazis 'empowering'? I don't – although admittedly she *does* sound like a woman who 'didn't need rescuing'. The real Coco Chanel was clever, prejudiced, talented, cynical – and interesting. The pale version of her boiled down to a feminist saint is not.

I can excuse that approach in a children's book, but it's alarming to see the same urge in adults. We cannot celebrate women by strip-ping politics – and therefore conflict – from the narrative. *Unfurl the bunting, and don't ask too many questions!* It creates a story of femi-nism where all the opponents are either cartoon baddies or mysteriously absent, where no hard compromises have to be made, and internal disagreements disappear. The One True Way is obvi-ous, and all Good People follow it. Feminists are on the right side of history, and we just have to wait for the world to catch up.

Life does not work like that. It would be much easier if feminist triumphs relied on defeating a few bogeymen, but grotesque sexists like Donald Trump only have power because otherwise decent people voted for them. There were women who opposed female suf-frage; women are the biggest consumers of magazines and websites which point out other women's physical flaws; there is no gender gap in support for abortion rights. People are complicated, and making progress is complicated too. If modern feminism feels toothless, it is because it has retreated into two modes: empty celebration or shadow-boxing with outright bastards. Neither deals with difficulty, and so neither can make a difference.

Women's history should not be a shallow hunt for heroines. Too often, I see feminists castigating each other for admiring the Pankhursts (autocrats), Andrea Dworkin (too aggressive), Jane Austen (too middle-class), Margaret Atwood (worried about due process in sexual-harassment accusations) and Germaine Greer (where do I start?). I recently read a piece about how I was 'problematic' for having expressed sympathy for the Supreme Court nominee Brett Kavanaugh. My crime was to say that his confirmation hearings had been turned into a media circus – and even those accused of sexual assault deserve better. The criticism reflects a desperate desire to pretend that thorny issues are actually straightforward. No more flawed humans struggling inside vast, complicated systems: there are good guys and bad guys, and it's easy to tell which is which. This approach is pathetic and childish, and it should be resisted. I want to restore the complexity to feminist pioneers. Their legacies might be contested, they might have made terrible strategic choices and they might have not have lived up to the ideals they preached. But they mattered. Their difficulty is part of the story.

Then there's the second meaning of 'difficult'. Any demand for greater rights faces opponents, and any advance creates a backlash. Changing the world is always difficult. At Dublin Castle in May 2018, waiting for the results of the Irish referendum on abortion law, I saw a banner which read: 'If there is no struggle, there is no progress.' Those words come from a speech by Frederick Douglass, who campaigned for the end of the slave trade in the US. He wanted to make clear that 'power concedes nothing without a demand'. In other words, campaigners have to be disruptive. They cannot take No for an answer. 'Those who profess to favour freedom and yet deprecate agitation are men who want crops without plowing up the ground,' said Douglass. 'They want rain without thunder and lightning. They want the ocean without the awful roar of its many waters.' Changing the world won't make people like you. It will cause you pain. It will be difficult. It will feel like a struggle. You must accept the size of the mountain ahead of you, and start climbing it anyway.

Then there is the difficulty of womanhood itself. In a world built for men, women will always struggle to fit in. We are what Simone de Beauvoir called 'the second sex'. Our bodies are different from the standard (male) human. Our sexual desires have traditionally been depicted as fluid, hard to read, unpredictable. Our life experiences are mysterious and unknowable; our minds are Freud's 'dark continent'. We are imagined to be on the wrong side of a world divided in two. Men are serious, women are silly. Men are rational, women are emotional. Men are strong, women are weak. Men are steadfast, women are fickle. Men are objective, women are subjective. Men are humanity, women are a subset of it. Men want sex and women grant or withhold it. Women are looked at; men do the looking. When we are victims, it is hard to believe us. 'At the heart of the struggle of feminism to give rape, date rape, marital rape, domestic violence, and workplace sexual harassment legal standing as crimes has been the necessity of making women credible and audible,' wrote Rebecca Solnit in *Men Explain Things to Me*. 'Billions of women must be out there on this six-billion-person planet being told that they are not reliable witnesses to their own lives, that the truth is not their property, now or ever.' When fighting for equal rights, women often face a hurdle of disbelief: does this problem really exist, if only women are talking about it? We know how unreasonable women are, after all.

Finally, there is another meaning of 'difficult' which I try to tease out in this book. Any history of feminism has to start by acknowledging that most revolutionaries are not . . . nice. And women have always been told to be nice. Girls are instructed to be 'ladylike' to keep them quiet and docile. (They are made of sugar and spice 'and all things nice'.) Motherhood is championed as a journey of endless self-sacrifice. Random men tell us to 'cheer up' in the street, because God forbid our own emotions should impinge on anyone else's day. If we raise our

voices, we are 'shrill'. Our ambition is suspicious. Our anger is por-
trayed as unnatural, horrifying, disfiguring: who needs to listen to the
'nag', the 'hysteric' or the 'angry black woman'? All this is extremely
unhelpful if you want to go out and cause trouble – the kind of trouble
that leads to legal and cultural change.

*

My favourite definition of feminism comes from the Nigerian author
Chimamanda Ngozi Adichie. A feminist, she said, is someone who
believes in 'the social, economic and political equality of the sexes'.
That sounds straightforward, but feminism is endlessly difficult. I
decided to write this book because I was tired of it. Looking back on
the 'Fourth Wave', the burst of activism which began in the early
2010s, it seemed as though we were congratulating ourselves on
'changing the culture', when there were few concrete victories to
report. And already the backlash was coming. Across the world,
from Vladimir Putin in Russia to Narendra Modi in India to Jair Bolsonaro in Brazil, populists and nationalists were pushing a return to
traditional gender roles. The US president grabbed women by the
pussy, because 'when you're a star, they let you do it'. The #MeToo
movement collapsed into a conversation about borderline cases and
did not lead to any substantial legal reforms. Abortion rights were
under threat in eastern Europe and the southern United States, and
had never reached Northern Ireland. Gang-rape cases convulsed
India and Spain. Free universal childcare was as much a dream as it
had been in the 1970s.

I had personal worries, too. It felt as though the feminist movement was more fractured than previous generations, making it
harder to achieve progress on any individual issue. It was more open
to some kinds of marginalised voices (those with social media
accounts, at least) but could feel hopelessly lacking in focus. Twit-
terstorms and a culture of instant outrage put the fear of God into
sexist advertisers and gaffe-prone politicians, but under all the

noise, were we really moving forward? 'Cancel culture' ensured that any feminist icon's reputation felt fragile and provisional. Often, we had barely anointed a new heroine before we tore her down again. 'Sisterhood is powerful,' the Second Waver Ti-Grace Atkinson once said. 'It kills. Mostly sisters.' Feminism often felt mired in petty arguments, and I noticed younger women casually denigrating the achievements of their predecessors. 'Cancel the second wave,' read one headline. When I talked at an event about the fights for equal pay and domestic-violence shelters, one twentysomething woman casually replied: 'Yeah, but all that stuff is sorted.'

I couldn't blame those women, because I was once complacent about the battles of yesterday. But as I read more, I understood the true scale of feminism's achievements and the challenges its pioneers had to overcome. I gained more respect for them, and extended more kindness towards the compromises they made. I tried to imagine what it must have been like to survive in a sexist office of the 1960s, fending off gropers and patronising put-downs. Would I have ended up growing a rhino-thick hide, and arguing that women needed to stop thinking of themselves as victims? Maybe. I tried to put myself in the place of the Victorian education reformers, trying to set up women's colleges. I decided that, like them, I would probably have emphasised the respectability of education, rather than painting it as a radical, liberating force. Would I have thrown a bomb or suffered force-feeding to get the vote? I doubted it. Would I have fallen out with other feminists? I was sure of it.

All this made me want to ask how we got here, in the hope it would help us decide where to go next. What works? What sacrifices are worth making for the greater good? What alliances are bearable in the service of a good cause? What do women need to do to be treated as full citizens, as independent human beings, as the protagonists in our own lives? We are still paid less. We still do more unpaid labour. We are still raped and murdered and abused by violent men. We are still taught to hate our bodies. We still die because research into sleeping pills and seat belts doesn't include us. We are still under-represented in politics. We still only make up a third of speaking characters in Hollywood films. Feminism has won many battles, but the war is nowhere near over.

A friend suggested a title to tie it together: *Difficult Women*. It was the summer when Theresa May ran for Conservative leader, and the veteran backbencher Ken Clarke was caught on a live microphone (admiringly) describing her as a 'bloody difficult woman'. It was used by the American feminist Roxane Gay as the title of her short-story collection in 2017. And it gave David Plante the title of his memoir of Sonia Orwell, Germaine Greer and Jean Rhys published in 1983, the year I was born.

Difficult Women were popping up everywhere. The word kept recurring as women tried to demonstrate how they were penalised for calling out sexism. The TV presenter Helen Skelton described being groped on air by an interviewee while pregnant. She did not complain, she said, because 'that's just the culture that television breeds. No one wants to be difficult.' The actor Jennifer Lawrence told the *Hollywood Reporter* that she had once stood up to a rude director. Afterwards, a producer took her aside and called her 'unruly'. The incident left her worried that she would be punished by the industry. 'Yeah,' chipped in fellow actor Emma Stone, mocking that criticism: 'You were "difficult".' All these people were edging towards the same idea, an idea which is imprinted on us from birth: that women are called unreasonable, selfish and unfeminine when they stand up for themselves. 'I myself have never been able to find out precisely what feminism is,' wrote Rebecca West in 1913. 'I only know that people call me a feminist whenever I express sentiments that differentiate me from a doormat, or a prostitute.'

*

A more conventional history of feminism would probably begin in 1792, with Mary Wollstonecraft's *A Vindication of the Rights of*

Women. But I'm not a historian, and this is not a conventional history. Like many women, I came to feminism through a pervasive feeling of wrongness with aspects of my life that I couldn't quite articulate. Feminism gave me the words to understand my experiences, and what I saw around me. It reassured me that I was not alone. It made me angry for all the women whose potential was lost and whose lives were restricted by unjust laws and unfair practices. It has introduced me to many of the best and most impressive people I know.

I want to take feminism apart and examine the machinery that makes it so powerful. By looking at a series of fights – for the vote, for the right to divorce, for the chance to go to university – I hope to show how change happens, and how much there is left to do. We will also see the tawdry compromises, the personality clashes and the backlash which accompanies any challenge to the status quo. In choosing my fights and my women, I have focused on Britain, where I live, but many of the patterns, arguments and controversies are universal. British feminism has been shaped by our lack of a written constitution, our parliamentary system and our official status as a Christian country, but also by wider currents such as immigration, declining birthrates and the entry of women into the workforce. I've stayed away from the obsessions of the online hot-take mill, such as arcane debates over vocabulary, because words matter less than actions. And I've chosen an eclectic selection of difficult women, who are all protagonists of the various fights. Each one has something to teach us, without us needing to airbrush the difficult bits out of their biographies.

No one can write the definitive history of feminism – there are many histories, and many feminisms. Even so, it feels daring to attempt any type of history at all. This is an exceptionally individualistic era, and women are often frightened to claim the authority to speak about any lives except their own. That might be prudent and safe, but it is also a misuse of privilege by those who have it. We

shouldn't talk *over* other women, but we can't just talk about ourselves either. A million memoirs don't add up to a history. To make
political progress, we need to treat women as more than a loose collection of individuals. We are a class, united by common problems as
much as we are divided by differences. Feminism must be broad
enough to deal with the fact that other identities – lesbian, immigrant, adulterer – might hold women back as much as their sex.
There is no one way to be a woman, and no universal pattern for
womanhood. Many of the biggest fights still raging are complicated
by the differences *between* women, as much as the differences
between us and men.

What's missing from this book? It's hard to know where to
start – which is the point. This is a partial, imperfect, personal history of feminism and my hope is that the gaps do not look like
deficiencies, but invitations. I can't wait to read others.

Let's start with me, in a restaurant, wondering how to get
divorced.

1. DIVORCE

You never really know a man until you have divorced him.

Zsa Zsa Gabor

I don't remember the day or the month, but I do remember where I was: a sushi bar in the Westfield Stratford shopping centre in East London. I was not yet thirty. I had just realised that I didn't want to be married any more, and I had finally told someone: my best friend Laura. There was only one problem. *How do you get divorced?*

After a few minutes of intensive googling, we found three relatively fast grounds: desertion, unreasonable behaviour or adultery. All of these involved one partner accepting the blame for the collapse of the marriage. If you wanted to get divorced without it being anyone's fault, you had to be separated for two years – or five years, if your partner contested the decision.

At the time, I was a twentysomething middle-class white woman with a degree and a magazine column; pretty much every characteristic which gives you sharp elbows and a sense of entitlement. My job had management responsibilities: half a dozen people reported to me, and I occasionally sent emails asking them to 'revert to me on that'. And yet I had entered a legal contract without bothering to discover how to get out of it.

I was extremely lucky – my now ex-husband is nothing but a gentleman, and we exited the relationship and the legal contract with as much dignity and as little friction as the situation allowed, helped by a lack of assets or children. But what I did in 2013 is something that the vast majority of women in history could only dream of doing, because getting divorced means something particular for women. It means that society considers you a full citizen, a person in your own right.

If I had my way, the history of divorce law would be as well known as the fight for gay marriage. Before the Married Women's Property Act in 1870, a woman's legal status changed at the altar, from 'feme sole' (Norman French for 'single woman') to 'feme covert' (a covered, or married, woman). She could no longer own property, sue or be sued, earn money of her own, execute a will or sign contracts. It took until 1926 before English women could own property on the same terms as men.

Under the traditional definition of marriage, there was 'marital unity' but not equality: a woman was a dependant with the same legal status as a child. As the English judge William Blackstone wrote in 1765: 'By marriage, the husband and wife are one person in law: that is, the very being or legal existence of the woman is suspended during the marriage, or at least is incorporated and consolidated into that of the husband: under whose wing, protection, and cover, she performs every thing.' A man could not grant anything to his wife, Blackstone added, because 'the grant would be to suppose her separate existence'.

*

Seventy years later, a woman called Caroline Norton made a similar observation. 'A woman has apparently no individual destiny,' she wrote in 1836. 'She is the property of those on whom she may reflect discredit.' Her husband George was refusing to agree a financial settlement which would have guaranteed their legal separation. During the marriage, he had beaten her so badly their servants had to intervene. After it broke down, he sold off her possessions and withheld access to their children. When she still refused to reconcile with him, he put her on trial for adultery – accusing her of sleeping with her old friend Lord Melbourne, the prime minister. The publicity around the trial exposed Victorian marriage as a form of ownership.

By all accounts, Caroline Norton was a lively, gregarious woman. She was friends with writers and thinkers; she wrote novels herself. Charles Dickens described her and her sister as 'sights for the gods';

the artist Edwin Landseer had a crush on her. Her husband George, by contrast, was a failure as a solicitor and as a person. He vented his resentment on his witty, popular wife. He initially encouraged her friendship with Lord Melbourne, reasoning that it would lead to jobs and favours, but then he got jealous. This is a known hazard when men feel they 'own' women, and try to control their bodies or brains to make money.* And so George put his wife on trial for adultery.

In *The Criminal Conversation of Mrs Norton*, the historian Diane Atkinson outlines the sexist dimensions of the case against Caroline. Her adultery would mean her husband was denied the 'domestic harmony and affections' to which he was entitled under the law. Effectively, George had exclusive rights to his wife's vagina, purchased through the marriage contract. Depriving him of that was an offence so serious that he asked for £10,000 – a million pounds today – in damages. The lawyers, judge and pamphleteers covering the case were all male; the only women involved were Caroline Norton's servants, who were called to testify against her. Caroline never went to court; she was hiding at her mother's apartment in Hampton Court Palace.

The lead counsel for George Norton, Sir William Follett, promised to air the couple's dirty linen in public – literally. Where the 1990s had Monica Lewinsky's blue dress, stained with Bill Clinton's semen, the 1830s had Caroline Norton's gown. According to Follett, it would show 'those marks which are the consequence of intercourse between the sexes'. One of her maids was summoned to testify that Caroline applied rouge before Lord Melbourne's visits. A coachman told the court that he had seen Caroline lying on the floor, exposing the 'thick part of her thigh' with the prime minister sitting on a chair nearby; the man was attacked by Melbourne's legal team

* Parts of Caroline's story remind me of Jenna Jameson's description of 'suitcase pimps', the boyfriend/managers of porn actresses, who veer between seeing their partners as meal tickets and resenting their stardom.

as a drunk with a grudge. (The defence relied heavily on the alleged untrustworthiness of servants when making its case.) The Attorney General Sir John Campbell argued that the Nortons were still sleeping together after the alleged adultery had taken place, when 'everyone knew that after a woman surrendered her person to a paramour, she looked down upon her husband with loathing and abhorrence'. After a trial in 1836 lasting nine days, the verdict came back at 11.40 p.m. – the jury ruled against George Norton. There would be no damages for him.

Caroline Norton's reputation, however, was stained for ever. There was no doubt that she had flirted with other men, including Lord Melbourne, even if she had not slept with them. Just as bad, the court case made it *harder* for her to obtain a divorce. She was now officially innocent of adultery, so she would have to prove that *George* had slept with someone else if she wanted a legal separation. 'They were stuck with each other until one of them died,' writes Atkinson. 'Estranged and living apart from her husband, Caroline had no automatic right to see her children, and he was immovable on that point. Caroline would not be able to change his mind, so she set about changing the law.'

In a way, we should thank George Norton. He seems to have been such a spherical bastard* that most of polite society quietly took Caroline's side. 'My husband is fond of paying me the melancholy compliment, that to my personal charms, and not to the justice of my cause, I owe, that all concerned in these wretched affairs take my part against him,' she wrote. Caroline was certainly the brains of the couple. When George claimed that she had no right to keep her own money, she began running up bills – then telling creditors to sue her husband.

Once the court case was over, Caroline wrote to the novelist

---

* The phrase comes from the Swiss physicist Fritz Zwicky, to describe people who are bastards no matter which way you look at them.

Mary Shelley, daughter of the feminist pioneer Mary Wollstone-craft, that she was angry at how 'a woman is made a helpless wretch by these laws of men'. The trial had made her a celebrity, in the most unpleasant modern sense. She was written about in newspapers, and parodied in cartoons, but unable to speak for herself. Unable to see her own sons – seven-year-old Fletcher, five-year-old Brinsley and three-year-old William Charles – she worried that her husband would treat the younger ones badly if he believed them to be Melbourne's children. She was asking, effectively, for joint custody; to see the boys for half their school holidays rather than the occasional hour sanctioned by her husband. Her requests were denied. When the boys were in London, she hung around St James's Park, hoping to see them. Once, when George was not at home, she managed to convince a footman to let her into the house. But in August, he took the boys to stay with his sister Grace in Scotland; Caroline went down to the wrong docks and missed waving them goodbye. When the children arrived at Grace's house, she beat the eldest, Fletcher, for reading a letter from Caroline. As a punishment for some small infraction, Brinsley was stripped naked, tied to a bedpost and whipped. George was using access to the children as a weapon against Caroline. He was punishing her for being 'difficult': for disobeying him, for flirting with other men, for exposing him to ridicule.

Throughout her unhappy marriage, Caroline had contributed to the family finances by writing novels with titles like *The Sorrows of Rosalie* and *The Undying One.* Now, she turned to producing pamphlets about her situation. 'I think it is high time that the law was known at least, among the "weaker" sex, which gives us no right to one's own flesh and blood,' she wrote to Mary Shelley. She was advised by her sister Georgy not to make her pamphlets too angry, but she worried that moderation and politeness made them sound weak.

In her second treatise on custody laws, Norton exposed how children were used as pawns by men. 'The law has no power to order that a women shall have even occasional access to her children, though she could prove that she was driven by violence from her husband's house and that he had deserted her for a mistress,' she wrote. 'The father's right is absolute and paramount, and can no more be affected by the mother's claim, than if she had no existence.'

Norton noted that 'bastard children' – whose parents were not married – were given to their mothers until the age of seven, but married men could forcibly seize their children, *'even should they be infants at the breast'* (the italics are hers). Because of that, a wife whose husband had cheated on her, beaten her, or otherwise made the marriage intolerable would still be reluctant to leave him. And even though being rejected by a woman might wound a man's pride, the law still made him both 'accuser and judge' in a divorce case. Such a man would be 'certainly angry, probably mortified, and in nine cases out of ten is *eager to avenge* his real or fancied injuries. To this angry man, to this mortified man, the law awards that which can rarely be entrusted to any human being, even in the calmest hours of life, namely, DESPOTIC POWER!'

*

In the years following the trial, George tortured Caroline by offering access to the children, only to withdraw it again. She saw them infrequently, as he continually changed the terms of his demands. Eventually, though, Caroline's pamphlets – and her lobbying – had an effect. Parliament began to debate a new law inspired by the Norton case. It would allow mothers custody of their children up to the age of seven, and guarantee access to them after that. The bill faced strong opposition in the Lords, where it was seen as an attack on the tradition of marriage – and therefore, the entire social system built around it. Caroline was described in a newspaper as a 'renowned agitatrice', to which she replied that she believed 'the beauty and devotion of a woman's character mainly to depend on the consciousness of her inferiority to man'. To get her bill passed, Caroline needed to seem respectable and unthreatening.

In 1839, MPs passed the Custody of Infants Act, which Diane Atkinson calls 'the first piece of feminist legislation in Britain'. Women who had not been convicted of 'criminal conversation' – adultery – now had a legal right to see their children after a separation or divorce. (Provided, that is, they were wealthy enough to establish that right in a court case.) Unfortunately, the law applied only in England, Ireland and Wales, and Caroline Norton's sons were in Scotland.

The couple's game of cat and mouse continued. Caroline rented a holiday cottage on the Isle of Wight in 1840, and George promised to send the children to her. They did not come. She wrote to him, and he suggested that she meet the children in London instead. They did not come. She found out they had been sent to an English boarding school, and travelled there to see them. She was not allowed inside. Then, in September 1842, her youngest son scratched his arm falling from a horse in the grounds of his father's home at Kettlethorpe Hall and developed tetanus. By the time Caroline arrived, the nine-year-old was already in a coffin. His last words to his father had been: 'I am certainly dying. I shall soon be strangled, pray for me.'

The death seems to have sparked some remorse in George, because Caroline was allowed to spend Christmas with her two surviving boys, and saw them more over the following years. Fletcher had tuberculosis, and was sent to Lisbon. Brinsley went to Oxford to study. Once they were adults, George could not keep them from seeing her. Still, she carried on campaigning, and the law kept moving. In 1857, the Matrimonial Causes Act allowed divorce cases to be heard in the courts, instead of requiring an Act of Parliament. But the law still favoured men, who could divorce their wives for adultery alone; women required another 'offence' such as incest, cruelty or desertion. That double standard was not removed until the Matrimonial Causes Act of 1923.

Further reforms followed throughout the early and mid-twentieth century and there are now more than 100,000 divorces a year in England and Wales, according to the Office for National Statistics. It isn't just people who have been divorced who owe Caroline Norton a debt; it's anyone who has ever had a wedding. Her campaign changed what marriage meant for women, moving it away from a purchase agreement and closer to a deal between equals.

Caroline Norton is a difficult hero for today's feminists. 'The natural position of woman is inferiority to man,' she once wrote. 'Amen! That is a thing of God's appointing, not of man's devising. I never pretended to the wild and ridiculous doctrine of equality.' She was, she said, her husband's inferior, 'the clouded moon to that sun'. Her arguments rested heavily on a traditional view of motherhood as self-sacrificing and sacrosanct, and on her class status. She wanted to be treated better than a housemaid, and better than the fallen women who had children outside marriage. Today, we would describe this as respectability politics – the belief that marginalised groups can protect themselves from discrimination by appearing 'respectable'. It is a dangerous tendency to indulge, because good behaviour tends to be defined by the group with power. Rights should be universal, not based on how sympathetic the people claiming them appear to the mainstream. Sorry, we would love to help you, runs the argument, but why must you be so difficult?

*

The end of my marriage was nowhere near as fraught as Caroline Norton's, but it was still a humbling experience. Despite a multibillion-pound wedding industry, the mechanics of divorce are not mentioned in bridal magazines and the kind of Internet forums where women call themselves 'FutureMrsX'. That is not because divorce doesn't generate revenue – I could show you the Regency town houses it has bought for specialist lawyers – but because it's still seen as shameful. A divorce is a failure.

I certainly felt like a failure when I got divorced: like I had taken a hammer and smashed the glass holding a perfect photograph of happiness. My parents were disappointed. Half a dozen friends never spoke to me again. I imagined that everyone could see that I had taken off my wedding ring, though I doubt a single person noticed. We had both taken each others' surnames, going double-barrelled, so I also had to change my byline. That felt like a public admission of a private shame.

When I got married again in 2015, there was no way I was going to take my new partner's surname. As far as any name can be yours, 'Helen Lewis' was mine. Yes, 'Lewis' is my father's name, passed down the male line, but it's also the one I've had since birth. It means *me*. And what other options do women have, anyway? The civil rights activist Malcolm X dropped his surname altogether, writing in his autobiography that 'for me, my "X" replaced the white slave-master name of "Little" which some blue-eyed devil named Little had imposed upon my paternal forebears'. But how many of us would contemplate something as radical as that? One couple I know mashed their surnames together to create a new one: that also solves the problem of what the children get called.*

The way that marriage has traditionally functioned as owner-ship is picked up brilliantly by Margaret Atwood in the naming conventions of *The Handmaid's Tale*: Offred, Ofwarren, Ofglen. These are patronymics, 'of' plus the name of a handmaid's com-mander. For Offred, her previous identity disappears along with her name when she is re-educated as a handmaid. She is now merely the property of Fred. But really, becoming 'Offred' is no different to becoming – as formal invitations still have it – 'Mrs John Smith'. In the late 1960s, the activist Sheila Michaels fought hard to reject Miss or Mrs in favour of 'a title for a woman who did not "belong" to a man'. She succeeded. Helped by the 1971 launch of *Ms* magazine, 'Ms' went from outlandish to commonplace in a generation.

The vision of Gilead presented in *The Handmaid's Tale* is

---

* Still, it's not a viable solution when Ms Hardman marries Mr Hancock.

shocking, but no more shocking than the fact that women with careers and bank accounts so readily yield up the most obvious marker of their identities. And that many find it romantic. 'We're a unit,' claimed one article I read. A unit of *him*. In countries which follow English naming conventions, taking your husband's surname erases your own family background, and your previous life, and nukes your Google results. It's also harder to trace women through parish records and historical documents than it is to trace men. Sometimes, all that's left of them is a stub: Mrs Smith, Mrs Tanner, Mrs Cartwright.

Traces of this erasure of women through marriage persist. Wedding registrars still ask for your father's profession for parish records, but not your mother's. Marriage certificates have a space for the names of the couple's fathers, but not their mothers. The children of single mothers and lesbians simply have to leave a blank. As did my husband and I: we declined to include one parent but not the other. The registrar looked pained, but accepted it.* Of course, all this doesn't *feel* shocking because it is widespread and widely accepted. But really, Mrs X is just a version of Offred. One of the hardest tasks of feminism is to expose how tradition gums up our vision, and makes us think that political choices are down to natural and immutable laws.

The idea of 'coverture' – of being a legal appendage to your husband, along with your children – sounds stoutly Victorian. But its effects persisted for a long time, and not just in marriage records. My mother, who was too busy cooking dinners and washing nappies in the 1970s to get her Greenham on, once told me how angry she was when she discovered her children couldn't go on her passport, only Dad's. Britain eventually solved this in 1998 by giving

---

* In 2018, the Registration of Marriage Bill had a first reading in the House of Commons. By making marriage registries digital, it would have allowed mothers to have their names recorded. Its further progress was halted by the dissolution of parliament for the 2019 general election.

children passports of their own, but even now, women with a different surname to their children are sometimes treated with suspicion at borders.

By the way, if you've changed your name and feel unfairly judged, let me say this: I don't think it makes you a bad person or insufficiently woke or whatever phrase we're using now. My feminist motto comes from Simone de Beauvoir: 'half victim, half accomplice, like everyone else'. If you hated your father, got fed up with people mis-spelling an 'ethnic' name, decided it was better for SEO purposes, or even just fancied an easy life, I completely understand. *Half accomplice, like everyone else.* Feminism should be less concerned with individual choices than the conditions in which they were made.

The history of divorce is the history of women's struggle to be treated as full citizens under the law. It is far from the only feminist fight with that aim: the vote, as we'll see, is an obvious example, but women have faced hundreds of other, smaller injustices too. Let's go have a drink in London in 1982. Mine's a white wine – oh, but I won't be able to get served at the bar. Because I'm a woman.

*

'It's a place where barristers and lawyers and journalists gather and exchange legal gossip at the bar,' said Tess Gill, cradling a cup of tea. 'You don't exchange legal gossip if you're a meek little woman sitting in the back at a table.' She was talking about El Vino on Fleet Street in London. The bar is just down the road from the Royal Courts of Justice, and at the time was next to the headquarters of several newspapers. Until Gill came along, El Vino had a curious rule. It insisted that women could not get served at the bar. They had to sit at the back.

Feminists were convinced that the rule violated the Sex Discrimination Act, passed in 1975. An early challenge was dismissed by a county-court judge as *'de minimis'* – not important enough to consider.* In 1982, Gill and the National Council for Civil Liberties decided to try again.

Throughout the twentieth century, it was common for pubs and working men's clubs to restrict where women could drink. 'When I used to go to Manchester,' Gill told me, 'the women would be sitting in the "offie", which was like a cubbyhole, which was outside; the men would be inside. The working men's clubs, sometimes they had ridiculous rules like there was lino round the bar, and the women could only stand on the carpet.' Gill had worked as a trade union official, and remembers threatening to phone the BBC when one bartender in Newcastle politely refused to serve her. He gave in.

Today it is the citadels of privilege which are most resistant to treating women as equals. Gentlemen's clubs like the Garrick and White's, student societies such as the Bullingdon Club and dining clubs such as Pratt's are exempted from the Equality Act, allowing their memberships to remain men-only.† Most Freemasonry lodges do not admit women (although trans women are allowed to stay members, post-transition). In 2019, Muirfield golf club finally invited twelve women to join after 275 years. Three years earlier, it had been deprived of hosting the Open championship because of its previous policy.

All these are meeting places for what you might call 'the establishment' – politicians, journalists, actors, judges – or at least, the bits of the establishment with dangly bits. My otherwise beloved Benedict Cumberbatch – who once wore a T-shirt proclaiming 'this is what a feminist looks like' – is regularly cited as a member of the men-only Garrick Club. Imagine being a senior female judge: you're already keenly aware of your minority status. Then you find out that

* He must have been unaware of what a totemic role challenging racial segregation at lunch counters played in the US civil rights movement.
† I hope it gives you as much joy as it does me that Iain Duncan Smith is a lifetime honorary member of Pratt's. Presumably he was blackballed by the Incompetent Twat dining club, his first choice.

your male peers are all hanging out somewhere that you're not allowed to go. Yes, there are a few women-only clubs and societies, but these have nothing like the history or exclusivity of their male equivalents. Trying to compare female-only swim sessions or the Women's Institute with the clout of the Freemasons would be funny if it wasn't such a regular tactic of sexists. In any case, abolishing the handful of women's clubs would be a price worth paying for changing the law.

Back in the 1980s, rules excluding women from particular spaces were much more common. Like the divorce laws, they codified their second-class status. That made them an obvious target for feminists. At the time, Tess Gill was active in London women's liberation groups, which usually met in someone's house because all the women had children. ('If someone didn't do what they were meant to do – we did keep minutes – at the next meeting, they had to make chocolate mousse as a penalty.') She and her friend, the journalist Anna Coote, worked out the best way to expose the absurdity of the El Vino rule and set up the grounds for a court case under sex discrimination legislation. They picked the morning, 11.30 a.m., so the landlord was unable to argue that they could not get served because the bar was busy. Two male witnesses went in first – 'we tried to get one of them to wear a kilt, but he refused' – and waited for the women to join them. They carried briefcases, which they put on the bar, because one of El Vino's arguments was that women would clutter up the space with their handbags. When Tess and Anna arrived, they greeted their friends, ordered their drinks, and were told to sit down. 'We said, no, we'd prefer to stand here, and I think they did begin to twig that something was going on.' Once the barman refused to serve them, they left. They had their evidence of sex discrimination.

Again, the county court ruled that the case was '*de minimis*'. The campaigners raised the money to take it to the Court of Appeal. The judges there had to confess that 'two of our brethren' drank in

El Vino, but the campaigners did not insist that they recused themselves. They won the case, and went down to the bar, trailed by cameras. They were *still* refused service on the grounds it would cause a breach of the peace, and went back to the Court of Appeal for an injunction which compelled the bar to give them a drink. 'At that stage, we said, "The last place we're going to have a drink is El Vino,"' Gill told me. The bar subsequently banned them for life, reckoning, in the words of one newspaper, that 'no one who cost £25,000 in lawyers' fees was a desirable customer'.

Gill faced a familiar kind of backlash: the issue was trivial. (Today, she would have been told that drinking in a bar was 'hardly FGM', or ordered to contemplate the plight of women in Saudi Arabia.) It wasn't just the county court who deemed the case too small to bother with; the press loudly proclaimed that it was a fuss about nothing, although that didn't stop *them* covering it extensively. Gill showed me the press clippings, which she has kept for more than three decades, spreading them out over her lap and the table in her cosy flat off Baker Street. I knew the words 'fairer sex' would appear, but there were also terrible puns: 'Wine, women and throng'. In the county court, a senior employment barrister tried to suggest that perhaps women didn't *want* to queue to get served. It's a well-worn, and deeply patronising, argument: women are better protected by men's kindness and chivalry than their own money and basic human rights. 'I'm sure you wouldn't want to be crammed in a bar,' the lawyer said to Gill. 'I do travel to work on the Tube every day,' came the reply.

Not all of the naysayers were men. One of the most vicious responses came from the 'First Lady of Fleet Street', opinion columnist Jean Rook. 'This week a hairy-voiced, bristling feminist rang me from a local London radio station asking me to celebrate at El Vino, the Fleet Street wine bar which, after banning women for forty years, has finally been cracked by court order,' she wrote in the *Daily Express*. 'All I can soberly say is that Women's Lib has reached the dregs when female journalists work themselves into a Bacchanalian frenzy over a triumph not worth a bunch of sour grapes.' The puns, I'm afraid, don't stop there. Gill and her friends 'made a bloody Mary nuisance of themselves', causing Rook to 'blush wine-red' because Fleet Street's feminists 'have scraped the barrel by splashing round heady headlines on How I Made History'.

Most of the column is a valiant attempt to pretend that there is no larger principle at stake. Of course, a woman who has succeeded in the existing system has an incentive to prop it up. But in the final sentence of her argument, Rook gave herself away: 'You made fools of yourselves, too. Now why not just get on with the job I've never had any difficulty taking from a man?' In other words, *how can systemic discrimination exist, when I personally have succeeded?* But the plural of anecdote is not data. Jean Rook represents another type of difficult woman – the kind who argues that her own personal experience is more important than all the evidence to the contrary. Her article is also a reminder that feminism is not a shorthand for 'what women think', but a political movement dedicated to the equality of the sexes.

Whenever feminists are attacked for focusing on a 'trivial issue', there is usually a bigger principle at stake. Tess Gill's and Anna Coote's inability to get a drink was a symptom of a world in which women were consistently treated as second-class citizens under the law. In 1974, they co-wrote a book called *Women's Rights: A Practical Guide*. It is full of quietly jaw-dropping examples. Governments assumed that men were breadwinners and women were homemakers, and therefore it was natural for men to have financial and legal control over their partners. Married women did not fill out their own tax returns; their income was noted on their husband's form. Any rebate due went to him. As a married woman, 'you will find, in practice, that ... hire purchase companies and landlords still ask for your husband's signature'. The 'cohabitation rule' meant that a woman living with a man had several state benefits withdrawn, even if he was not financially supporting her. The contraception chapter records that 'it is still the policy of most clinics to ask for your husband's consent if you are having a coil fitted or an operation for sterilisation. Their excuse is that the doctor must be protected from being sued by an irate husband who might demand compensation for loss of his ability to have children'. And, of course, 'your husband cannot normally be prosecuted for rape if he forces you to have sexual intercourse against your will . . . As far as the law is concerned, when you marry a man you consent to have sexual intercourse with him while you are married.'* Male immigrants could bring their wives into Britain as dependents, but female immigrants were only allowed to bring in husbands under 'exceptional circumstances'. There was, however, a special type of visa open only to women: a twelve-month stay was permitted for 'au pair girls' living with a family and doing domestic work. ('No mention of au pair boys,' note the authors.)

All of this overt discrimination happened within living memory. My mother's generation were often asked to find a responsible man to countersign their mortgage applications. In 1974, Gill's and Coote's book noted that 'building societies are getting rather more enlightened in their attitudes these days and few will admit to discriminating against women'. Which would have been legal, of course; this was the year before the Sex Discrimination Act. Three out of twenty-five institutions surveyed said they might require a 'guarantor' for a female loan applicant. One refused to lend to single women at all, citing 'quota restrictions'. It was also harder to get a mortgage with a low-income job – and, guess what, the majority of low-income jobs were held by women.

I wonder how many younger women know about this. The Second Wave of feminism in the late 1960s and 70s is often now derided as privileged and blinkered. But it swept away the legal framework which enshrined women's second-class status. Gill's and Coote's

* This was only changed through a court case in 1991, the year the Hubble telescope was launched and the first website went online. Madness.

handbook offers advice on dealing with immigration services and how to visit your partner in prison. Tess Gill worked with lesbians whose children were taken from them by the divorce courts. This was not a ladies' lunch club. If it looks like that in hindsight, it's because the work of thousands of women has been largely forgotten, and the fierce opposition to it has been forgotten too. As a feminist, victory is often bittersweet: the new reality quickly feels normal, obscuring the fight required to get there. Progress erases struggle.

All these Second Wave advances made the same point as the fight for divorce. Without independence – legal and economic – women were reliant on men giving them whatever they felt was appropriate. In marriage, women were left at the mercy of drunkards, gamblers and abusers. At work, they were grudgingly accepted, as long as they didn't make trouble or ask to be paid the same. At the pub, the story was the same. Women were not really people.

*

In 2010, a group of judges ruled on a case known as 'Radmacher', involving prenuptial agreements. These are used by rich people to protect their assets if they get divorced. Many see them as unfair: it is usually the richer spouse (or their family) who employs the lawyers needed to draw one up. The poorer spouse might not be able to employ their own advisers, and might feel pressured to go along with whatever document is put in front of them.

In Radmacher, the homemaker and poorer spouse was a man, but in most similar cases it would be a woman. In the ruling, that fact led to the closest thing that senior judges get to a Paddington Bear-style 'hard stare'. The object of a prenup, one of the judges wrote, 'is to deny the economically weaker spouse the provision to which she – it is usually, although by no means invariably, she – would otherwise be entitled'. And then came the *coup de grâce*: 'In short, there is a gender dimension to the issue which some may think ill-suited to decision by a court consisting of eight men and one woman.'

The sharpness was justified. Today, more than 180 years after Caroline Norton's divorce trial was an all-male affair, our laws are still firmly in the hands of men. And a particular type of man, at that. More than seventy per cent of senior judges are privately educated, compared with seven per cent of the population of a whole. As of 1 April 2018, only 6.8 per cent of judges came from a black or minority ethnic background. Two-thirds of MPs, our lawmakers, are male. By April 2018, only 29 per cent of all court judges were female. The Supreme Court has three women and nine men.

The judge who wrote that opinion was the first female law lord. She came up through academia rather than the traditional judges' circuit. In September 2017, she became the first female president of the Supreme Court. Her name is Brenda Hale.

Reading Lady Hale's biography, two things stand out to me. First, she calls herself a feminist: her coat of arms bears the Latin inscription *Omnia Femina Aequissimae* (Women are Equal to Everything). Second, she has been divorced.

In person, Brenda Hale is quietly terrifying. I met her at the Supreme Court's headquarters on Parliament Square, where she has an office filled with porcelain frogs: an in-joke with her second husband, whom she has described as her 'frog prince'.

Her career is a reminder of the speed of change. She graduated in law in 1966, when divorce law was still built entirely around the idea of guilt and innocence. Difficult women were treated more harshly when marital assets were divided. The assumption, Lady Hale told me, was that a woman 'had to be innocent to get anything out of her husband, or if she was less than wholly innocent, what she needed to be provided with would be reduced by the extent to which she was less than wholly innocent'. Any wife painted as an unreasonable nag risked getting a lower settlement. I asked her if she would accept the characterisation of divorce law as a punishment, to make the couple involved feel like failures. 'No, I wouldn't put it that way,' she said. 'Marriage is meant to be a lifelong commitment, so you could only divorce somebody if they had basically committed a fundamental breach of the marital contract, and you, as the innocent party, were therefore permitted to seek a dissolution against the guilty party. So there was certainly an innocent party and a guilty party.'

It wasn't until 1969 that separation – a neutral term – was added to the list of possible grounds for divorce, and the idea of 'matrimonial offences' was abolished. The trouble now, Lady Hale believes, is the legacy of the older system. It *looks* as if a divorce is based around fault, but in reality the system 'makes no attempt to allocate blame accurately, none at all. And that's what makes a lot of people feel that it's unjust.' A couple must decide between themselves that one of them will agree to be legally deemed 'unreasonable' or adulterous, even when both have slept with other people or both have contributed to the failure of the marriage.

Lady Hale's view is that there should be 'no-fault divorces' where the couple agree that the relationship has broken down. After a waiting period of six months to a year, they make a joint statement reaffirming that belief. No reasons have to be given, so there is no wrangling over who left whom, who slept with whom, or who treated whom worse. The divorce is then granted.

Doesn't that sound like the current grounds of separation? Well, no. There is no burden of proof attached to no-fault divorce. If you currently use 'separation' as the grounds, you have to demonstrate that you *have* separated, perhaps using mortgage letters and bank statements and other paperwork, and your partner can contest it. Flicking through my 1970s feminist handbooks, I was shocked to discover that one woman was refused a divorce because her husband was still living in the spare room and she was cooking his meals for him. Her kind attempt to resolve the breakdown of their relationship with minimum disruption to their children was used as a reason not to dissolve the marriage.

No-fault divorce is an idea whose time has come. Then again, it has felt that way for nearly thirty years. In 1990, a Law Commission report strongly recommended reforming the grounds for divorce, calling them 'confusing and misleading'. Couples did not understand the artificial categories used, particularly if these had little to do with the actual reason for them breaking up. The lack of no-fault divorce was 'discriminatory' because separation – the only grounds which did not involve blame – was difficult for poor couples. Take a couple with a council-house tenancy, which cannot be reallocated until the divorce is finalised. How do you prove separation if neither of you can afford to move out? Couples were being asked to maintain 'separate households' under one roof, which was 'a most unnatural and artificial lifestyle'. In reality, 'a young mother with children living in a council house is obliged to rely upon fault whether or not she wants to do so and irrespective of the damage it may do'. The current law provoked 'unnecessary hostility and bitterness', just as it had done in Caroline Norton's time. It also did nothing to save marriages, and made life harder for children.

These recommendations were criticised, says Lady Hale, 'on the basis that it was an attack on marriage and you needed to maintain the fault basis of divorce because otherwise divorce would be too easy, or not moral'. However, she points out that divorce is currently 'easy' in legal terms if both parties agree on the grounds. It is fast, too, if one side will admit to adultery.*

*

When I got divorced, I was in my late twenties, with good friends, a loving family and a decent job. And yet it was still a profoundly lonely experience. I made the decision to leave in December, and then

---

* Civil partnerships and same-sex marriages cannot be dissolved on grounds of adultery. According to our law, the only kind of sex that's sexy enough to end a legal contract is good old penis-in-vagina. This is, as we'll see later, part of an outdated conception of what 'normal' sex is. But in the meantime it's great news for fans of cunnilingus and remaining married.

immediately faced the question: what about Christmas? Who ends their marriage just before Christmas – and how could I find somewhere else to live during the holiday season? So I stayed until January. But that brings its own horrors. When you know you're going to leave, it poisons all your interactions with your partner: you are lying to someone who loves you – and someone who part of you still loves.

Next, the practical considerations. I had virtually no savings – just enough to put down the deposit on a rented flat after sleeping in a friend's spare room for a couple of weeks. The same friends met me at my old place with a taxi to take my stuff away. All I wanted, I had said, were my clothes and books. I was the one who'd screwed this up, after all. In my first night in my new flat, I could see the platforms of Highbury station through the window. The flat hadn't come with curtains. I got undressed in the dark, hoping there wasn't a pervert with night-vision goggles lurking in the houses opposite. I kept thinking about all the other women who had done what I just did. How much harder it would be to leave with children. How much harder it would be to sneak away in the daytime from a violent, controlling partner. How much harder with only a joint bank account. How much harder without a bank account at all.

The Second Wave feminists fought hard for women's economic independence, and that battle is not over. Universal Credit – Iain Duncan Smith's flagship welfare reform, which rolls together six benefits into one – is a backwards step. It automatically goes to the 'head of the household', which contradicts decades of campaigning by feminists. In 1975, when child benefit was brought in – replacing family allowance – the Labour politician Barbara Castle ensured that it went to mothers. In the Commons, she called it 'a new universal, non-means tested, tax-free cash benefit for all children, including the first, payable to the mother'. There were arguments at the time that it would be 'simpler' to include it with the payslips of the family breadwinner. That would mean, in almost every family of the time, the man. Castle rejected that idea, saying that the money would be a great relief to women whose 'shopping money' had run out by the middle of the week. The benefit belonged in the purse, not in the wallet. It would give women who didn't do paid work a little money to call their own.

We often talk now about the anguish of men who have seen manufacturing and other traditionally male jobs disappear. We should be honest, though, about where some of this anguish comes from: the loss of status and control that came from being head of the household and arbiter of its cashflow. It was easier to stop your wife being 'difficult' – scolding you, contradicting you, questioning your priorities – when you could cut off her income.

Barbara Castle lived in a world where a woman who stayed at home was a supplicant. If her partner was paid weekly, she might have to wait for him to give her the 'housekeeping' – money for bills and food – with the rest kept for him. Under this system, women had no expectation of any money to spend on themselves, while their partners perhaps retained a few pounds for the pub or the bookies. It was also harder to leave. When I wrote about Universal Credit, I was overwhelmed by stories about 'running-away money'. One man told me that when his mother died, the family found a stash of money hidden in a drawer. Thankfully, she had never needed it – but she was always aware that she might do. There is little mention of the phrase on the Internet. It's an artefact of an earlier age, in which a woman who worried that her partner's temper was worsening, or his drinking had begun to cloud their lives, or even simply that she no longer loved him, would find it hard to escape.

In January 2016, Paulette Perhach wrote in *Billfold* about her generation's version of running-away money. She described one road a young woman with a decent job might take: running up credit card bills, buying expensive lunchtime sandwiches, letting your nice boy-friend cover the rent while you get yourself together. And then: your boss gropes you, and your boyfriend overhears you talking to another

man, and grabs you hard enough to send you crashing into the coffee
table.

> He seems so sorry, cries, even, so that night you lie down in
> the same bed. You stare up at the dark and try to calculate
> how long it would take you to save up the cash to move out.
> Telling yourself that he's sorry, convincing yourself it was an
> accident, discounting this one time because he didn't hit
> you, exactly, seems much more feasible than finding the
> money, with what you owe every month. The next time you
> go out as a couple, his arm around your shoulders, you look
> at all the other girlfriends and imagine finger-sized bruises
> under their long sleeves.

Perhach wanted young women to have a different story. If they
wore cheap clothes, worked extra shifts and lived within their
means, they could build up savings. That would mean they could
quit the job with the groping boss, and dump the possessive, violent
boyfriend. She called the money a 'fuck-off fund'.

Her essay went viral, and alongside the positive reactions came
a welter of complaints. How do you build up a fuck-off fund when
your job is insecure, when even cheap clothes mean you have to
resort to a credit card, and – in America – when a simple chest infection or broken finger can land you with a huge medical bill? The
criticism wasn't wrong. Not everyone can build up a fuck-off fund
(although if you can, you should). The state has a role to play, too.

That idea now seems faintly radical even in Britain – never mind
hypercapitalist America. The British feminists of the Second Wave
grew up in a much more collectivist society, with the foundation of
the NHS and the welfare state still fresh in the public memory. They
probably assumed that legal changes would continue, and society
could be pushed to restructure itself further. But there is always a
backlash. Both here and in the US, we have seen the demonisation of

'welfare queens' and 'benefits scroungers', with single mothers por-
trayed as parasites leeching off the taxpayer. There is widespread
opposition to state benefits on the right of politics, and not just
because of their cost to the Treasury. There is also an ideological
point about supporting lifestyles (such as single parenthood) that
social conservatives dislike. Today, some politicians use welfare policy to punish women who are 'difficult'. That is, women who don't
'make the marriage work', who want more from a relationship than
the bare minimum of a roof above their head, or who dare to fall in
love with someone else.

*

The right to divorce might seem like a strange place to start our story.* But feminism is ultimately about independence: control of our
bodies, and control of our lives. In the 1800s, the law treated women
like children, to be looked after by men. That arrangement persists
today in Saudi Arabia, where the 'guardianship' system means
women have to seek permission from their father, husband or near-
est male relative to apply for a passport, travel abroad or study. The
'reforming' government there graciously granted women the ability
to vote in 2015 and drive in 2018, but has since imprisoned activists
for challenging the guardianship system. Saudi Arabia also demonstrates how legal and financial control is used to enforce other
restrictions on women's lives, such as 'modest' clothing standards.

    In nineteenth-century Britain, the series of feminist legal
reforms which began with the Custody of Infants Act and the Married Women's Property Act allowed women to become increasingly
independent – and increasingly 'difficult'. By the turn of the twentieth century, women like Caroline Norton could no longer be held

* You'll have to forgive me, in this chapter, for focusing on heterosexual relationships.
With gay marriage only introduced in Britain in 2013, the US and Ireland in 2015, and
Australia in 2017, there is little research on same-sex divorce.

hostage by their partners, and treated like possessions rather than people. They could dream of building up the nineteenth century equivalent of a fuck-off fund. They were harder to blackmail into submission. They were beginning to be free. It all came too late for Norton herself, though. She won her adultery case, but not her independence. In the end, what legally separated her from the unbearable George was his death in 1877. She too was dead within three months.

Divorce is now legal in every country in the world, except the Philippines.* But these reforms are often very recent, uncomfortably fragile and limited in scope. Ireland did not vote to legalise divorce until 24 November 1995, and even then the referendum was won by just 50.28 per cent of the vote. Clearly, women as well as men feared change to the status quo.

Our divorce law still needs to be reformed. The presumption that mothers are the primary carers is being gradually eroded, which will inevitably affect 'access' to children after divorces. A less adversarial system, which favours dialogue over assigning blame, would benefit parents and their children. The old argument that making divorce less needlessly unpleasant would encourage the break-up of families is obsolete. Divorce rates have been falling for years. In April 2019, justice secretary David Gauke announced that he would bring forward proposals for 'no-fault divorce'. There was barely a squeak of backlash. 'While we will always uphold the institution of marriage, it cannot be right that our outdated law creates or increases conflict between divorcing couples,' said the Conservative MP.

For centuries, marriage was used to control women – to suppress their difficulty, to stop them being unruly and independent. Divorce laws have traditionally done the same. They have encouraged us to put women's behaviour on trial, in the knowledge that

* The only legal way to end a marriage in the majority Catholic country is annulment. Muslims can obtain a religious divorce but not a civil one.

they will always be judged more harshly for their imperfections than men. They have made leaving a relationship carry a heavy social and economic cost – one which falls harder on women.

Feminists fought to ensure that the institution of marriage could no longer be used to control women, and to ensure that divorces did not leave us destitute. The law no longer installs men as our protectors, deforming their love into a form of ownership. I am glad I got divorced, and I no longer feel ashamed that my marriage ended. Instead, I feel gratitude to the women who fought so that they – and I – could be free to make our own choices.

And once women gained a little more control over their lives and their money, they were better placed to fight the other laws and practices which made them second-class citizens. Our next story takes us to Manchester in 1905, where two young women are tired of asking nicely. They want the vote, and they mean to get it – even if that means using violence.

2. THE VOTE

I am not going to discuss the wisdom or the unwisdom of the tactics of what are known as the militant suffragists, but I will make this general remark in passing, that in spite of the sneers of Hon. Members behind me, if the same degree of courage, the same devotion to a great cause, was being shown on the field of battle, or under other circumstances, those exhibiting it would be held up as heroes for national admiration.

Keir Hardie MP, 1913

Christabel Pankhurst was frustrated. After half a century of petitions, peaceful demonstrations and pleading, women still did not have the vote. At a Liberal Party meeting in Manchester in October 1905, she watched as the male speakers droned on from the platform, and decided that a new tactic was needed. Women could no longer ask politely for their rights and be ignored, as she felt the law-abiding suffragists were. The twenty-five-year-old law student was ready to begin a new type of campaign. A militant one.

If you have heard of the suffragettes, you will probably have heard of Christabel Pankhurst. But for now, it is the figure sitting next to her who should interest us. In photographs, the first thing you notice are her eyes – sharp and clear, with a birdlike inquisitiveness. She is the fifth of eleven children, born to a family of Lancashire mill workers. She was no great shakes in school, which she only attended for a few years. Her strong northern accent separates her from the genteel Pankhursts, and later in life she will become anxious that she has been caricatured because of it. As Christabel's patience runs out, a large white banner reading 'Votes for Women' goes up, and the twenty-six-year-old is pushed forward to speak. Her question – 'Will the Liberal government give women the vote?' – is ignored by a young politician called Winston Churchill. Men try to pull her back down into the crowd, and a steward puts his hat over her face. She is thrown out of the meeting and Christabel spits on a police officer, ensuring that they are both arrested. At the court, Christabel tells the (male) prosecutors and the (male) magistrates that their rowdiness is understandable: 'We cannot make any orderly protest because we have not the means whereby citizens may do such a thing; we have not a vote; and so long as we have not votes we must be disorderly . . . if we were citizens we should be law-abiding.' The young woman beside her tells the court that she represents thousands of factory women: 'We are determined that something shall be done.' She refuses to pay a fine and goes to prison instead. The resulting publicity is so overwhelming that she becomes a kind of celebrity. It is the first of thirteen times she will be jailed for the cause.

Meet Annie Kenney.

*

The way I learned about the suffragette story at school left me with a vague impression of bonnets and prison sentences. I knew that after decades of peaceful campaigning, women turned to window-smashing in the years before the First World War. If pressed, I could have identified the movement's leaders as Emmeline Pankhurst and one or more of her daughters. In fact, there were three: Sylvia, Christabel and Adela (their two brothers died young). Christabel is the most famous, because she was the one who came up with the organisation's militant policies. Together with her mother, she commanded the Women's Social and Political Union, which had its offices on St Clement's Lane, near Aldwych in central London.

Various people who crossed either Emmeline or Christabel were thrown out of the union. By the end of 1913 this included two of its greatest supporters (and greatest donors), Fred and Emmeline Pethick Lawrence, as well as Sylvia and Adela Pankhurst. Anyone who disagreed with the WSPU's use of violence was forced out; others left after realising there was no place for democracy in the movement. The role of men also caused ill-feeling: from the start, only women could be WSPU members. Nonetheless, around forty men were arrested for militant actions in support of the union, and several, including Fred Pethick Lawrence, were force-fed.

Alliances with other political movements were also tightly

controlled. Sylvia Pankhurst's close friendship with Keir Hardie, an MP from the newly founded Independent Labour Party, was always regarded with suspicion. Sylvia's final crime in the eyes of her mother and sister was to appear on a platform with George Lansbury – a man and a Labour politician, a double insult – in support of strikers in Dublin. Members of the WSPU were supposed to focus exclusively on votes for women. Sylvia had already drifted away to her own East London Federation, focusing on working-class women, but in January 1914 she was kicked out of the WSPU completely. Today, she is the 'presentable Pankhurst' – her flirtation with communism is more acceptable to many modern feminists than other suffragettes' later interest in fascism. Sylvia was also more alert to what we would now call intersectionality – the idea that different oppressions intersect with one another. She later became involved in the anti-colonial movement.

Christabel Pankhurst feels far more like a product of her age. She saw the fight for the vote as part of a 'sex war' which justified violence. That stance drove away the more moderate suffragists. You get some idea of the strength of Christabel's personality from her letters, some of which I read in the library at the University of East Anglia. After the Second World War, when she had moved to America, she sent airmails back to Annie Kenney on large sheets of irregularly shaped paper, with the corners folded inwards to form an envelope. Every inch of space is crammed with writing, zigzagging in every direction. She was still brimming with zeal.

Autocratic, single-minded and ruthless: Emmeline and Christabel Pankhurst were undoubtedly difficult women. But what about their followers? How did they persuade so many women – just over a thousand of them – to join the militant cause, risking injury, imprisonment, torture and death? And how did their foot soldiers feel about the great struggle for the vote?

Annie Kenney fascinated me for a reason she would have hated later in her life: she was working-class. There is now a caricature of the suffragettes as ladies-who-lunched-and-occasionally-committed-arson; think of the dippy absent mother in *Mary Poppins*. This is something which often happens to women who challenge the status quo: any whisper of personal privilege is used to paint their concerns as piffling, a sideshow to other, greater oppressions. OK, OK, *some* women have a rough time, runs the patronising logic, but what do *these* ones have to complain about? You might think the struggle for the vote – the struggle to be recognised as a full citizen – would be immune to this kind of denigration. But you would be wrong. The fight for female suffrage ran alongside the fight for suffrage to be extended to men under thirty, and the fight for Irish Home Rule. The proponents of the latter causes both decided, at different times, to screw over women's suffrage campaigners to boost their own chances of success. Women are expected to put their own needs last.

Annie Kenney also intrigued me because I wanted to know what the relationships *between* women were like in the WSPU. The WSPU is a rare revolutionary organisation which was founded and run by women. It offered its militants a chance to relate to each other in ways that previous generations would have found unthinkable. 'No cause can be won between dinner and tea, and most of us who were married had to work with one hand tied behind us,' wrote suffragette Hannah Mitchell in her memoir. That meant many of those who joined were unmarried and childless. These recruits gained a kind of economic independence unimaginable to their mothers and grandmothers; the WSPU paid its organisers enough for them to rent their own flats in London. For the first time, women's ability to organise politically was not destroyed by their caring responsibilities and economic dependence on men. 'Looking back on my own life, I feel my greatest enemy has been the cooking stove – a sort of tyrant who has kept me in subjection,' wrote Mitchell.

For the suffragettes, the vote was *the* cause; they were not general do-gooders who could be distracted by other social reforms. Nor would they waste their freedom on pursuing pleasure. 'Nuns in a convent were not watched over and supervised more strictly than were the organisers and members of the Militant Movement during the first few years,' writes Kenney in her 1924 autobiography, *Memories of a Militant*. 'It was an unwritten rule that there must be no concerts, no theatres, no smoking; work, and sleep to prepare us for more work, was the unwritten order of the day.'

This austere existence shaped the suffragettes into something approaching an army, forging strong bonds which could weather persecution by the state. What they perhaps did not expect from their new world was exhilaration. 'The changed life into which most of us entered was a revolution in itself,' adds Kenney. 'No home-life, no one to say what we should do or what we should not do, no family ties, we were free and alone in a great brilliant city, scores of young women scarcely out of their teens met together in a revolutionary movement, outlaws or breakers of laws, independent of everything and everybody, fearless and self-confident.'

It is easy to see why the suffragette movement appealed to Kenney, who might have expected a life like the one her mother had, perpetually pregnant and bonded to her home town. While campaigning, Kenney visited Australia, America, France and Germany. She was carried into packed meetings on a stretcher, waving a handkerchief like a martyr. She went on the run from the police. She might even have had a romantic relationship with Christabel Pankhurst: one historian pointed to the accounts of Annie regularly sharing a bed with other women at the Blathwayt family home near Bristol and told me the explanation was either 'very exciting or very boring'.

The suffragette movement also appealed to other types of women, like the one Kenney met at the Green Lady hostel in Littlehampton in 1908. 'Tall, majestic, noble, to me she looked what she was – one of England's great noblewomen,' wrote Kenney in her memoir. 'She always wore long flowing coloured scarves which reminded me of a bunch of lavender enveloped by clouds of delicate, varied hues. Her voice was quiet with a depth of feeling, and, to me, a touch of sadness ... Her passion and devotion for the working-class women in the Movement was quite out of the ordinary. She loved them and they loved her.'

The tall, majestic woman was Lady Constance Georgina Bulwer-Lytton, and for her the suffragette movement represented a different kind of salvation. For 'Lady Con', it meant freedom from a tediously genteel life of looking after her mother, reading Russian classics and pining for an absent fiancé.

In letters written in her twenties and early thirties, Lytton complains of shooting parties where 'the men are quite astonishingly the same'. She created an alter ego, Deborah, who was more liberated than she could be. 'What would they do if I suddenly unbuttoned and shook out Deborah upon them in one of her maddest moods?' Lytton asked her sister Emily after a dull party. 'But far from having the courage to do this, I can't even find the buttons, and I feel as if I had been sewn up for years, or rather never had an opening, any more than an apple dumpling.' Stuck at home, she fell prey to 'suicidal mania'. Her physical health was delicate too, with her heart causing her endless concern. Above all, she appears to have been bored. It all felt, as she wrote to her eldest sister in 1899, like '*waiting, not actually living*'. The suffragette movement made her feel alive. Ultimately, though, it nearly killed her.

*

It's a strange Saturday night when you find yourself contemplating what a 'non-zero risk of death' might be. Crossing the road carries a risk, as does taking Ecstasy or paragliding. But choosing to suffer, when you know the risks, is different. Reading Diane Atkinson's biography of the suffragettes, *Rise Up Women*, I couldn't shake the descriptions of force-feeding from my mind. Use of the procedure started in 1909, when suffragettes began to go on hunger strike to protest being treated as ordinary criminals rather than political prisoners. Four years later, the government tried to stop it by passing the Cat and Mouse Act, allowing prisons to release women who were dangerously malnourished – and then jail them again as soon as they recovered. 'The authorities believed that force-feeding would act as a deterrent as well as a punishment,' writes Lyndsey Jenkins in her biography of Constance Lytton. 'This was a serious miscalculation: it actually had the opposite effect. Seeing the gaunt bodies of their comrades and hearing their horrific stories galvanised the suffragettes.' Hunger strikers received medals from the WSPU with purple, green and white ribbons; the suffragette newspapers carried striking illustrations of the procedure, describing it as torture.

'The feeling was that the tube was absolutely choking you, and when it was withdrawn that it dragged after it the whole of your inside,' Laura Ainsworth, one of the earliest victims, told a meeting. In her prison diary, Emily Davison described 'feelings of suffocation and sickness' which made her cough and retch. 'Twice every day, four, five or six wardresses come in as well as the two doctors,' Sylvia Pankhurst wrote to her mother in February 1913. 'I am fed by a stomach tube. They prise open my mouth with a steel gag, pressing it in where there is a gap in my teeth. I resist all the time and my gums are always bleeding. I am afraid they may be saying about me that I am not resisting but, believe me, my shoulders are bruised with struggling whilst they hold the tube into my throat and force it down. I used to feel I would go mad at first and to be pretty near to it, as I think they feared, but I have got over that and my digestion is the thing that is most likely to suffer now.' As a Pankhurst, Sylvia's condition was watched closely by the government. A letter from the prison doctor to the Home Secretary – released only in 2005 – records that she resorted to 'wilful vomiting' after each feed.

Force-feeding is still used today, and it is still contentious. In 2015, the Israeli parliament legalised the process for use on Palestinian hunger strikers, but doctors there have repeatedly refused to be involved. 'The message we wish to convey to physicians is that forced feeding is tantamount to torture and that no doctor should take part in it,' Dr Leonid Eidelman, head of the Israeli Medical Association, said in May 2017. Was there any way to show people what the British state did to women who wanted the vote? Could I be force-fed? I emailed Dr Alexander Scott, an intensive-care specialist at South Tees hospital in northern England. That's when he mentioned the 'non-zero risk of death'. His email was businesslike. 'I have no doubt that unconsented and forceful insertion of an NG [nasogastric] tube constitutes torture,' it began. It was sometimes necessary to anaesthetise patients to get a tube in, he said. If they were awake, they could help the doctor by swallowing a glass of water as the tube passed through the muscle which seals off the larynx (which leads to the lungs) and opens up the oesophagus (which food goes down, into the stomach). In a confused or non-compliant patient, the feeding tube itself had to force open the muscle, bruising or tearing the delicate lining of the throat. 'If the patient is thrashing their head from side to side or otherwise resisting, there is a higher chance of the tube passing into the trachea through the vocal cords,' Dr Scott wrote. 'This can happen anyway through bad luck. If that happens the patient will experience severe and distressing coughing, pain, and difficulty in breathing – the vocal cords and upper trachea are very sensitive to being touched to protect the airway. If you've ever had a drink "go the wrong way" imagine that sensation but much amplified – the sensation is caused by the vocal cords spasming and shutting off the airway to prevent your drink ending up in your lungs.'

A force-feeding tube incorrectly inserted can collapse a lung. Inhaling the feeding solution can cause a fatal infection. Dr Scott dug out the account of Lilian Lenton, who contracted pleurisy from the 'intolerable and intense' procedure. Her inflamed lungs sounded like the result a nasogastric tube ending up in a lung. He signed off: 'I'm not sure how this could be done by a doctor legally in the UK for the purpose of a demonstration.'

Let that sink in. In the twenty-first century, it was too dangerous for a qualified medical professional, with access to cutting-edge equipment, to insert a nasogastric tube into an uncomfortable but essentially compliant patient. The tubes used on the suffragettes were larger and less flexible than modern ones; the doctors less highly skilled; and the women were often held down by four or six prison warders while all this went on. The tubes were not always cleaned between feeds, and *pints* of liquid were poured down their throats, producing a sensation of fullness to the point of bursting. And all this happened against their will, when they were often already dangerously weak from hunger striking. I could not be force-fed, even for demonstration purposes, because of the 'non-zero risk of death'. The suffragettes faced far worse odds.

Kitty Marion, a German-born actress who became an arsonist, was force-fed more than 200 times. In 1909, she wrote a letter to *The Times* alongside Constance Lytton and Emmeline Pethick Lawrence. 'We want to make it known that we shall carry on our protest in our prison cells,' it read. 'We shall put before the Government by means of the hunger strike four alternatives: to release us in a few days; to inflict violence upon our bodies; to add death to the champions of our cause by leaving us to starve; or, and this is the best and only wise alternative, to give women the vote.' After being released from prison in December 1909, Marion received a hunger strikers' medal from the WSPU. Then she went off to do the Christmas panto season.

*

Constance Lytton's doubts about the suffrage cause evaporated as soon as she began talking to Annie Kenney, Annie's sister Jessie and Emmeline Pethick Lawrence. She imagined a heavenly light shining from them, like a stained-glass window. 'One evening, after incessant rain, Annie Kenney and I marched arm-in-arm round the garden, under dripping trees,' Lytton wrote later. 'I explained that though I had always been for the extension of the suffrage to women, it did not seem to me a question of prime urgency, that many other matters of social reform seemed more important, and I thought class prejudice and barriers more injurious to national welfare than sex barriers.'

Kenney – as a working-class woman – disagreed. When she had started work in the mills at the age of ten, she had handed over her wages to the family purse. She got far less back as pocket money than her brothers. She spoke about how women's lives were shaped by 'the glorious act of motherhood and the tending of little children. Was there anything in a man's career that could be so honourable as this? Yet how often is the woman who bears humanity neglected at such times, so that life goes from her, or she is given no money to support her child.' The vote would ensure that needy women could not be ignored. Her manner won over Lytton, who was a decade older. 'One little line to lay my thanks at your feet for all the glow and life you put into me from your glowing, living self in these few hours we have been together,' Lady Con wrote to the younger woman in April 1909.

Although she quickly supported the cause, Lytton was a slow convert to militancy. She asked Emmeline Pethick Lawrence in 1908 whether there was anything she could do to help *except* appear on a platform with other suffragettes. There, she said, she would feel duty-bound to distance herself from tactics such as obstructing the police and would feel like 'a traitor in the camp'. She was asked instead to use her political contacts to lobby for the suffragettes to be treated as political prisoners. She tried an MP she knew, who contacted the Home Secretary, Herbert Gladstone. He refused to intervene. Then she marched to Bow Street police court, and asked to see the head officer. She was greeted with 'nothing but smiles, graciousness and unduly easy access'. It is hard to imagine Annie Kenney, with her plain outfit and Lancashire accent, receiving such a reception. Lytton's brother Victor was in the House of Lords, and her aristocratic heritage gave the suffragettes more respectability – as did the presence of Queen Victoria's god-daughter, the Anglo-Indian princess Sophia Duleep Singh.

Kenney was useful in a different way. The Pankhursts gave her the role of standard-bearer for working women. In 1913, she led a deputation to David Lloyd George. It included a 'fishwife', a 'pit-brow lassie', a 'laundress' and a 'tailoress', who told the assembled MPs how the 'girls worked for 3 1/4d an hour, whilst the men were paid 6 1/2d an hour for the same work'.

Lytton was first held for stone-throwing on 24 February 1909. 'I and two of my children went to greet her at the doors of the prison on her release on March 24,' wrote her sister Betty in a letter. 'As soon as I saw her, I realised as I had not done before that she no longer belonged to us. She belonged to her union, and nothing else really counted.' Her other sister Emily felt the same, telling their aunt in March 1909: 'We cannot disguise from ourselves that our old Con has gone for ever.'

Newly militant, Lady Con was prepared to be arrested again. But something nagged at her: she couldn't shake the feeling that she was receiving unfairly soft treatment because of her class. When she was arrested a second time, she was ready to be force-fed, and stood waiting by the door with her fingers blocking her mouth and nostrils. But she was released instead. She felt guilty because the other women arrested with her suffered enormously. One was tied to a chair with a sheet and held down by three wardresses to be fed. Each woman could hear the screams of the others through the walls. 'The altogether shameless way I had been preferred against the others at Newcastle,' Lytton wrote, 'made me determine to try whether they would recognise my need for exceptional favours without my name.' She had once longed to be unbuttoned, liberated 'Deborah'. She now became 'Jane Warton' instead. On a trip to a department store, she bought new, cheap clothes; she was fitted for a pair of pince-nez spectacles and an unfashionable hat, and carefully unpicked the embroidered initials from her underwear. The surname came from one F. Warburton, who had written her a supportive letter when she came out of prison, and the first name from Joan of Arc.

In January 1910, she was arrested for a third time, this time as

Jane Warton, for throwing stones in Walton, Liverpool. The ruse was nearly discovered during the strip search as her handkerchief had 'Con' embroidered on it; however, she managed to throw it into the fire without anyone noticing. In the police cell, other prisoners laughed at her for looking like such a *'Punch* version' – the satirical magazine's stereotype – of a suffragette. She was sentenced to a fortnight in the third division, as an ordinary criminal. She wrote a quotation from Henry David Thoreau's essay on civil disobedience on the wall: 'Under a government which imprisons any unjustly, the true place for a just man is also a prison.' She added in brackets, 'or woman'.

Then she started her hunger strike. After eighty-nine hours, the prison doctor and wardresses fed her without checking her heart or even feeling her pulse. She found the experience horrifying. The mixture was milk, eggs, brandy, sugar and beef tea (Lytton was a vegetarian) and the pouring stopped only when 'the vomiting [became] excessive'. The doctor assumed that she was exaggerating her distress; she realised that while a lady's complaints were listened to, the terror of a working-class woman was not. 'Suddenly I saw Jane Warton lying before me, and it seemed as if I were outside of her,' Lytton writes in *Prisons and Prisoners*. 'She was the most despised, ignorant and helpless prisoner that I had seen. When she had served her time and was out of the prison, no one would believe anything she said, and the doctor when he had fed her by force and tortured her body, struck her on the cheek to show how he despised her! That was Jane Warton, and I had come to help her.'

After her seventh force-feeding, she cried for the first time. She was hallucinating and constantly cold, wrapped in blankets. She was eventually released after being force-fed once more; a rumour had reached the Press Association that there was no 'Jane Warton'. The governor had also suspected something, and had contacted the Home Office.

Lytton's weight loss was given as the medical reason for her release. As 'Jane Warton', her troublesome heart had never been tested. At five foot eleven, she now weighed just seven and a half stone. She had lost two pounds a day, despite the force-feeding, and her legs were so thin it was painful to sit down. Back at home, she had to eat her meals kneeling on a cushion. One of the crowns on her teeth fell out; it had been damaged by the gag. A month later, her legs were infected and swollen, with her weak heart unable to maintain her circulation. The prison authorities still maintained they had checked Jane Warton's heart before feeding her, and the Home Office line was that she had refused a proper examination. Therefore, she deserved everything she got.

But Constance Lytton, unlike Jane Warton, had powerful friends. Her brother Victor wrote a letter to *The Times* backing up her story, and the new Home Secretary Winston Churchill – a friend of Victor's – was told about it. The truth could not be suppressed. Not only were employees of the government choking, slapping and nearly asphyxiating political prisoners, they were treating working people worse than their own class. The impact of Lytton's story was enormous. The government's breezy assurances that force-feeding was a safe, well-supervised medical procedure were blown apart. 'The experience in prison this time was intensely grim and dreadful, but now the reward seems undeservedly great,' Lytton wrote to fellow suffragette Dr Alice Ker, from her sister's flat in London. 'To think that I who have suffered by far the least of all the "forcibly fed" should be making people wake up more than all of them.'

Any middle-class feminist trying a similar stunt today would undoubtedly be accused of class tourism – taking the spotlight for herself rather than raising up the voices of marginalised women. But only an aristocrat could have shamed the ruling class. And because the press reaction at the time was so strong and the whole episode was so embarrassing for the government, the story of Constance Lytton's time as Jane Warton is usually boiled down to a straightforward triumphal narrative. But peer into the cracks and there are hints that other suffragettes were resentful of her class privilege, even then. As Emily Lutyens wrote to Betty Balfour, the prison doctor 'told me that his suspicion has first been aroused by the ill-concealed delight of one of the other suffragettes at hearing Warton was being fed'.

*

Reading dozens of suffragette letters on microfiche in the LSE archive left me desperate to see the real thing. It's strange, isn't it, the communion that can only be had with physical objects? I wanted to hold the same paper that Constance Lytton and Annie Kenney had held; see the handwriting they must have recognised, with joy, when they picked up an envelope; to feel the energy and rhythm of their pen strokes. So: a train to Norwich, and specifically, the University of East Anglia, which holds Kenney's archive. It came up from storage in brown boxes and buff folders, and was full of minor treasures. Her London Library pass; a national registration card with the occupation given as 'suffragette'; and her letters. There was a whole folder from Lady Con.

There was another reason I wanted to see these sheets of paper in the flesh, as it were. Chugging through the microfiche archive, I had found a gap after Constance Lytton's letter to her friend Alice Ker on 4 May 1912. There was a reason for that: 4 May is the last day she wrote anything with her right hand.

Her health had never been good. Even before joining the suffragettes, she ate very little and worried a lot. After suffering from shingles, and a seizure, Lytton missed 'Black Friday' – 18 November 1910 – when suffragettes were beaten and sexually assaulted by police as they tried to storm the Houses of Parliament.* The next year she and Annie Kenney went to see the Tory politician Arthur

* One of those arrested on Black Friday was Rosa May Billinghurst, the 'cripple suffragette', who was paralysed from childhood polio. She charged the police in her tricycle. They let her tyres down in revenge.

Balfour – Kenney gave him a flower wrapped in paper – and she was arrested for window-smashing. Lytton spent eight days in prison (without force-feeding) before an anonymous donor paid her fine. Another suffragette jailed alongside her got a longer sentence. Lytton wrote a letter to the government in protest; Emily Davison, who always went further than anyone else, set fire to a postbox.

As 1912 dawned, Lytton – dressed in purple, white and green – attended the wedding of the suffragette Una Dugdale. The ceremony made the newspapers because Una refused to 'obey' her husband. She was told that if she did not, the marriage would not be legally recognised.* On 5 May, though, Lytton's body betrayed her. A stroke paralysed her right arm, and crippled her right leg and foot. She was found in her rented flat on the Euston Road, incapable of movement or speech. There was no question of smashing more windows or daring the authorities to force-feed her again. She had to retire to the countryside.

Lytton left the suffragette campaign as it entered its extreme militant phase. 'Both Christabel and her mother were against the taking of human life,' wrote Annie Kenney in her memoir, 'but Christabel felt the times demanded sterner measures, and burning she knew would frighten both the public and Parliament.' In February 1913, Emmeline Pankhurst was arrested for conspiracy to bomb an unoccupied house recently bought by the chancellor, David Lloyd George. She admitted inciting the action and was sentenced to three years in prison. She immediately went on hunger strike.

The conviction provoked a wave of violence, and four months later a camera recorded Emily Davison as she was trampled to death by horses at the Derby. During her lifetime, Davison had been

* The Church of England scrapped mandatory obedience in 1928, but the tradition endured. Princess Elizabeth promised to 'love, cherish and obey' Prince Philip at their wedding in 1947, and the word's non-appearance at the wedding of Prince Harry and Meghan Markle prompted news stories in 2018.

regarded as something of a liability by the WSPU. She had little regard for her safety, once throwing herself head-first down the stairs of a prison. But in death, she became a martyr. Her funeral became an unforgettable spectacle, a sea of women in white, purple and green, captured on postcards and film reels.

At the peak of the militant campaign, women set fire to the teahouse at Bellevue Zoo in north Belfast, attacked the jewel cabinets at the Tower of London, cut telegraph wires in Dumbarton and left phosphorus in postboxes in Dundee. They poured acid on the greens of Knock golf club and tried to place bombs on trains in Lancashire. Annie's sister Jessie plotted an arson campaign; incriminating papers were found in the flat they shared. In 1914, 'Slasher' Mary Richardson attacked the *Rokeby Venus* in the National Gallery with a meat cleaver, shattering the glass and leaving deep lacerations across the goddess's naked back. 'I have tried to destroy the picture of the most beautiful woman in mythological history as a protest against the government for destroying Mrs Pankhurst, who is the most beautiful character in modern history,' she wrote in a statement published in *The Times*.*

Even today, the sheer scale of suffragette bombings, arson and other militant activity is not widely known. The suffragettes did far more than smash windows, although they always claimed that they were not aiming to kill people. The historian Fern Riddell has suggested that from the 1920s, the Suffragette Fellowship – an influential collection of resources gathered to 'perpetuate the memory of the pioneers' of women's suffrage – deliberately downplayed their violence. With victory assured, there was no need to show the divisive means used to achieve it.

But understanding the use of violence is vital to understand how the suffragettes were aiming to change women's lives – and smash

---

* Richardson later became head of the women's section of the British Union of Fascists. She left after realising the BUF was not that into women's rights.

the habits of subjugation and subservience drummed into women from birth. In June 1912, Christabel Pankhurst used the *Votes For Women* newspaper to defend militancy on practical and moral grounds. Between equals, she argued, reason was better than force. But men and women were not equals: 'it is a case of one sex being held in bondage by the other sex'. And there was another reason for encouraging violence. 'Militant methods have been good for the souls of women,' she wrote. 'They have swept away the evils of "lady-ism", of timid gentility, of early Victorian effeminacy as distinct from womanliness.' The vote had to be *taken*, not given. Women needed, she said, to shake off their 'slave spirit'. As Emmeline Pankhurst wrote in her autobiography: 'We threw away all our conventional notions of what was "ladylike" and "good form", and we applied to our methods the one test question: will it help?'

There were clear class-based overtones to this fight. When Christabel Pankhurst and Annie Kenney were arrested in 1905, the *Guardian* court report observed: 'If the evidence was to be believed, the defendants' behaviour was such as one was accustomed to attribute to women from the slums. It was regrettable that such a charge should be brought against persons who ought, at least, to be able to control themselves.' Young middle- and upper-class girls were socialised to be docile – not to be difficult – by invoking the spectre of unruly working-class women. 'Without doubt I myself was one of that numerous gang of upper-class leisured spinsters, unemployed, unpropertied, unendowed, uneducated,' Constance Lytton wrote in *Prisons and Prisoners*. For such women, 'a maiming subserviency is so conditional to their very existence that it becomes an aim in itself, an ideal. Driven through life with blinkers on, they are unresentful of the bridle.' Lady Con decided that she would rather risk dying than live the sheltered half-life of a useless spinster.

The use of violence, then, was designed to turn genteel ladies into Difficult Women. The Pankhursts and their followers felt that all the polite, civil – and legal – methods of campaigning for the vote were exhausted. Their success confronts us with a difficult question: does terrorism work? Instinctively, I want to believe that extreme militancy was a dead end, the final spasm of a fracturing movement. But perhaps only the outbreak of the First World War – which prompted Emmeline Pankhurst to suspend the militant campaign – prevented women like the Kenney sisters killing dozens or even hundreds of people. Perhaps it took an epidemic of female violence to shake the government out of its apathy.

In 1924, the social campaigner and suffragist Eleanor Rathbone claimed that militancy 'came within an inch of wrecking the suffrage movement, perhaps for a generation'. The resolutely non-violent Millicent Fawcett took a more nuanced view. The extreme militant phase repelled her so much that she severed ties with the suffragettes, and while followers of the Pankhursts plotted to bomb and burn, Fawcett led 50,000 women on a march to London. Still, though, in her 1924 memoir *What I Remember*, she noted that Annie Kenney's 'perfectly proper and legitimate political question' had been ignored at that 1905 meeting in Manchester. 'We had become quite accustomed to holding magnificent meetings in support of women's franchise with every evidence of public sympathy and support, and to receive from the anti-suffrage press either no notice at all, or only a small paragraph tucked away in an inconspicuous corner.'

The arrest of Kenney and Christabel Pankhurst, however, changed 'the withering contempt of silence' to 'columns of hysterical verbiage directed against our movement'. The suffragettes were easy to condemn, but hard to ignore. Their actions also boosted donations to peaceful, law-abiding suffragist societies. Many of those who claimed to be repelled by the militants were what we would now call 'concern trolls' – pretending to care about the success of a movement they had never supported anyway. In 1906, Fawcett recounted, 'an old friend of mine called out to me across the table at a dinner party that after the outrageous conduct of the militants he would never again do anything in support of women's suffrage. I retorted by asking him what he had done up to that moment.' She got no answer.

*

In the militant phase, while Annie Kenney was interviewing potential arsonists in the flat she shared with her sister Jessie, Constance Lytton was trapped at home. She was supposed to limit her exposure to news for the sake of her heart. When her letters resume, the handwriting is completely transformed, because she had to learn to write again with her left hand. No more looping cursive; the characters are angular and jerky. Her entire memoir, with reflections on the state of the English prison system, was written like this, 'slowly and laboriously', as her sister Betty puts it. (Later, she acquired a typewriter.) The book is extraordinary, telling not just the story of the suffragette prisoners but other women who suffered at the hands of men and a male-dominated legal system. One was abandoned by her lover with a young child, a baby and no means of support. The woman strangled the baby rather than let it starve, and was sent to prison.

Lytton's response to this shocking story was ahead of its time. She proposed a system of child support, paid by the state and reclaimed from fathers. In 1911, she wrote, legitimate children under one year old died at half the rate of illegitimate ones, suggesting that many in the latter group succumbed to disease or starvation. To Lytton, the lack of a child-support law demonstrated how women's interests were ignored by a political system run by men. The woman who killed her baby was released on the same day as her, and Lady Con handed over her address, scribbled on a slip of paper. But she never heard from the mother again. After the first women got the vote, a series of laws and commissions – including the Married Woman (Maintenance) Act 1920 and Finer Report of 1974 – helped to create the modern concept of 'child support'.

During the same jail sentence, Lytton saw an activist from the Women's Freedom League, Mrs Macdonald, slip and break her leg.

The prison authorities carried Macdonald back to her cell, refusing to let her see a doctor and have the limb reset immediately – a decision which left her with a permanently shortened leg. For years afterwards, Lytton campaigned for proper compensation for this injury. On the way to Walton Prison, she sat with a prostitute, shivering in a thin dress and fake fur boa. But where was the other half of the transaction, the man who paid for sex, she wondered? Certainly not in prison. Everywhere she looked, Lytton saw women being unfairly punished in a world designed by men.

Prisons and Prisoners was released in 1914, while the campaign for the vote was still not yet won, and so it reads as polemic. Lytton knew she had to take control of the narrative: the government was still happy to smear her as a fantasist, or bury her story completely. By then, it had abandoned force-feeding as a policy. Instead, it played 'cat and mouse' with hunger strikers.

Annie Kenney was soon caught up in this game – and she played it far better than the hapless officials she was pitted against. She went to recuperate between prison sentences at the home of a painter called Marie Brackenbury. It was soon nicknamed the 'Mouse Castle'. The suffragettes often refused to hand themselves in once their recovery leave from prison expired. They became outlaws, elusive and thrilling figures who drew huge crowds when they appeared in public. Kenney once disguised herself as an old lady to sneak out of the Mouse Castle without being arrested. 'I looked at myself in the glass,' she wrote in her memoir. 'I was no longer Annie Kenney – I was Annie Kenney's grandmother!' Another time, to avoid the policemen waiting outside, she hid in a hamper and had herself delivered to a meeting. She also claimed to have escaped the Mouse Castle dressed in a black bathing suit, black stockings on her arms and legs, and a black veil with eyeholes. 'I just looked like the Black Cat of the pantomime.'

Newspapers found these stories irresistible. In one picture from 1909, the Australian campaigner Muriel Matters poses in a basket hung below an airship, from which she planned to scatter Votes for Women leaflets across London. A year earlier, Flora Drummond had hired a boat so she could shout at MPs on the parliamentary terrace from the River Thames. In 1911, the suffragettes disrupted the census, reasoning that if women didn't count, they shouldn't agree to be counted. Emily Davison hid in a cupboard in Parliament so she could give her address as 'the House of Commons'.* Others went roller-skating all night at a rink near the WSPU headquarters in Aldwych, so their location could not be recorded at all. For all the censorious thundering which accompanied such spectacles, young women across Britain, trussed up in corsets and heavy skirts, must have seen the pictures and thought: *that looks like fun.*

*

The start of the First World War interrupted the suffragette movement. As Emmeline Pankhurst suspended militancy, the government released all WSPU members from prison. But the issue was not forgotten. The Speaker of the House of Commons, James Lowther, had come round to female suffrage after years of protests in Parliament. In late 1916, he began to hold twice-weekly meetings with MPs and peers on electoral reform. They realised that holding the next general election under the old rules – which would have excluded many soldiers from voting, because they were under thirty or did not own property – would be incredibly controversial. It was time to overhaul the voting registers. The 'Speaker's Conference' ruled that the vote should be extended to men of all ages, and to female property owners over the age of thirty. Given the number of deaths in the Great War, truly universal suffrage would have meant female voters outnumbered male ones.

The suffragist leader Millicent Fawcett led a delegation of women

* During his time as a Labour MP, Tony Benn snuck in and put a plaque there, dedicated to her. You can see it there today, but you have to shut yourself in the cupboard to do so.

war workers to the prime minister backing the idea in March 1917. 'We would greatly prefer an imperfect scheme that can pass to the most perfect scheme in the world that could not pass,' she said. Emmeline Pankhurst also spoke at the meeting, saying that she wanted female suffrage 'with as little disputes and as little difference as possible'. Although hoary old dinosaurs tried to introduce wrecking amendments until the bitter end, the legislation expanding the voting rolls received royal assent on 6 February 1918. Fawcett and Pankhurst had been right to accept the compromise. Just as civil partnerships led to gay marriage, so partial votes for women led to truly universal suffrage in 1928.

My time in the archives helped me understand a nagging question about the suffragettes: why does it feel like they disappeared? Even the Pankhursts failed to impose themselves on British public life in any great way after 1918, although Emmeline unsuccessfully stood for Parliament several times. These women had suffered force-feeding, imprisonment, sexual assault and surveillance by the British state, then lived through one of the most bloody, wasteful wars ever fought. Oh, and there was the small matter of the Spanish flu, which killed 228,000 people in Britain. It's a miracle the country didn't descend into anarchy. In the 1920s, feminist campaigning continued on birth control, divorce reform and other issues, but many of the suffragettes were knackered.

Annie Kenney said she left the movement 'as I joined it, penniless'. She lived in St Leonards with her fellow suffragette Grace Roe, and studied theosophy, a quasi-religious mystic tradition. After taking part in Christabel Pankhurst's unsuccessful attempt to run for Parliament in Smethwick in 1918, she faded from public life. That year, while staying at a hotel on the Isle of Arran, she met James Taylor. They married on 24 April 1920, with the bride given away by her brother Reginald. She suffered from undiagnosed diabetes, leading her to gain weight. The close network forged during the militant years dissolved.

For Constance Lytton, too, there was no question of any more campaigning. She was too ill to attend a suffrage celebration in the Albert Hall in 1918, though she desperately wanted to go. She did what she could, however, lending her name to a 'Mother's Clinic' set up near Holloway Prison by a fellow suffrage campaigner called Marie Stopes. She and Annie lost touch during the war, but she wrote in 1920 to congratulate her friend on her marriage and to ask her to visit. Like many of the other suffragettes, she had trouble adjusting to calling her friend Mrs Taylor – after all, several couples from the WSPU days had taken each other's surnames, such as Frederick Lawrence and Emmeline Pethick, who became the Pethick Lawrences.* Similarly, many of Christabel's letters are addressed to 'Annie Kenney Taylor' or 'A. K. Taylor'. It feels as if she didn't want Annie's *nom de guerre* to be lost. And when Betty Balfour wrote to Kenney after her marriage, the letter begins: 'My dear Mrs Taylor, (I should like to call you Annie Kenney)'.

In July 1920, Lytton sent Annie a brooch of white sapphires, saying that although it was not worth much, it had sentimental value because she 'always wore it above my hunger strike medal'. She ended with a touching postscript, acknowledging Annie's pregnancy: 'Oh! How happy I am to think you have already a secret! The book will be . . . better if it waits for that.' The baby, christened Warwick, was born on 4 February 1921 by Caesarean section. Annie was forty-one. She had always believed that motherhood was part of a woman's calling, and now made her only child the centre of her life.

In the years after the war, Constance Lytton began to feel slightly better: the result, she told Annie's sister Jessie, of visiting a physiotherapist. 'It seems like a miracle after being for ten years ½

---

* To hyphenate or not to hyphenate? Emmeline used the unhyphenated form in her letters. But, ludicrously, peers can have only one-word names in their titles, so when Fred was ennobled he became Baron Pethwick-Lawrence. (This is why Andrew Lloyd Webber is Lord Lloyd-Webber.)

dead.' However, her heart was still enlarged. Once again, she tried to live independently, moving out of the family home and renting a flat in Paddington. She died there at 4 p.m. on Tuesday in Whitsun week, 22 May 1923. She was fifty-four years old.

As with Emily Davison, her suffragette comrades saw Lytton as a martyr. She might not have given her life in one eye-catching act, but she sacrificed her health to show the world how the British state was treating the difficult, demanding women who campaigned for the vote. At Lady Con's funeral, Emmeline Pethick Lawrence placed a palm leaf on her casket. Alongside it was a note which read: 'Dearest Comrade, you live always in the hearts of those who love you and you live forever in the future race which inherits the new freedom you gave your life to win.'

*

Annie Kenney outlived her friend by thirty years. As time went on, she and her family became resentful of the way she was written out of the suffragette story by its louder, more privileged members. 'Just as the coral reef is the work of millions of polypi, so the structure of our Movement was the work of thousands of women, who laboured, silently, alone, and unacknowledged,' she had written in 1924. But later she began to wonder why the histories gave the Pankhursts all the credit, while she was reduced down to a 'mill girl'. After all, when Christabel Pankhurst had been forced to escape to France, she had run the WSPU.

She was egged on in her grievance by Christabel, who had moved to America and thrown herself into religion. 'My only consolation is the thought that what is now happening in the world corresponds to the fore-warnings of the prophecies in the Bible,' reads a typically apocalyptic sentiment crammed tight on to airmail paper. 'It seems a strange thing that when Annie is ever mentioned by Sylvia and other people in connection with the Suffrage campaign one would think that the only meritorious thing Annie had ever done in her life was work in a cotton factory!' wrote Annie's sister Jessie to Christabel in 1935. 'Now Christabel, you know Sylvia – and I know Sylvia. I know as you know her consuming jealousy of you and other suffragettes, especially Annie.'

Christabel encouraged this narrative, writing with careless snobbishness to Jessie in 1957: 'People might suppose that Annie lived in her working dress, whereas I never once saw her in it, and she and all of you were nicely dressed like everyone else out of working hours. Moreover, as I always say you Kenneys were not typical factory people. It would be very well for the country if they were all like you . . . but that unfortunately is not the case.'

Inevitably, Annie Kenney's relationship with the Pethick Lawrences was coloured by the different directions their lives took after the First World War. Fred Pethick Lawrence became an MP for Leicester West, financial secretary to the Treasury, and leader of the opposition to the wartime coalition. He was made a peer and was involved in negotiating independence for India. Annie, meanwhile, lived a simple life in Letchworth.

The rich couple seem to have been aware of this; their letters often contained a stamped addressed envelope, saving Annie the cost of replying. When Fred Pethick Lawrence asked for Annie's contribution to some articles Emmeline was writing for the *Sunday Graphic*, he gently suggested that Annie was well aware of the propaganda value she had to the movement. 'We are afraid that we do not see eye-to-eye with you over all this,' he wrote. 'We do not think you should feel so sensitive about your background. I glory in the fact that my grandfather was a carpenter . . . It is of course an essential part of the story that women of all classes were in the movement, and that while Lady Constance represented the nobility, you in your turn regarded yourself as representing working women.' Still, he did not offer to pay her for contributing to the piece.

A radio play written in the early 1950s, *The Women's Rebellion*, brought matters to a head. Annie, now past seventy, was not sent the script by the producers, who did not know she was still alive. According to letters written by her son Warwick Kenney Taylor to various BBC managers and the scriptwriter Jill Craigie, she was heartbroken by her depiction as a lower-class clod with a broad accent. 'I feel it is high time that the exploitation of the "stunt" value of my mother as a "mill girl" was finished,' he wrote to BBC controller Donald Stephenson. The BBC promised not to broadcast the play again, and Craigie vowed to stay away from the subject, telling Warwick, 'there are so many people and conflicting interests that one would spend more time in dealing with this than in the actual writing'.

The deep and unanswerable question in all this was how much Annie Kenney herself felt this way – and how much were others being indignant on her behalf. In her papers at the University of East Anglia, there is a signed note in shaky writing which reads: 'I, Mrs Ann Taylor, formeley [sic] Miss Annie Kenney, by reason of ill health, do hearby [sic] vent on my son Warwick Kenney Taylor power to act on my behalf in all matters connected with the public presentation of my name or the part I personally played in the suffragette movement.'

Flicking through the loose papers, there was another intriguing discovery. Uncatalogued, unsigned, the sheet of paper started: 'This is very private . . . only for the family or for anyone who would write a proper life of Annie.' The contents were as inflammatory as that covering letter promised, although I couldn't match the handwriting to any of the brown folders before me. Was this by Jessie? Or Annie's daughter-in-law – Warwick's wife? 'When Annie first met the Pethick-Lawrences they said the most flattering things about her,' it read. 'After they left the movement, it seem their pens cannot move to say anything in their books worth reading about Annie.' According to the letter-writer, this was their revenge on Annie for siding with Christabel Pankhurst against them. Worse, the Pethick Lawrences were now demanding that Annie help them with articles

Emmeline was writing for a newspaper, even though they had three secretaries of their own. 'And Annie who has no servant, has to do her own housework, and myself still having to look after my own living must set to and do this for them, because they were either insincere about Annie before they left the Movement, or because they have never forgiven her for not going with them. This is a thing to remember in all this tangled web of relationships.'

The bitterness felt horribly familiar from my own time in the feminist trenches. Even the suffragettes found the memory of their great triumph soured by personality clashes. Still, the letter highlighted quite how improbable their success was. For just over a decade, the campaign had brought together dozens of Difficult Women, from fishwives to aristocrats, mill girls to Indian princesses. Their alliance had held together long enough to change women's lives for ever, by giving them the vote – and a voice. Politics would now have to respond to women's concerns, or face their disapproval at the ballot box.

Today, Parliament is still dominated by men. Only a third of MPs elected in 2017 were female, and women make up just a quarter of the House of Lords. There are still ninety-two hereditary peers in the Lords – bonkers enough by itself – and most of their titles are passed down to the eldest son rather than eldest child. So ninety-one of those remaining peers are male – meaning that institutionalised sexism remains in Parliament itself.*

That male dominance makes female MPs' lives harder. In 2010, a newly elected Stella Creasy was stopped by a man from getting into the lift reserved for MPs in the Commons. He couldn't believe that she was also an MP. In 2017, the *Daily Mail* covered a meeting between the prime minister Theresa May and the Scottish first minister Nicola Sturgeon with the front-page headline: 'Never mind

---

* In 2018, five peers' daughters took the government to the European Court of Human Rights to challenge the principle of primogeniture, where men inherit first.

Brexit, who won Legs-it?' Women still make up a minority of the lobby journalists who work in Westminster. It took until 2018 for the first statue of a woman to join Gandhi, Churchill and nine other men on Parliament Square. It was of the suffragist Millicent Fawcett, who was depicted holding a sign with her words on the death of the suffragette Emily Davison: 'Courage calls to courage everywhere.'

The picture is not all grim. Parliament now has a nursery, new parents can vote by proxy, and sitting hours have been reformed to make them more family-friendly. Women can now vote in every country in the world – although it took Switzerland until 1971 to make that happen.* The British suffragettes were part of a long, rolling but ultimately unstoppable wave which turned women into a political force. Once they were established as independent citizens in the public realm, women were able to agitate for greater private freedoms – such as access to birth control.

Annie Kenney died on 9 July 1953, aged seventy-three. Her burial certificate records her name as 'Ann Taylor'. As I walked away from the library, I felt sad about that final erasure. But ultimately, does it matter? Ann Taylor might be buried, but the memory of Annie Kenney lives on. She was part of an extraordinary generation – including our next Difficult Woman, who supported the suffrage movement . . . in between cataloguing the tenderness of her breasts and having orgasms through the power of thought alone.

Are you ready? Let's talk about sex.

---

* Technically, women can't vote in Vatican City. But then again, no one except cardinals can vote in Vatican City.

3. SEX

On the day when it will be possible for woman to love not in her weakness but in strength, not to escape herself but to find herself, not to abase herself but to assert herself – on that day love will become for her, as for man, a source of life and not of mortal danger.

Simone de Beauvoir, *The Second Sex*

'As an erotic sensation, penetration of the vagina by the penis can leave a lot to be desired,' write Anna Coote and Beatrix Campbell in *Sweet Freedom*, an account of the women's lib movement. 'In other fields of market research, similar data about the extent of customer dissatisfaction might have led to withdrawal of the product.' The authors marvelled that, at the end of the Swinging Sixties, so many women were still bored in bed. Perhaps they only reached orgasm through masturbation. Perhaps they hated their bodies so much they couldn't enjoy sex. 'Everybody was supposed to be having such a terrific time and yet . . . fucking was a let-down.'

Of all of feminism's unfinished revolutions, the right to good sex is among the most intractable.* You can campaign for legal reforms – like the right to vote – through protest marches, civil disobedience, petitions and newspaper columns. But so much of feminism is bound up with our unruly female bodies, and with the messy realm of personal relationships. These fights are difficult for other reasons. Despite the best efforts of exhibitionists and swingers, most sex happens between two people, in private. The boom in online porn might have alerted us to the staggering breadth of human sexual activity, but it has not led to a new era of openness. Instead, the proliferation of 'tube' (aggregator) sites means that audiences see endless iterations of narrow sexual scripts and an equally narrow range of bodies. In Britain, school sex education is still woefully poor. Teachers are still terrified to talk about pleasure. We know that women suffer

* This chapter focuses on straight relationships. Any lesbians or bisexual women feeling left out: the 'Love' chapter is for you.

from an 'orgasm gap'. Only 65 per cent of straight women 'usually or always' climax during sex, the Kinsey Institute found, compared with 95 per cent of straight men. We have become more liberal, but not more satisfied. And the Permissive Era brought new pressures: Coote and Campbell wrote that women were pressured to *'do it*, and impose no conditions. The more they did it, the more "liberated" they were deemed to be.'

Today, that ideology persists. Young women worry about being called frigid, and young men feel pressured to be 'up for it' at all times. Having a low sex drive is seen as uncool, even close to a moral failing. Teenagers on Tumblr have invented words like 'demisexual' (attracted only to people you're in love with) or 'sapiosexual' (attracted only to intelligent people) to excuse themselves from the obligation to fancy everyone. The permissive society is OK with people having as much sex as they want, with whoever they want, but feels free to look down on anyone 'saving themselves for marriage'. It feels oddly daring to say that, as a woman, you are more likely to have good sex with someone you respect and can talk honestly with, which rules out most one-night stands.

Decades after the pill reliably separated sex from reproduction, too many of us still aren't getting what we want. So why isn't sex working for women? The answer begins a century ago.

*

What is sex? It sounds like a trick question. In the 1990s, after it was discovered that Bill Clinton was getting blow jobs in the Oval Office, he infamously claimed: 'I did not have sexual relations with that woman.' Was he lying? It depended on your definition of 'sexual relations'. A survey found that only 40 per cent of college students thought oral sex 'counted'. That is not surprising, because our law regards vaginal penetration by a penis as a special category of sex, both in divorce cases (where it alone counts as adultery) and rape (which English law distinguishes from 'assault by penetration' with any other object).

In the Britain of the 1910s, however, the question was even more urgent. *What is sex?* For thousands of people, the basic mechanisms of intercourse were a mystery. Without any clue how conception worked, women were powerless to prevent it.

Not Marie Stopes, though. Born in 1880, she was raised by parents who were happy to educate their daughter, and she gained a degree and then a doctorate in botany. By the end of 1910, she had turned thirty – without a husband or children. This did not bother her too much, because she believed that intellectual, middle-class women were late sexual developers, but she was still on the lookout for a likely contender. On Boxing Day 1910, she found one: a Canadian geneticist called Reginald Ruggles Gates, two years her junior. By New Year's Eve, they were engaged. By March, they were married.

When Gates came to live with Stopes and her sister in her house in Hampstead, he received a series of shocks. The first was that Marie hated housework and expected her husband to share the load. She announced she would be keeping her name. She was, somewhat presumptuously, already working on a book about love and marriage, which was not going well. She soon received a letter from her friend, the novelist Maurice Hewlett, advising her that an early version was . . . well, let's hand over to diplomatic Maurice. 'It is a kind of first sketch of a thing which, when complete, might be romantic, poetical, philosophical . . . The verses are not really part of the book.' A sex manual with *poetry* ? The horror, the horror.

Stopes duly burned much of the manuscript and started again. This time, the writing was better, although her marriage was already getting worse. 'The sex life of Dr Stopes and Dr Gates was a complete flop,' writes her biographer June Rose. 'In public, he embarrassed her by fondling and caressing her, even putting his hand in her dress.' Although Gates pawed her in public, Stopes claimed later that he could not maintain an erection. He was also jealous of her success, unimpressed by her bluestocking friends, and isolated as a foreigner in London. He became possessive.

In December 1912, Marie met fifty-four-year-old Aylmer Maude, a biographer of Tolstoy, who was himself trapped in a sexually unsatisfying marriage. After two months of flirting and taking him to dances, she moved him into the house in Hampstead, with her husband's (perhaps unwitting) blessing. She started to write Maude letters saying that Gates was a 'spoilt and undeveloped child' and complaining about their lack of intimacy.

A divorce would have been difficult, unless she confessed to adultery, making her the one at fault. (As a woman, if she wanted to be seen as the wronged partner in a divorce case, she would have needed to prove that Gates cheated on her *and* committed another marital offence, such as cruelty.) An annulment, which would declare the marriage had never been legally valid, would be easier. The way she told the story later, her marital problems drove her to read medical treatises in the 'cupboard' – the restricted-access section of obscene books – at the British Museum. It was only then, she claimed, that she realised that they hadn't really been having sex. Gates was impotent, 'so limp as he struggled to enter that he pushed it in with his fingers'. That description, when recounted to a court, was enough to get her marriage annulled.

By early 1914, her personal life was a mess. In May, as the suffragettes marched on Buckingham Palace, she packed up her things and moved out of the house in Hampstead. She went to live with friends, then pitched a tent alongside the coast in Northumberland for the summer. Gates eventually got the hint, left the house and sailed back to Canada.

As her marriage was disintegrating, Stopes had begun to keep a sex diary – or as she called it, a 'Tabulation of Symptoms of Sexual Excitement in Solitude'. Written in her neat longhand, the word 'solitude' is double-underlined. 'The many tendernesses and excitements that may occur when one is with a man in partial or complete sexual embrace are not included in this scheme,' she noted, briskly. She recorded days where she felt tired and overworked, although she still managed 'one or two orgasms during these days, but they were clearly induced by thought'.

Over the course of a month, her breasts had quite the thrill ride. Their sensitiveness varied; at one point she felt 'so that one is conscious of their shape', at another 'they feel definitely heavy and as if straining at a leash'. Later, she noted that 'the nipples are responsively sensitive if touched', finishing the month with the faintly incredulous 'they are actually larger than usual'. Her 'sexual parts', meanwhile, variously 'throb slightly', 'throb definitely when stirred by memory' and 'force one to touch them until orgasm occurs'. All of this was tabulated and cross-referenced with her menstrual cycle.*

Unfortunately for Marie Stopes, the small matter of the First World War damaged her efforts to share this knowledge with the world. She spent the war years in a whirlwind of writing: pamphlets, plays, articles, novel drafts, letters to Aylmer Maude. Her fiction was, and I really can't stress this enough, absolutely dire. I tried to read *Our Ostriches*, her 1923 play performed at the Royal Court, and had to give up. It was simply unbearable. After reading another of Stopes's scripts, George Bernard Shaw wrote to her: 'Short of rewriting this play, I can do no more with it than cut 20 pages just to shew [*sic*] you how you should cut the rest. You haven't used your brains one bit.' I find it impressive and horrifying in equal measure that Marie kept plugging on regardless.

Stopes also worked on her sex manual, *Married Love*. She was not a woman to let her personal tragedy go to waste. She knew that the story of an innocent, middle-class graduate 'virgin wife' helplessly watching her marriage fail was irresistible. In the preface to

* The current generation of women, with access to period trackers, is probably the first since Marie Stopes to have such a keen understanding of why their tits hurt and they just cried over a video of a Labrador making friends with a budgie.

Married Love, she wrote that she had 'paid such a terrible price for sex-ignorance that I feel that knowledge gained at such cost should be placed at the service of humanity'. She began to send the manuscript to friends. One suggested that it should be published in French, restricting its readership to the middle and upper classes, so she would be less likely to be prosecuted for indecency. But Marie was determined that her message should reach as wide an audience as possible.

Other correspondents gave a different reason against publishing the book. Keeping women in the dark would preserve their essential innocence (read: ignorance) of the 'nasty' aspects of life. The idea that a woman might have desires – needs – of her own was alarming to them. After all, a sexually knowledgeable, and therefore sexually demanding, woman is definitely a Difficult Woman. 'Marie dismissed the idea that "nice" women have no spontaneous sexual impulses,' writes June Rose. Her research 'led women to understand that they had a right to sexual impulses and need not feel ashamed of them'.

Eventually, *Married Love* found its way into the hands of the philanthropist Humphrey Roe, then a lieutenant in the Royal Flying Corps. He agreed to donate £200 anonymously to support its publication. The book came out on 26 March 1918, a day that Marie spent visiting Humphrey in hospital. His plane had crash-landed after a bombing raid on the Western Front and he had been sent home to England. Their courtship was even quicker than her pursuit of Reginald Ruggles Gates. Within weeks they were deciding the name of their first (as yet unconceived) child, as Marie had declared that she wanted to marry and get pregnant before Roe returned to the battlefield. At that point, he confessed that he was already engaged. The jilted fiancée turned up at Marie's house and demanded that the new couple wait six months before she would break off the engagement and allow them to marry.

The thought of any delay irritated Stopes. At thirty-seven, she felt that her chances of having a baby were slipping away from her.

Married Love, by contrast, was a roaring success, selling 2,000 copies in its first fortnight on sale.

*

The book could not have come at a better time. The First World War brought new freedoms for British women as they moved into the workplace and began to mix socially with men. The spectre of so many deaths at the front seems to have loosened the taboo on pre-marital sex.

Marie Stopes's sexual revolution accompanied an economic one, a pattern which was repeated in the 1970s. In *Sweet Freedom*, Anna Coote and Beatrix Campbell recount asking women what drew them to feminism: 'We were struck by how many mentioned in almost the same breath the Ford strike and a paper written by an American, Anne Koedt.' The 1968 Ford strike at Dagenham saw female machinists walk out of the factory, angry that their jobs were classified as less skilled than male roles. It was a radicalising moment in public life. The paper by Anne Koedt, by contrast, offered a private revolution. It was called 'the myth of the vaginal orgasm'.

To understand the impact Koedt's work had, we have to rewind to the start of the twentieth century. In 1905, Sigmund Freud had outlined a model of female sexual development which ran like this. In girls, sexual arousal depends on the clitoris, which is stuffed full of nerve endings, but a grown woman's pleasure should instead derive from the vagina. And what's a vagina for? The clue is in the Latin name, which means 'sheath for a sword'. So while foolish little girls fixated on the body part which was obviously capable of producing orgasms, the mark of a sophisticated adult woman was instead to derive pleasure from heterosexual intercourse. 'With the change to femininity,' Freud wrote, 'the clitoris should wholly or in part hand over its sensitivity, and at the same time its importance, to the vagina.'

Unfortunately, the whole premise was garbage. The inside of the vagina has very few nerve endings compared with the clitoris. The

'G spot' is more elusive than the Loch Ness Monster.* Only 30 per cent of women orgasm reliably through penetration alone, without added clitoral stimulation. Freud's theory led to decades of women feeling like failures. A sexual script where penetration was supposed to lead inexorably to climax left them wondering what was wrong with their bodies. For some writers, even giving nature a helping hand, as it were, was cheating. 'Consider the woman who plays with her clitoris during the act of coition,' wrote the philosopher Roger Scruton in 1986. 'Such a person affronts her lover with the obscene display of her body and in perceiving her thus, the lover perceives his own irrelevance. She becomes disgusting to him, and his desire may be extinguished.' Got that, ladies? Don't try to have an orgasm, for heaven's sake. It will make him feel bad.

Aha, I know what you're thinking. What if you have penetrative sex and the penis just sort of accidentally bumps the clitoris a bit? Might that not be the answer we've all been looking for? Unfortunately not. For many women, the clitoris is simply too far from the entrance of the vagina to be stimulated as a side effect of penetration. We have a French princess, of all people, to thank for this useful bit of knowledge. Marie Bonaparte was the great-grand-niece of Napoleon and a friend and patient of Sigmund Freud. As a child, she had been caught masturbating by her nurse, who told her that the practice would kill her and made her wear a nightgown with drawstrings at the bottom. Banned from studying for the baccalaureate because she was a girl, Marie spent the rest of her life conducting independent research into sexuality. One of her subjects was herself. Having given up clitoral masturbation, she discovered that she couldn't come from sex in the missionary position with her

---

* The name comes from the gynaecologist Ernst Gräfenberg, although it was coined by a woman, Beverly Whipple. In fact it's amazing how many parts of the female genitalia are named after men: Gabriele Falloppio got the tubes, Caspar Bartholin the lubricating glands, and James Douglas got the pouch between the rectum and the uterus, which frankly he is welcome to.

(admittedly gay) husband, or any of her lovers.* So she decided to test her pet theory. She measured the genitals of 243 women and published the results in an academic journal in 1924, entitled 'Notes on the Anatomical Causes of Frigidity in Women'. Around a fifth of her sample were *téléclitoridienne*, 'women with distant clitorises' more than 2.5 cm from the urethra. These women found it extremely difficult to orgasm from penetration alone. Her measurements have been validated by later research: if your clitoris and vagina are more than a thumb's width apart, you will struggle to climax purely from intercourse. Marie Bonaparte had a drastic solution. In 1927, she had her clitoris surgically moved closer to her urethra by asking a surgeon in Vienna to cut the ligaments which held it in place. She tried again in May 1930 and January 1931. It didn't work.

I read about Marie Bonaparte in Mary Roach's history of sex research, *Bonk*. The way Roach tells the story, it's very funny. But it's also sad. First, Bonaparte assumed that there was something wrong with *her*, not with how she was having sex. She spent years trying to fit the Freudian idea of 'mature' female sexuality, trying to climax through intercourse alone. In the end, she had surgery to correct a problem that didn't exist, all to uphold a model of sexual pleasure which centred men and the Great Almighty Cock. An easier option would have been to try a few different positions, such as her on top, or even just to tell the men in her life to be more creative.

As a side note, in the 1940s Bonaparte interviewed two women in Egypt who had undergone female genital mutilation because their societies believed it would help women 'graduate' to vaginal pleasure. However, they had not experienced some magical conversion, as Freud suggested might happen. 'Both women – though they did report having orgasms from intercourse – still masturbated clitorally, on their scars,' writes Roach.

---

* On their wedding night, her husband said: 'I hate it as much as you do. But we must do it if we want children.' Now that's foreplay.

Swirling around all this is a male fear of redundancy and failure. If penises are . . . not irrelevant, exactly, but secondary to women's sexual pleasure, that presents a challenge to our conventional idea of what 'sex' is. It should also provoke compassion for men trying to prove their virility in the face of impossible odds: they aren't bad at sex because their partners don't come through penetration; they just need to expand their sexual vocabulary. This was Anne Koedt's mission in the 1970s. She wanted couples to abandon 'normal' ideas of sex – based around reproduction and the primary importance of the penis – and find out what worked for both of them. Why was the 'missionary' position seen as the default, when it offered so little clitoral stimulation to women? 'We must begin to demand that if a certain sexual position now defined as "standard" is not mutually conducive to orgasm, then it should no longer be so defined,' she wrote. 'Men also seem suspiciously aware of the clitoral powers during "foreplay", when they want to arouse women and produce the necessary lubrication for penetration. Foreplay is a concept created for male purposes, but works to the disadvantage of many women, since as soon as the woman is aroused the man changes to vaginal stimulation, leaving her both aroused and unsatisfied.'

Of course, it can be hard to find out whether or not sex is working for women, for one simple reason. Sometimes, we lie.

*

I am one of those liars. Like many women I know, I have faked dozens of orgasms. I have agonised about admitting this in print. *Oh, sorry, we thought you were a Serious Person. Now we see you're a Sex Person.* Let's quietly move this book from the 'history' section – alongside the wars and kings – to somewhere it will feel more at home. Lifestyle? Self-help?

Feminism deals with our most intimate experiences – sex, childbirth, housework, family – as well as our public ones. That brings its own difficulties. Accounts of men's lives are seen as containing universal truths, while women's lives are niche, specialist subjects. Try to imagine the plays of Arthur Miller, say, with female protagonists. Would the troubles of a 'Jane Proctor' or 'Lily Loman' have the same grandeur? That's one reason literature and art must encompass women's voices and experiences. We cannot just be seen from the outside. We have to speak in our own right. We have to be protagonists, in literature and in our own lives. We can't be reduced to planets orbiting the great male sun. 'One of the elements of male chauvinism is the refusal or inability to see women as total, separate human beings,' wrote Anne Koedt. 'Rather, men have chosen to define women only in terms of how they benefited men's lives.'

So yes, it's important to tell you that I have been a faker. Because what the hell? I was a fraud: not just to my partners, but to myself and to the readers of my articles on feminism. How can you claim to be an empowered, independent woman if you can't be honest with the person closest to you? But it wasn't just me. The blame also rests with the male-centred ideas of sex that surrounded me as I grew up.

In February 2018, I went to talk to an Oxford college feminist society. What did these young, highly educated women (and a handful of brave men) want to talk about? It turned out many of them had read the same article about 'the female price of male pleasure'. In it, Lili Loofbourow asked whether men and women were using the same term – 'bad sex' – to mean different things. She suggested that for men, 'good sex' generally meant an orgasm and 'bad sex' meant the absence of one. 'But when most women talk about "bad sex", they tend to mean coercion, or emotional discomfort or, even more commonly, *physical pain*.' Around 30 per cent of women reported pain from vaginal intercourse, she noted, and 72 per cent from anal sex. Something clicked for me. My female friends often talked about stopping sex because it hurt – they weren't sufficiently aroused, they had just removed a tampon, they had recently given birth, they were getting towards menopause. Were men having all these problems too, or was their blunt instrument ... well, a blunt instrument?

Loofbourow suggested that because women generally expected less from sex, their standards for what counted as a good time were lower. We are more easily pleased, because we are used to not being pleased at all. And while there are 2,000 clinical trials studying erectile dysfunction on the research database PubMed, there is much less research on female sexual problems. These are seen as more difficult to understand – and perhaps less lucrative to address.

The young women at Oxford asked me, earnestly, whether 'bad sex is a feminist issue'. My answer was yes. Almost anything is a feminist issue when the world is so deeply structured around sex differences. But that doesn't make this all men's fault. When I mentioned my fakery count to a male friend, he asked me: 'Don't you get performance anxiety if you fake an orgasm?' I'd laughed, and then blushed, because he'd got it exactly the wrong way round. By and large, I think, straight women fake orgasms *because* they have performance anxiety. They fake orgasms with nice guys, guys they like, guys they think would want them to 'have a good time'. They don't feel confident enough to explain that no, *that* isn't working, or – sorry, this isn't going to happen as a happy by-product of penetration. (Shout-out to the *téléclitoridiennes*.) They don't want to bore their partner. They are worried about being, in Caitlin Moran's glorious phrase, a 'hand-wearier'. All this springs from a belief that their pleasure is secondary, a bonus, not a shared primary objective of a sexual encounter with a man. They don't want to be too demanding, too difficult – and they don't want to leave their partner feeling hurt or diminished. Nice girls don't ask for too much.

During sex, women are too often trying to give pleasure without expecting to receive it. That's not helped by sexual scripts which come from porn, and from Hollywood. Ninety-four per cent of film directors are men, and perhaps as a result, movies push what Dr Jen Gunter called 'the three-strokes-of-penetration-bite-your-lip-arch-the-back-and-moan routine'. As a gynaecologist, once she started to see how sex is influenced by sexism, she couldn't stop. 'Consider vaginal discharge,' she wrote in the *New York Times*. 'Even though urinary incontinence is far more common a problem, it's discharge that brings women to the office in tears . . . One or two millilitres of normal discharge – a sign of a healthy vagina, and production during intercourse is unquestionably a good thing – is somehow taboo, while men's ejaculate, which comes out of the very tube from which they also urinate, is often glorified, especially in pornography.' Gunter also saw patients who fretted about whether they were too 'loose', or if their inner labia were too big. Brace yourself for something you would never know from watching porn: in 50 per cent of women, the inner labia protrude beyond the outer ones.

In 2005, five female scientists wrote a paper which I have begun to brandish at parties, explaining why I don't get invited to parties. 'There are surprisingly few descriptions of normal female genitalia in the medical literature,' explained Jillian Lloyd, Naomi S. Crouch, Catherine L. Minto, Lih-Mei Liao and Sarah M. Creighton in the obstetrics and gynaecology journal *BJOG*. 'In contrast, measurements for male genitals are widely available and were published as early as 1899.' And so they replicated the work of Marie Bonaparte eight decades earlier, measuring the genitals of fifty women. Their subjects had an average age of thirty-five. Some had no children; some had never had sex. The majority were white, but the study included black, Asian and mixed-race women too.

What they found was astonishing. Clitoris size ranged between 5–35 mm – from the size of a pea to the width of a passport photo. The distance between the clitoris and the urethra was 16–45 mm. The inner labia ranged in length from 2–10 cm, and from 7–50 mm in width. Let me repeat that: some of the women had labia *five times longer* than others. In forty-one of the women, the genitals were darker than the surrounding skin. The accompanying photographs are a trip. You might struggle to pick a particular penis out of a line-up, but the differences between women are obvious. Some had tiny strips of inner labia, others had full-on flower petals. And yet, the researchers noted, this was not reflected in the scientific literature. Surgical guidelines stated that women with inner labia which measured more than 4 cm from base to edge were deemed worthy of corrective surgery. 'However, we found that labia minora dimensions displayed much greater variation,' the researchers wrote. 'None of the women in our study had expressed any personal difficulty or sought cosmetic surgical alteration.'*

The lack of awareness of this natural variation, even among doctors, has unfortunate consequences. Women are requesting labiaplasty – having their labia trimmed – because they conclude from porn and from their partners that their genitals look abnormal, even freakish. That surgery is not 'cosmetic', because the inner labia contribute to sexual stimulation, and reaching orgasm. Jen Gunter was horrified: 'Can you imagine a man getting a penile reduction so that it looked more presentable to his female partner or better in yoga pants?'

*

It took me ten minutes after meeting Lesley Hall to start talking to her about penetration. The archivist is a striking figure, with a streak of neon green in her grey hair. As she led me through to the Wellcome Library in Euston, I told her about the last time I was there, writing about its collection of tattooed human skin. 'Yes,' she replied. 'Henry Wellcome collected what we might technically call . . . some weird shit.'

Hall has been researching the life and work of Marie Stopes for decades. She wrote her PhD thesis on men's letters to the contraceptive pioneer, which are full of their anxieties about premature ejaculation and impotence and mismatched sex drives. When I told

---

* One group of women does sometimes need labial surgery: professional cyclists. Saddles (designed for men) can cause friction, which in turn causes swelling, chafing and fatty tumours called lipoma.

her that my friends were surprised to hear that a significant percentage of women cannot come through penetration, she threw up her hands in exasperation. 'Did Alfred Kinsey die in vain?'

Kinsey was, of course, one of the most influential sex researchers of the twentieth century. A biologist by training, he started his research on gall wasps.* Moving on to human subjects, he conducted hundreds of confidential interviews, discovering that masturbation, premarital sex and affairs were all far more common than previously thought. He created the 'Kinsey scale', presenting sexuality as a spectrum from very straight to very gay. 'The world is not to be divided into sheep and goats,' he said. He also disputed the existence of the vaginal orgasm, calling it a 'biologic impossibility'.

His work had several important conclusions. The data about women's masturbation debunked the idea that they had inherently slower sexual responses than men. The only reason it looked that way was because of 'the ineffectiveness of the usual coital techniques'. In other words, a model of sex that worked far better for men than women – the same problem identified by Marie Bonaparte. 'Many males,' Kinsey wrote, 'basing their concepts on their understanding of coitus and upon their conceit as to the importance of the male genitalia in coitus, imagine that all female masturbation must involve an insertion of fingers or of some other object into the depths of the vagina.' He discovered that it did not. He also questioned the diagnosis of 'frigidity' handed out by psychiatrists, and suggested that most women were capable of orgasm. Most previous sex research, he noted, had been done by men.

Like Marie Stopes's *Married Love,* Kinsey's work was an immediate commercial success. His first volume, *Sexual Behaviour in the Human Male,* sold 200,000 copies in two months. It created a whole discipline: sexology. But his work on the myth of the vaginal orgasm received relatively little attention until Virginia E. Johnson and

* A 2003 play about his life is called *Fucking Wasps,* a title I wholeheartedly applaud.

William H. Masters confirmed many of his findings in the more liberal 1960s. 'One suspects that although many marriage counsellors and sex therapists grasped the implications of the new findings regarding female orgasm, few were prepared to discuss them in print,' wrote Regina Markell Morantz in *American Quarterly* in 1977. 'Kinsey's evidence implied that intercourse was not the most efficient method for women to achieve pleasure. Indeed, his statistics on female homosexuality suggested that lesbians were more likely to achieve orgasm consistently.' It is sometimes said that every generation thinks it has discovered sex. The truth is that every generation seems doomed to discover that conventional ideas about sex are wrong. And then to forget that fact.

None of Kinsey's fine-grained data was available to Marie Stopes in 1918. That's why she had to chart her own sexual responses in such vivid detail. She and Humphrey Roe were married on 16 May 1918, three weeks after he promised his previous fiancée Ethel that he would wait six months to make a decision. His new wife was not a woman who was easily resisted. She asked Aylmer Maude (now sixty and still as enamoured of her as ever) to be a witness to the union. Just as tellingly, he agreed. Maude even gave her away when she insisted on repeating her vows at a church ceremony the next month. A photograph shows Marie striding out of the church with a determined expression, an umbrella held over her head by Roe.

She quickly became pregnant, and instructed Humphrey to remain near her room in the nursing home as she gave birth. His diary records him leaving the room at 5.23 p.m. – fathers were then barred from attending births – followed by Marie's increasing moans and pleas for pain relief. At 11 p.m. on 16 July 1919, he recorded that the doctors had come out of the room. 'They tell me they cannot hear the child's heart.' The baby, a boy Marie called Henry, was born dead an hour and a half later. Marie was furious with how she had been treated by the medical staff. She had wanted to give birth on her knees, allowing gravity to assist the process, but 'was hauled about, my hands and wrists and finally my legs were held, till I felt like a trapped and frenzied creature ... As they allowed me no support, not even the bars at the top and foot of the bed, there was nothing to lever against.'

Her experience was typical of the medicalised world of childbirth in the early and mid-twentieth century. With the laudable aim of reducing the number of dead women and babies, the (male-dominated) medical establishment had decided that there was a correct way to give birth: lying on a bed, on your back. Stopes was angry at being overruled by men who thought they knew better than her. The doctors probably thought she was just being difficult. 'Today the Active Birth Centre promotes a "more natural" posture and Marie could have found midwives and doctors to allow her to give birth the way she chose,' writes her biographer June Rose. 'In her desire to have her child in the age-old kneeling or squatting position, Marie was paradoxically too far ahead of her time.' Women's bodies did not fit the male model, in sex or medicine, and they suffered for it.

After the publication of *Married Love*, Stopes became famous. In 1921, she opened her first Mother's Clinic – the one supported by Lady Constance Lytton – and spread the word about the 'Pro-Race cap', her preferred method of contraception. This was a rubber dome which fitted over the cervix, preventing sperm from reaching the egg. Where she had once condemned the 'lower classes' for being 'thriftless, illiterate and careless', she now agreed with other reformers that access to birth control was a potent way to reduce poverty. The clinic was based in Holloway, North London, then a deprived area. Marie Stopes insisted that it was staffed by women, with nurses on the front line and a female doctor available to see trickier cases. Many patients were reluctant to give their names. There was little coverage in the media.

Not all the reaction to her preaching was positive. One psychiatrist called her work 'practical handbooks of prostitution'. Other readers called it filthy and immoral, worrying that it roused the imagination in ways that God-fearing citizens would not be able to control. But the vast majority of the letters received by Stopes's publisher were positive, even adoring. Forty per cent were from men.

Some of the letters are heartbreaking in their desperation. 'Could you be kind enough to tell me the safest Means for Prevention of Children as my age is 37,' one letter begins. With fourteen children – nine still living – aged between seventeen and six months, the woman had been told that 'I have a very Weak Heart if I have any more it might prove fatal my inside is quite exausted [sic] I have a Prolapsed Womb, it is wicked to bring children into the world to Practicly [sic] starve.' Another woman recounted how her efforts to avoid pregnancy through abstinence were leading her husband to penetrate her anally: 'He says if you won't let me at the front, I will at the back. I don't care which way it is so long as I get satisfied. Well Madam this is very painful to me, also I have wondered if it might be injurious.' To desperate women like this, Marie Stopes sent advice about fitting a contraceptive cap. Then in 1924, after years of advising women how *not* to have babies, Stopes had one of her own: a son, Harry. She was forty-three.

Her views now seem an odd hodgepodge of progressive and reactionary. She was prone to snobbish pronouncements about the working class, yet replied diligently to the semi-illiterate women who wrote to her asking for help. She was a Conservative and a supporter of women's suffrage. She was at ease with casual anti-Semitism, and sent a volume of her poetry to Hitler in 1939 with a fawning cover letter saying 'love is the greatest thing in the world'. *Married Love* did not mention homosexuality, and she once referred to lesbianism as a 'disease'. Stopes also admitted to something which has haunted generations of middle-class feminists: that their freedom depended on domestic help from other women.* She

* My own take: there is nothing wrong with having a cleaner or a nanny as long as those jobs are fairly paid. Historically, they have not been. And if a straight couple

wrote in the *Sunday Chronicle* in 1920 that 'civilisation would fall to pieces' without it.

It can also be hard to separate her opinions from her strategic decisions. *Married Love* carries forewords by a professor and a Jesuit priest to invest it with scientific and moral authority. Stopes was in favour of birth control, but publicly opposed to abortion. During her lifetime, clinics with her name on them did not give advice about terminations. They now do, which makes them controversial. In December 2017, the Marie Stopes Clinic in Belfast closed. It had regularly attracted large protests, and women using the service needed escorts in and out of the buildings. In the five years it operated, its oldest patient was fifty-two and its youngest was thirteen. The teenager had been raped by a relative.

*

Married Love is written in a style that is – there is no other word for it – bonkers. There are acres of purple prose about portals of desire interspersed with the realest of real talk. 'Plucking lavender and violets . . . Then: here's how to stimulate the clitoris,' is how Lesley Hall describes it. The tonal shifts are enough to give you whiplash.

Like her views, Stopes herself was a mass of contradictions. She presented herself as a naive sex-starved wife. In reality she was determined to get her own way. In 1922, her fellow birth-control advocate Stella Browne wrote to Havelock Ellis to say 'it is going to be very difficult for anyone to work with her at all. I can't give you a detailed description of her behaviour at our recent Birth Control Meeting but I assure you it was a pitiful exhibition of temper and insolence and made a most unfortunate general impression. Moreover she seems to be getting quite unbalanced in her egomania and conceit . . . she is making fresh enemies daily.' In her paper

---

both work, why is it deemed to be the female half that's employing the cleaner, anyway?

'Situating Stopes', Hall's own judgement is brisk: 'Marie Stopes did not play nicely with others, failed to give credit where it was due, was unsupportive of other campaigners when they fell foul of the law and officialdom, and was unable to work in harmony or even tactical solidarity with the rest of the movement.'

Many historians now believe that Stopes's great personal tragedy – her sexless marriage to Ruggles – was a lie. June Rose's biography is sceptical. There are surviving letters asking Stopes for birth-control advice during her first marriage, indicating that she was not completely ignorant of the subject. She was also interested in biology from her teens. I suspect poor Reggie did struggle to get it up occasionally, but this was not the only reason their marriage failed. His own testimony remained locked away for decades, but in papers left to the British Library, he claimed that Stopes was 'super-sexed to a degree which was almost pathological'.

The biggest blight on her legacy is her interest in eugenics. Before researching her work, one of the few concrete facts I knew about Marie Stopes was that she tried to forbid her son Harry from marrying a woman who was short-sighted enough to need glasses. That, I thought, went well beyond 'difficult' and straight into 'indefensible'.

In the 1920s and 30s, eugenics was a common interest among intellectuals. In a more paternalistic age, the idea that other people's fertility was the business of an educated elite was seen as a respectable position. There was also a certain naivety about where such ideas would lead before the 1930s, when it became clear that Nazi Germany was sterilising and killing those with learning disabilities, epileptics, schizophrenics, gay men, lesbians and other 'degenerates' as part of its pursuit of an Aryan 'master race'. The regime copied the sterilisation programme from a similar initiative in California.

As a researcher, Lesley Hall does not acquit Stopes of the charge of being a eugenicist – and does not feel the need to do so, in order to find her worth studying. But she does place Stopes within the context of her time, when families of ten or more were crammed into a couple of rooms. 'Movements to control reproduction do fall into two halves,' she told me. 'One is people who are telling other people you should either be having more babies of the right kind, or we should be stopping those people having babies . . . [The other is] people who are trying to empower people to have the children they want, in the numbers they want. And Marie is on that side.'

Lesley Hall also thinks that Stopes's objection to her prospective daughter-in-law was a cover for her desire to control him. 'Can we say Jocasta complex?* She was very bound up with him. She would have found *something*. It was very difficult to find something to object to about Mary Wallis. She was an intelligent young woman, she was highly educated, she was attractive. She wore glasses – right. Strike her out.' Stopes did exactly that: she cut Harry out of her will. When she died in 1958, she left her clinics to the Eugenics Society. She had, perhaps inevitably, fallen out with the Family Planning Association.

It is impossible to untangle the personal and political selves of Stopes, and to attribute her actions neatly to one or the other. Does it make me feel better to learn that her jeremiads against her future daughter-in-law were driven not by eugenic excesses but maternal overprotectiveness? I'm not sure. But it complicates the picture, as does learning that her opposition to abortion in the 1910s and 20s was a tactical calculation, much like the suffragettes' demand for limited female voting rights. History suggests that Stopes made the right decision: once birth control was accepted by the medical establishment, and then the Church of England, the battle lines moved forward. Once it had been established that women should have control over their bodies, the fight for abortion rights became easier.

There is an impulse to tidy away eugenics from the story of contraceptive pioneers in the UK and US, because it provides

* Lesley Hall is referring to Oedipus' wife. And, it turned out, his mother.

ammunition for anti-abortion advocates in America, and those opposed to funding contraceptive distribution in the developing world. I was once dumbfounded by a black American conservative woman who told me that I supported 'the murder of millions of black babies' because I was pro-choice.* In the developing world, religious conservatives have tried to depict birth control as a tool of imperialism and colonialism, an imposition from the West which disrupts traditional family structures. We cannot deny the unpalatable views of Stopes and fellow birth-control advocates such as Margaret Sanger. But we can put them in context. What they believed has nothing to do with the modern reproductive justice movement. The organisation which now bears Marie's name was founded in 1976, after her own clinics folded a year earlier.

The battle started by Marie Stopes continues today. How much did her difficulty contribute to her achievements? She got contraception and female sexual desire discussed at the tea-tables of polite English society. In 1923, she brought a libel case against an obscure Catholic doctor who accused her of obscenity, and the resulting publicity saw birth control mentioned in the same newspapers which had refused to take adverts for her clinics.† Her legal costs were considerable, but attendance at her clinics rose. Like the suffragettes, she had discovered that being thunderously condemned was better than being politely ignored.

Lesley Hall compares Stopes to Germaine Greer, the radical, outrageous, funny, fearless, infuriating, awe-inspiring and often unsisterly feminist pioneer. 'In the early 70s, inside the movement people thought she was a bit of a nightmare and difficult to deal with, but she was a public face who got a lot of excitement going

---

* Black and Hispanic women have significantly higher rates of abortion than white women in the US, according to research by the Guttmacher Institute.
† Another court case around birth control appears to have spurred Stopes to sue. If there was going to be a free-speech martyr on the subject, Marie was determined that it would be her.

about feminism, in the way that Stopes got people thinking about birth control,' Hall says. At the same time, others were doing the thankless work of setting up task forces and lobbying politicians. But any movement needs both provocateurs and pragmatists. Just as in the fight for the vote, 'you did need the Pankhursts out there being militant, but you also needed Millicent Fawcett doing the really boring stuff of sitting on committees and getting small incremental changes to laws, gradually changing hearts and minds'.

We don't need to *like* Marie Stopes to value her. She gave women (and men) the gift of knowledge, helping them to understand their bodies and their desires, and to feel more in control of both. To get an idea of the vast expanse of normal. It has never been easier to see how other people have sex. But that has brought its own difficulties.

*

Here's what sex meant to me, as a teenager: foreplay, penetration, male climax, FIN. You really had to *work* to find porn in the 1990s – one of my boyfriends got busted by his mum for having a PRINT MAGAZINE under his mattress.* But that was the story it told. The increasing availability of Internet porn has reaffirmed that three-step programme as 'the' way to have sex. And in a strange quirk of fate, where Anne Koedt worried that missionary was the default way for her generation to have sex, it appears rarely in porn, because you can't see what the hell's going on.

We now fancy ourselves as much more liberated and experimental than either Marie Stopes's generation or the feminists of the Second Wave. But the explosion (ew, sorry) of Internet porn has created a new sexual script which is equally narrow – and just as unlikely to work for women. Porn is rarely just everyday sex with a camera pointed at it. It is choreographed, staged, shot and edited. But we don't talk about its tropes and clichés because it is consumed

* This feels so antiquated that it would be like recording a sex tape on a gramophone.

(largely) alone, and because there is no canon which everyone is assumed to share. And unlike with say, theatre or television, there is no class of people employed as 'porn critics', unpicking its clichés and stock characters. All that means it can *look* like real sex, when it's incredibly artificial. And, of course, it is largely made by men, for men.

In the last few years, there has been a fashion for 'sex positive' feminism. It's good to spread the word that sex is normal and natural, not something shameful and secret. But too often, feminists, particularly younger ones, have been scared to make criticisms of the sex *industry* – where desire meets capitalism. They fear being attacked as dried-up old prudes if they criticise the excesses of porn or prostitution.* There is a temptation to depict sex itself as inherently cool, interesting or worthwhile. It is not: hearing dull people bore on about their kink is usually about as fun as watching a slideshow of someone else's holiday. The edginess of sex is overrated, too. Your parents did it. Your grandparents did it. Your grandparents might be *doing it right now.* Ultimately, two groups are invested in making women worry about being 'frigid': people who want to sell them overpriced lingerie, suspenders or other sex-tat, and people who want to coerce them into sex they don't really want to have. Sex is great. But so is rock-climbing. Neither defines your worth as a person.

It always troubles me that we subject other forms of culture to intense scrutiny – 'Is *Girls* racist?', 'Is *The League of Gentlemen* transphobic?' – and leave porn untouched. It often traffics in lurid ethnic stereotypes: lascivious, 'jungle bunny' black women; subservient Asian schoolgirls; pure, untouched white virgins. There's often a curious whiff of homophobia about male-male-female threesomes, with the two guys avoiding eye contact as if the whole shagging-the-same-woman thing is an awkward coincidence and it's easier to

---

* The answer to this line of argument is simple: hey, I like sex so much I *have it for free*!

pretend the other dude isn't there. On many aggregation sites, 'inter-racial' is a separate category – as if having sex with someone of a different race is equivalently unusual to a threesome or being peed on. Escort services still gleefully advertise 'shemales' and 'chicks with dicks'. The assumption here is that you get an exemption for using offensive language if you have an erection. Is it like a note to get out of school sports?

The porn actor and director Stoya, who has been shooting adult films since 2007, is one of the most insightful critics of her industry. 'When they put it on the tube sites it's "teen whore gets fucked", which is not great language to be introducing a human with,' she told me. Stoya believes that what she's doing can be positive – young women tell her she's a role model, young men ask her for sex advice – but she is frustrated by the economics of porn. After lawyers' fees and tax advice and mandatory sexual-health checks, most adult per-formers make very little. Their careers tend to be short, and it can be hard to find other work afterwards.

Although porn performers are sharing their most intimate moments, they have no control over where their scenes end up, or how they are presented. Stoya might shoot a scene which involves sadomasochism, and make sure the performers explicitly discuss their boundaries on camera beforehand. But what ends up on the tube sites is a short clip of the sex itself: *teen whore gets fucked*, even when the 'teen whore' is actually twenty-seven, and owns the com-pany making the film. Imagine being reduced to a misogynistic caricature of yourself, naked, on the Internet. Such clips are literally dehumanising: names are stripped from the descriptions, because that would make it easier for performers to find them and pursue a copyright claim against the aggregators.

All Stoya's criticisms are familiar to me from complaints about ad-funded web journalism. If people won't pay for your work, then to run a viable business you either need to produce content at very low cost, or rip off the work of others. Where journalism has lurid clickbait headlines – 'you won't believe how bad this 90s star looks now' – porn has descriptions which demean and dehumanise. That affects female performers more, because the imagined audience is male.* The gif previews of videos can also be brutally reductive: here's a girl in airport security; the girl with her head forced on to a table, face contorted towards the camera; the girl with legs behind her head as a disembodied penis shoots its load over her gaping ass.

Without getting full Marie Stopes about the 'invisible glories of the wavelengths of the soul', none of this does justice to what it's like to have sex with someone you love. It reminds me instead of Philip Larkin's glum misanthropy: that sex is like 'asking someone else to blow your nose for you'. But most people don't want to talk about it, because they worry criticisms of the sex industry look like prudishness. This is dumb. Questioning the supply chain and employment practices of a fast-food giant doesn't mean you hate burgers. And you don't get excused from having ethics just because you have an erection. Personally, I don't watch porn.† But if you do, then for fuck's sake take an interest in the people making it.

In the middle of all this, Stoya is trying to go her own way. She doesn't have the conventional porn-star look: no breast implants, no blonde hair extensions, no lip fillers. She practises aerial acrobatics, so she has strong arms, and something close to a six-pack. Sometimes she has armpit hair. I admire her for all that. She shoots queer scenes, sells them individually through an independent website, and publishes essays alongside them. She also tries to stay away from the standard heterosexual foreplay-penetration-popshot script.

---

* Pornhub's eye-opening 2018 year in review claimed that twenty-nine per cent of the site's 92 million daily visitors were female, up three percentage points from 2017 – although it should be noted that measuring Internet users' genders is rarely an exact science. The number-one search term among women was 'lesbian'. For men, it was 'Japanese'.

† That's partly an ethical decision, and partly because the sofas are so hideous.

That's difficult. 'I'm under the pressure of capitalism: dick sells,' she tells me. I find her attempt to turn people into ethical masturbators almost heroic. 'Of course, if someone just wants porn, like, just wants to see someone getting fucked, then they can ignore all the writing and skip past the introduction. But I try to put it in there.'

Stoya makes the bulk of her income from her branded Fleshlight – a silicon-lined tube in a can, with the business end modelled on her labia. The idea is that when you're tired of just watching your favourite porn star, you can get that little bit closer to having sex with her. I find the whole thing stalkerish – you can buy lotion for your replica vagina in a can – but for Stoya, it's good money. The Fleshlight sales subsidise her other work.

The feminist case against the porn industry usually focuses on its effect on women, but it is having a big effect on men, too. Where are the spaces where guys can talk to each other about the difference between what they see on screen and their own sex lives? Men ask Stoya the questions they can't ask their friends, she tells me. It's the strange paradox of masculinity: rock-hard but also paper-thin. If I told my female friends about a sexual or relationship problem, I am confident they would respond with sympathy, humour and good advice. I'm not sure that most men could talk to their friends in the same way.

The flip side is that I'm annoyed that the only constructive pressure on the porn industry to *change* (as opposed to attempts simply to repress it) seems to be coming from feminists – from women. Given that men are the biggest consumers of porn, why isn't the onus on them to change it, to make it less misogynist, to make sure its performers are fairly treated and paid? Sometimes I look at the feminist movement and think: *how did we get landed with this?*

Down the line, Stoya said she wanted to end on a positive note. When the #MeToo movement exploded in late 2017, there were some long-overdue conversations about power and consent and coercion. But there was, occasionally, an assumption that sex between men and women was inherently unequal. Men are not psychic, and their partners owe it to them to be honest. If we don't like something, we need to say so. Otherwise, we are unwittingly tipping back into the model of sex which Marie Stopes worked so hard to smash: the male aggressor, pursuing a passive, receptive female. At Barnard College in the US, Stoya said, a young woman asked her: ' "What do I do when my boyfriend wants something that I don't wanna do, because that's not fair to me?" And I'm like, "Well, is he trying to force you, is he trying to coerce you? No? Then you have to remember that he's a person too with his own desires." '

She paused. 'My hope is that, even though there is a literal gender war playing out, that we will be able to remember that every interaction with the opposite sex does not have to be a battle.'

I hope that too. I hope the *téléclitoridiennes* find out there's nothing wrong with them. I hope that in the future, no one frets about a mythical vaginal orgasm that is never going to arrive. I hope that women realise that their bodies and desires aren't difficult, just different. I hope that teenagers don't think the standard menu of foreplay-penetration-popshot is all there is. I hope this generation of sex educators succeeds where Marie Bonaparte, Marie Stopes, Alfred Kinsey and the rest failed, and we finally overturn the persistent myths about what 'normal' looks like.

I hope that one day, for more women, sex won't be such a fucking let-down.

4. PLAY

Girls just wanna have fun(damental human rights)
Women's March slogan

'She had a kick like a mule,' her teammate Joan Whalley recalled. 'She was the only person I knew who could lift a dead ball, the old heavy leather ball, from the left wing over to me on the right and nearly knock me out with the force of the shot.'

In her day, Lily Parr was a phenomenon. At fourteen, when she started playing for a local team, she was 'hauntingly beautiful in a sullen, dark way, just out of school – if she'd ever bothered to go', according to her biographer Barbara Jacobs. She was also 'foul-mouthed, never without a Woodbine in her mouth except when she was playing, a kid who took her chances to pocket anything left lying around'.

The year was 1919. While Marie Stopes was educating women about their bodies, another group of women were using theirs to do something new – play football. At its peak, Lily Parr's team played in front of a crowd of 50,000, more than the number of spectators who watched England's opening game in the most recent women's World Cup. In their day, the 'Dick, Kerr Ladies' also travelled to France to compete and they became celebrities thanks to Pathé newsreels shown in cinemas. Their success suggests the path that women's sport could have taken throughout the twentieth century: well funded, well attended, well loved. Instead, the Football Association snuffed out Lily Parr's career, and women's football as a whole. As women like the US captain Megan Rapinoe finally become house-hold names, the sport is only just beginning to recover.

Women playing football had always been controversial. Before the First World War, the game was seen as alarming and unfemi-nine. 'A man charges with his chest and shoulders, and checks with his hip. Will the doctors tell us that these portions of a woman's body are fit for such rough purpose?' asked a letter-writer to the Sheffield *Evening Telegraph and Star* in February 1895.* 'A woman sometimes waddles like a duck and sometimes like a chicken – it all depends on her weight,' another keen amateur physiologist wrote to the *Pall Mall Gazette* a few days later. 'I don't think lady-footballers will ever be able to "shoot" goals.'

These two letters come from Tim Tate's *Girls With Balls*, which tells the story of several difficult women. And they needed to be difficult. Throughout history, women have been deliberately and repeatedly excluded from sport. Only men could compete in the ancient Olympic Games. Women were barred from the Boston Marathon until 1972. They did not receive equal prize money at Wimbledon until 2007. The lag is greatest in team games, which are still less well funded, less prestigious and less popular than the male versions. One of the problems is that in sport, women are not arguing to be treated exactly the same as men. There is no woman in the world who could get selected for a Premier League team, or beat an elite male athlete over a 100-metre sprint. We need our own leagues and sex-segregated competitions, because testosterone gives men such a physical advantage.

But the idea of women playing together and competing against each other has often attracted a backlash. As organised sport gathered strength in the nineteenth century, the first women's football teams faced financial and social pressure to give up. Pioneers included the Scottish suffragist Helen Matthews, of 'Mrs Graham's XI', whose players were repeatedly chased off the pitch by angry men in the early 1880s, and Lady Florence Dixie, who founded the British Ladies' Football Club a decade later. (In her youth, Lady

---

* Sir, if she can push an eight-pound baby through her pelvis, it can probably handle bumping into the opposing winger. Also: you guys have TESTICLES swinging around down there. Get a grip.

Florence had skipped the London season of balls and tea parties and gone big-game hunting in Chile, returning with a pet jaguar called Alfums, poor bastard. She was that kind of woman.)

Early female footballers were castigated for the amateurishness of their games, even though their matches regularly had to be cancelled because of threats of violence. They were treated as freaks rather than athletes, attracting big, unruly crowds who came to gawp. Several used pseudonyms, allowing them to disappear if things got too rough. But they kept chipping away at the idea that women could play football. We know too little about them, but what we do know is intriguing. One of the teams led by Helen Matthews fielded a black player called Emma Clarke – described by the *South Wales Daily News* as 'the fleet-footed dark girl on the right wing' – at a time when there were only two black players in the men's league.*

Two things allowed women's football to achieve wider popularity: trousers and war. In the late nineteenth century, campaigners argued that women should be freed from their corsets and crinolines. In 1881, the Rational Dress Society was founded. One of its demands was that the weight of women's undergarments should be halved, from fourteen pounds to seven pounds – still the weight of a newborn baby.† When you imagine early feminists doing anything – marching, leafleting, tying themselves to railings – remember that they were doing it in extremely heavy, uncomfortable clothes.

The rational-dress movement explicitly linked women's restrictive fashions to their restricted lives. Women's clothes were designed

---

* Emma Clarke was previously misidentified from team sheets as goalkeeper Carrie Boustead, and the mistaken identity lingers on. In 2017, the poet Sabrina Mahfouz wrote a play about her, saying, 'The fact that there's so little to be found about [her] is part and parcel of the lack of documentation over the years to do with anything outside of the white, male experience.'

† I just weighed my underwear – let my commitment to feminism never be questioned – on the kitchen scales. Thanks to modern lightweight fabrics and the disappearance of petticoats and corsets, my knickers, socks and an underwired bra clocked in at just 5.5 oz (156 g).

to be looked at, not lived in, and strong taboos on genteel women getting sweaty or dirty were an effective way to immobilise them. Opposition to reform was fierce. Amelia Bloomer – who gave her name to loose trousers as an alternative to a floor-length skirt – went back to conventional dress in 1859 after nearly a decade of widespread ridicule. In America, several states had laws forbidding women from wearing trousers. But the idea that women could break free from their cumbersome skirts was slowly gathering force, helped by the growing popularity of the bicycle. 'Bicycling has done more to emancipate women than anything else in the world,' said the American campaigner Susan B. Anthony. 'I stand and rejoice every time I see a woman ride on a wheel. It gives women a feeling of freedom and self-reliance.'

The second game-changer was the First World War, which ate up young men's lives, and spat the survivors back out injured and shell-shocked. The Heart of Midlothian football team enlisted together – as men were encouraged to do – and six of its eleven men died in 1916. The absence of so many men left Britain's munitions factories short-staffed. Women were employed to fill the gaps – on half the pay, of course, for the same grinding twelve-hour shifts, six days a week. The work was dirty and dangerous, with 'munitionettes' filling explosive shells by hand. Their skin turned yellow from the chemical base of the TNT they used, so they were nicknamed 'canaries'. But their pay packets gave them independence, which is always threatening. 'The press wallowed in a frenzy of disapproval,' writes Barbara Jacobs in *The Dick, Kerr Ladies*. 'Sensational stories were written of the excesses of these young women – a munitionette entering a pub and pulling out a wad of notes from her knicker leg, demanding drinks all round, in front of two of her noble heroes, wounded soldiers who were down to their last shilling. And another entering a department store and buying a fur coat off the peg (how dare she!).' And as women entered the munitions factories in the mid-1910s, they began to do what men had done – kick a ball about during breaks. The Dick, Kerr & Co. factory in Preston, named after its founders W. B. Dick and John Kerr, had its own sports pitches, and soon a rough women's football team had formed.

Changing fashions reflected the changing times. In October 1917, two women were dismissed by the Metallurgical Company in Newcastle for wearing trousers outside the factory gates, according to the National Archives. All seventeen women in the factory stopped work, calling for their two colleagues to be reinstated. Instead, all the women were dismissed. But the reforms gathered pace, and they proved vital for female athletes: it would have been impossible to thunder up and down a pitch for ninety minutes in a bustle. In 1900, women footballers wore 'knickerbockers' – baggy shorts gathered at the knee – along with thick stockings. By around 1920, recognisably modern shorts had been introduced.

Women had legs – and they weren't afraid to use them.

*

The chances of getting Lily Parr into a dainty, ladylike outfit would have been minimal, football or no football. She was born in 1905 in St Helens, which is now part of Merseyside. Her birthplace is just thirty miles away from Annie Kenney's, born quarter of a century earlier. Like Kenney, she came from a large, working-class family: John, Lizzie, Bob, Lily, George, Bill, Elsie and Doris. Her eldest brother was born when their mother, Sal, was nineteen; her youngest sister when Sal was forty-two. Her family home was dirty – with chickens and a pigsty at the back – and noisy, with hefty portions of food on the table and a babble of children around it. Lily smoked incessantly, nicked anything left lying around, and cracked morbid jokes. 'When the older players were getting ready for a match, there were elastic stockings going on knees and strapping up of ankles, there were bandages here there and everywhere,' Joan Whalley said later. 'Then Parr walked in, and she stood looking around at them all and said, "Well, I don't know about Dick, Kerr Ladies football team, it looks like a bloody trip to Lourdes to me." '

Lily's older brothers John and Bob were keen footballers, and she quickly picked up the habit. By her teens, she was six foot tall, an agile, left-footed winger. She was often underestimated because of her sex: there's a well-known story about her taking a kick from the edge of the penalty area, and breaking the (male) goalkeeper's arm.

During the First World War, factories had promoted their women's football teams as fundraisers for good causes. The FA had suspended the men's league, so there was no competition for spectators or grounds. Into this landscape strode Lily Parr. Alfred Frankland, a manager at the Dick, Kerr factory in Preston, had seen the teenage Lily play against his own team. He knew how powerful she was, and how fast. After some wrangling with her mother, Lily moved to Preston to play for Dick, Kerr Ladies. She even got her own room, where she smoked Woodbines in bed.

Local matches were all very well, but Frankland had grander plans. He arranged for his girls to play against a French team in 1920. By all accounts, the French girls were delicate and chic; the presumption was that the Lancashire lasses they would play against were not.* At the hotel for lunch, Lily Parr declared she was so hungry that she could 'eat a buttered frog'. At the Dick, Kerr canteen that night, Lily refused to join in the waltzes, but did end up leading everyone in the hokey cokey (cigarette in mouth, obviously). Trips to the countryside and Blackpool and London followed, with games of football in between, including one at Stamford Bridge. The French team taught Lily how to pronounce 'merde' properly. The reception from the crowds, and from the newspapers, was generally positive. After all, these girls were raising money for charity.

---

* Pleasingly, instead of caps, the French team went on to the field wearing berets.

Once the matches against the French team were over, the Dick, Kerr Ladies made their way back from London. On their journey home, the first serious women's football team in British history ran into the first women's strike in British history – a sight that would have been unthinkable a generation earlier. The female workers of John Lewis, who wanted the right not to live in hostels provided by the company, were part of a new mood of militancy, encouraged by the trade unions and the Labour Party.

*

'Until the Dick, Kerr Ladies, working-class women had never been admitted to the ranks of those who did good works of which the nation could be proud and for which the nation was deeply grateful,' writes Barbara Jacobs. 'Somewhere in there is a shifting of power. And it could be thought dangerous, couldn't it?'

Over the next year, the women played exhibition matches at home. Lily Parr was described in the *Daily News* as a 'fifteen-year-old girl back who is said to kick like a first-division man'. Then it was off to France for the return matches. Lily's teammate Alice Woods was shocked by what she saw in the country's north: line upon line of graves, 11,000 in all. Her diary records climbing the Arc de Triomphe, and that Lily fell asleep during a lecture on military gymnastics at Les Invalides. Their first match ended with an unfriendly pitch invasion, and the girls had to run back to their dressing room. To reach the next game, they crossed the barren battlefields of the Somme, where so many of the Heart of Midlothian team had died four years earlier. The area was still pocked by barbed wire, bombed-out buildings and derailed trains. Then on to Versailles, where Alice recorded in her diary: 'I have stood where peace was signed.' They won 6–0 at Le Havre and 1–0 at Rouen and then boarded the ferry home. Just before Christmas, the girls played a game at night – until then, an impossibility – as the Dick, Kerr engineers asked the War Office for two surplus searchlights. The request was approved by the secretary of state, Winston Churchill.* It was watched by 12,000 people, and footage was broadcast in cinemas across the country.

Then came the pinnacle of women's football in Britain. On Boxing Day 1920, the Dick, Kerr team were scheduled to play their great rivals, St Helens, at Goodison Park, home of Everton. It had a capacity of 53,000.† Some 67,000 people turned up, so thousands were turned away. The gate receipts were £3,000 – half a million in today's money. In the New Year, the team played up to three matches a week, and by August they were taking the St Helens team with them to the Isle of Man. It was a punishing schedule, managed alongside work or study. The women who worked in the factory at least had an understanding employer; others, such as nursing student Florrie Redford, had to make up lost wages by working at night.

The success of women's football had begun to attract hostile attention. Mixed-sex teams had already been banned since 1902 (and are still banned today for over-eighteens). Women were forbidden from acting as referees. During the war, when the men's season had been suspended, the women's game provided a diversion for those men left at home working in 'starred' (protected) occupations, the wounded and those on leave from the front. But the FA restarted the men's league in the autumn of 1919, by which time more than 2 million British men had been discharged from the army. The country they returned to was heavily indebted, and still full of Victorian slums and factories. There were fears about the birth rate following the death of so many young men.

The returning Tommies had to come first, the government decided. The lack of jobs was causing riots from Liverpool to Cardiff. 'Official papers from the period show that the government was seriously worried that unemployment among the millions of

---

* The first searchlight failed during the match. Then one of the operators pointed the other directly at two players by accident, temporarily blinding them.

† For comparison, the modern Wembley Stadium holds 90,000.

demobilised servicemen would cause widespread labour unrest and a potential Bolshevik takeover,' writes Tim Tate, referring to the revolutionary movement which had just ended the godlike power of Russia's royal family. 'There was an obvious focus for much of the anger amongst demobilised servicemen on women doing "their" jobs, in "their" factories.' A government-backed committee stated that a woman's work should not 'interfere with her service in bearing children . . . She must be safeguarded as homemaker for the nation.'

This new mood was devastating for many of the 1.5 million women who had joined the workforce during the war. Some went back into the home, others returned to 'women's work' such as laundry or dress-making. Any woman who refused a domestic service job could have her unemployment benefit withdrawn. In any case, women were entitled to a lower amount than men. Middle-class occupations such as teaching and the Civil Service introduced 'marriage bars' – requiring women to leave the workforce on marriage. Many of these were not lifted until the next world war broke out, in the 1940s.*

By 1921, politicians were seriously worried that the old order could not reassert itself. A new weekly magazine, the *Football Special and Sporting Pictorial*, carried a column by 'Football Girl' which warned that women players were becoming obsessive. 'A girl in her teens and early twenties should have many interests in life, and it is not good for her to bother with just one thing,' it added. 'Usually she thinks she is being noble and all that sort of thing when she gives up her other pleasures for football, but as a matter of fact she is being nothing of the kind – she is simply being short-sighted and selfish.'

That word 'selfish' is a telling one. After all, what are women supposed to be? Caring, nurturing, supportive. Selfless. Life's supporting characters. No wonder that exceptional women – whether in sport, literature, art or elsewhere – so often get described as

---

* Lloyds bank, for example, permitted married women to keep their jobs only from 1949.

'difficult'. By demanding attention for themselves, they are violating a deep taboo.

Our uneasiness about women controlling their own lives also applies to writing, art, music and other creative pursuits – any form of play. 'A book is made out of small selfishnesses,' wrote Claire Dederer in an essay for the *Paris Review* in November 2017. 'The selfishness of shutting the door against your family. The selfishness of ignoring the pram in the hall. The selfishness of forgetting the real world to create a new one. The selfishness of stealing stories from real people. The selfishness of saving the best of yourself for that blank-faced anonymous paramour, the reader. The selfishness that comes from simply saying what you have to say.'

Perhaps that sentiment also lay underneath the growing horror of women's football. These women were unruly and unfettered. They belonged to themselves and to each other, rather than slotting into the neat, man-adjacent boxes – daughter, wife, mother – society had ready for them. Being exceptional requires a thousand small selfishnesses, and the world was not ready for women to be that difficult. It is still not ready.

*

By 1921, the fundraising power of the Dick, Kerr Ladies team – once a propaganda boost to the war effort – had become more contested. In March, the government ended its control of the coal mining industry, and the mine owners responded by cutting wages and increasing hours. Strikes swept the north of England, and the women's fundraising activities moved from supporting wounded Tommies to the men picketing their employers.

Once women's football was no longer a harmless novelty, it came in for harsh criticism. 'With women who take up athletics the tendency is to overdo it,' the runner W. G. George told the *Nottingham Evening Post* in April 1921. 'As for women's "soccer" football, I scarcely think it conforms to the average woman's ideal of modesty, especially when staged as a public exhibition.' By this time Lily Parr was still only sixteen, and columnists worried tenderly about the effect of football on such a delicate young girl.* There was an undertone of classism here, too. Should 'young ladies' play the 'working man's game'?

This publicity made the Football Association nervous. Its leaders started to question the finances of the women's game, and in October 1921 it decreed that any (men's) club which hosted a women's match had to handle the accounts arising from it. The women's teams could not be trusted to run their own books. The suggestion was that they were corrupt.

Then, on 5 December, the FA crushed the sport altogether. 'The Council feel impelled to express their strong opinion that the game of football is quite unsuitable for females and ought not to be encouraged,' its ruling stated, adding that there were concerns over 'the appropriation of receipts to other than Charitable objects . . . The Council requests the clubs belonging to the Association refuse the use of their grounds for such matches.' Suddenly, women were banned from playing on any professional pitch in Britain, and referees and other officials could not assist in their games. It was a killer blow.

The FA marshalled (male) doctors to back up its case. One claimed the 'jerky' movements of football were bad for women. 'The game of football is not a woman's game,' said Frank Watt, secretary of Newcastle United. 'It was permitted on professional grounds as a novelty arising out of women's participation in war work and as a novelty with charitable motives. The time has come when the novelty has worn off.' The manager of Arsenal, A. L. Knighton, was concerned that injuries sustained on the pitch might mean 'their future duties as mothers would be seriously impaired'.

Watt's statement illuminated something for me. The 'wave' model of feminism depends on the idea that there were two great

---

* In the best tradition of op-ed columnists, clearly they had never met or spoken to her.

bursts of activity in the movement; the first in the 1910s, when women got the vote; the second in the 1970s, when equal pay legislation was passed. What happened in between? The suffragettes were exhausted – that I could understand. But the FA ban on women's football showed the extent of that other great anti-feminist force: backlash.

Thanks to the First World War, 1.5 million women had joined the workforce. Once they began to work like men, they could spend like men, and play like men. But now the real men were coming home, shell-shocked and wounded, having made a huge sacrifice for their country. They wanted their jobs back – and, frankly, I expect they wanted their tea on the table. And so there was a concerted effort to re-establish the old order. That was what the 1919 Restoration of Pre-War Practices Act, which ordered women out of the factories, was intended to do. And that was also what the FA's ban did. 'Leisure' only makes sense as a concept in opposition to 'paid work'. It takes place in public: in betting shops, at sports grounds, at museums, theatres, concert arenas. By restricting women's access to professional sports, the ban reasserted the public sphere as men's domain.

Alfred Frankland vowed that the Dick, Kerr Ladies would play on, 'even if we have to play on ploughed fields'. Their next game was hosted by a rugby club. They won 3–1. Lily Parr scored two of the goals. But at sixteen, her semi-professional career was over. By the end of the year, she had lost her job at the Dick, Kerr factory – now called English Electric – and started work at the Whittingham hospital.

*

I was surprised that I had never heard of Lily Parr. But then, why would I? Like many of the women I know, I have never loved sport. I grew up thinking it wasn't for me.

Even now, it's shocking how often 'sport' means 'men's sport'. Look at the newspapers: the football section is the *men's* football section. The rugby section is the *men's* rugby section. The usual excuse is that the women's game is simply less exciting, with the underlying implication that it's because the female body is weedier. But come on. Snooker on television is *men's* snooker, and there's no reason women can't hold a stick and wear a waistcoat. Darts is *men's* darts, even though there's no physical reason women shouldn't be able to grow ponytails, drink pints of bitter and have absurd nicknames. The 'male default' is extremely strong in sport. The website where I buy running gear has two categories: running shoes and women's running shoes. Many races hand out free T-shirts – in men's sizes only. The London Marathon, where half the runners are women, offers a 'unisex' finisher's shirt, which many say is far too big for them.

Yes, there are exceptions to the male domination of play. Serena Williams has become one of the best known athletes in the world – albeit at the cost of enduring constant, racially inflected suggestions that her muscles and power somehow make her unwatchably unfeminine. There are even disciplines where women's achievements have overtaken those of men. In January 2019, the ultra-runner Jasmin Paris won the 268-mile Spine Race across the Pennines in eighty-three hours and twelve minutes. She beat the men's record by twelve hours. She was still breastfeeding her fourteen-month-old daughter Rowan, and had to stop to express milk along the way. In endurance events such as ultra-marathons, men's greater speed and strength is less of an advantage.*

Still, the assumption that sport is a male arena persists. 'Team sports in particular are seen as really against the grain,' says sports journalist Anna Kessel, author of *Eat Sweat Play: How Sports Can Change Our Lives*. 'That's bound up in latent homophobia, this idea of women as a group is really threatening.' I hadn't considered this before. Where women have become superstars, it has often been

---

* Here's an injustice for men's rights activists to get stuck into: only women are allowed to compete in synchronised swimming and rhythmic gymnastics in the Olympics. Then again, only men can do Graeco-Roman wrestling.

through individual achievements. Of all the female athletes I can instantly name, none come from team sports. Flo Jo, Simone Biles, Martina Navratilova, Billie Jean King. Without athletics and tennis, I'd be drawing a blank. But I can name umpteen male footballers, even though I know so little about the game I once spent half a season of *Championship Manager* accidentally playing Ian Wright in goal.

Things are slowly getting better. In 2019, matches from the women's football World Cup were shown on BBC1. The *Telegraph* started a dedicated women's sport pull-out – and hired Anna Kessel to write for it. The reflexive sneering about the lower quality of women's sports is diminishing. That does not mean that progress will be a straight line. The FA's ban was a symptom of the backlash against women's sports in the 1920s. A century later, I feel something similar in the pockets of homophobia, racism and misogyny still festering in football culture – and in the reluctance by the sport's governing bodies to take them seriously. In 2015, the Chelsea men's team doctor Eva Carneiro received an apology and settlement from the club after being subjected to wolf whistles. 'She ran on to the pitch to look after a male player, as you do as a doctor, and people started chanting,' says Kessel. 'One person said: show us where you piss from, you slut. This is a doctor tending to a patient on the field.'*

Here's the thing: I would bet some of those who hurled abuse at Carneiro work in offices where HR would crack down on sexist banter in a heartbeat. But at a football game, fans can lose themselves in a crowd. They feel liberated from their daily lives. For a small number, that provides an excuse to indulge in grim, sexist behaviour. 'People still make this argument that football is a working man's game, they've worked hard all week, now here's their space, why are

* Carneiro accepted a multi-million pound pay-off and a confidentiality agreement after a tribunal. Chelsea apologised 'unreservedly to her and her family for the distress caused'.

you trying to change it,' says Kessel. A similar dynamic operates on video-game voice chat and on social media. It is comforting to think that trolls are all basement-dwelling losers, but many turn out to be 'respectable' men and women with families. Anonymity gives them a chance to let rip. And perhaps those spaces can be so sexist precisely because sexism is now so unacceptable elsewhere. I guarantee there will be the odd man who reads this and goes: *For God's sake woman, you've taken everything else! Why can't you leave football alone?*

The idea of football as a men's game has unfortunate consequences for women. One of the most persistent irritations of life is what I call the Seriousness Gap. It goes like this. Things that men do, things that men like, things that are dominated by men = serious, mainstream, worthwhile. Things that women do, that women like, that are dominated by women = silly, trivial, niche. As a quick thought experiment, remember the complaints over the *Today* programme covering London Fashion Week, a creative industry which generates millions in revenue for British businesses. Then contrast it with the way my Twitter feed is taken over every Saturday by men talking about the latest 1–1 draw. Both fashion and football are fun – if expensive – hobbies. But interest in the former is a black mark against being perceived as a Serious Person, because fashion is designated as a female interest. Men are serious, and women are not.

There is another feminist dimension to this argument. I don't begrudge the joy that many people – including my mother-in-law, an avid Spurs fan – get out of the game. But I do find something uncomfortable about the way that it functions as a networking system and small-talk generator for (mostly) men. *Come to the game with me,* says your boss. *Did you see that goal?* says your co-worker. *Oh, an Arsenal fan? My sympathies,* says the man you've never met before. Women are largely locked out of this rich seam of banter, while the men who Speak Football get a career boost. 'Your male peers are flirting with their male bosses constantly,' writes Caitlin Moran in *How to Be a Woman.* 'The average workplace is like fucking

Bromancing the Stone. That's basically what male bonding is. Flirting. They're flirting with each other playing golf, they're flirting with each other going to the football, they're flirting with each other chatting at the urinals – and, sadly, flirting with each other in after-hours visits to strip clubs and pubs.'

The idea of football being a bastion of unfettered masculinity is reflected in how the industry approaches female employees. 'Clubs and players say they don't feel comfortable having a female medic in a male dressing room. They feel it would disturb the atmosphere, men wouldn't feel comfortable, they wouldn't be able to talk openly, they would have to "behave",' says Kessel. But the same diktats do not apply in the women's game. 'It's mostly men that are running women's sport. I see male coaches, mostly male medics. They manage alright; they knock on the door when women are getting changed.' The head coach of the England women's football team is a man, Phil Neville, who played for Manchester United for a decade. His presence – and his experience in the men's game – means his team are taken more seriously.

In football, the women's game lags far behind the men's version, thanks to that FA ban from 1921. The Women's Super League – the equivalent of the Premier League – was launched only in 2011. Until then, female footballers were still working in other jobs alongside their training commitments. That makes it impossible to say yet how exciting and skilful women's football can be. Yes, women's football does not currently attract the ticket sales or television viewing figures of the men's game. But give it a century of investment and infrastructure, and then we'll talk. Kessel was astonished when her elder daughter arrived at reception class aged four, and the boys in her class were already saying that 'girls can't play football'. She asks: 'How can they already know, at four, that this cultural norm exists? It's because it's so entrenched.'

The picture in rugby is similar. The Netherlands became the first country to award professional contracts to women's sevens players in

2011. England followed in 2014. It took another four years to bring in professional contracts for fifteen-person squads. The decision came after English women were paid to train for nine months in the run-up to the 2017 World Cup. They reached the final – and then faced losing their salaries immediately after the final whistle. In tennis, there are still complaints that women play three-set matches at Grand Slam tournaments, while men play five. As Anna Kessel points out, most female players are perfectly happy to play for longer; it's the tennis authorities who don't seem keen, for reasons of tradition and court scheduling. Elite women played five-set matches in both the US National Championships of the 1890s and the WTA tour finals of the mid-1980s. "We women are strong, ready, willing and able," said Serena Williams in 2014.

Kessel is fervent in her belief that sport and exercise should be open to more girls. 'Women being physical is still a radical thing that makes people uncomfortable,' she says. And the belief that boys are naturally 'sporty' has unfortunate side effects for many of them, too. I know plenty of men who feel just as left out by banter about clean sheets and the trouble with the back four as I do. They feel, in some way, that if they cannot Speak Football, then they cannot Speak Man. That adds to the stigma around boys who like art, music, literature or dance, suggesting that these are effeminate pursuits, or that straight men shouldn't enjoy them. If we expand the idea of what women can do, we do the same for men.

*

Talking of men, Ama Agbeze gets mistaken for one with unnerving regularity. 'It happens so often that I'm like . . . I just have a complex,' she tells me. I find it baffling: the thirty-six-year-old captain of the England women's netball team has long pink braids, and doesn't look remotely masculine to me. She presumes it's her height, but adds: 'I'm not even that tall! In netball, I'm just average!'

Agbeze is six foot in bare feet, but when we meet, she's wearing low heels. As a sworn opponent of teetering shoes, I'm surprised to find that pleases me. At nine inches taller than the average British woman, and three inches taller than the average man, Agbeze must feel the full force of Chimamanda Ngozi Adichie's observation that we 'teach girls to shrink themselves, to make themselves smaller'. Yet she is not afraid to stand out.

Her career shows the effect of starving women's sports of funding. The *Sunday Times* compared her to the captain of the England men's football team, Harry Kane. Where he earned close to £200,000 a week from Tottenham Hotspur, she earned around £600, mostly from Sport England, topped up by her club London Pulse. Where he took a blacked-out limousine after twisting his ankle, she turned up to the newspaper interview on crutches, having taken the Tube. Where Kane had a £7 million house, she lived between her parents' home in Birmingham and a shared flat in London. Where his two children barely interrupted his playing career, the thirty-six-year-old ruefully admitted to me that a baby would mean the end of her time in professional sports.

Agbeze is an exceptional athlete, but she had to leave Britain to fulfil her promise. She grew up near Birmingham, the daughter of two Nigerian immigrants who wanted her to focus on her education. 'They obviously had to work for those things when they were younger and earn them all: even if you wanted to have an education, you might not have been able to afford it,' she said. At school, she played at county level, and by the time she got to university, where she studied law, she was playing for England. After her master's degree in 2008, she was asked to play professionally by a team in Australia, where women's netball is much better funded and supported. Unlike her equivalent athletes in male sports, she never imagined she could make a career out of professional sports. 'I always thought it was going to be I'd play that one season, and then I'd come back to the UK and, as my mum said, find a proper job,' she said. 'Then it kind of just kept on happening . . . Every year, I thought, *oh, this is the last year I'm going to do this.*'

The biggest crowd she has played in front of in Britain is 10,000 – a fifth of the number who turned out for Lily Parr and her teammates in 1920. She tells me that the Harlequin Ladies rugby team has been trying to drive up attendance with a special match called a Game Changer. In 2018, it attracted a record number of spectators: 4,500.

I find these figures faintly depressing. They will only improve, surely, if women's sports get greater publicity. In Australia and New Zealand, every netball game is broadcast live and then repeated. Here, Sky has the rights to the Super League and shows a few games a week on its Sports Mix channel, which is available to all customers. There has long been an argument about keeping the 'crown jewels' of sport such as the Ashes on the BBC, where anyone can watch them. For all that Sky's investment in women's netball is welcome, I wish that the Super League was on a free-to-air channel. When the England versus Scotland game in the 2019 women's football World Cup was shown on BBC1, viewing figures peaked at 6 million. Given more publicity, women's national teams can become part of the national conversation.

Agbeze says that most people she meets are surprised to hear that there is such a thing as a professional netball player, even though 'probably 90 per cent of females played netball at school'. I confess that I didn't know such a thing existed, even though I was (briefly, pre-puberty) a solid goal attack. Agbeze plays goalkeeper or goal defence, the watchful strategist's positions. Like many elite athletes, she projects an aura of relentless professionalism. She is evangelical about the benefits of exercise at any level: better mental health, learning to work in a team, improving your focus and discipline. She thinks it's a shame that women fall out of the habit of playing team sports. 'I feel like loads of people lose track of their friends because life just gets busy . . . [but if] every Friday at five o'clock we go and have a kickaround, it links you together.' She had been joking with her husband, she said, that she needed to learn golf, 'because loads of networking happens over golf'.

Yes, she worried as a teenager about what she looked like when exercising – 'If it had been in the days of Google, I'd probably have been googling "How can I stop sweating?"' – but it was never enough to put her off. And yes, she worries about having children: how do women juggle caring and working out? Imagine 'if a gym had a crèche which was free', she said. Hmm, I thought. I can't imagine that in a swanky city-centre gym designed for office workers. However, it did cheer me up to hear that Agbeze doesn't like ultra-macho gyms any more than I do. 'I've been to some gyms that are really, really intimidating, and I'm – well, a professional athlete.'

Finally, I asked her, are you a feminist? 'No,' she said, 'I shy away from labels.' Then she qualified that. 'I do believe that I want everything to be equal and everything should be fair and everybody should have an equal opportunity.' She was shocked, she said, about the divisions in the world. 'I'm black, and I know that ethnic minorities aren't favoured, and I'm a woman, and women – I just, it's so crazy.'

But her idea of a feminist was . . . 'Charlie Dimmock'.

I made a face. Charlie Dimmock? The presenter of the BBC gardening programme *Ground Force*, who notoriously did not wear a bra?

Agbeze laughed. 'Maybe that's in my mind, like I'm associating burning your bra with not wearing a bra,' she said. 'And so I feel like, in my head, those are feminists.'

It was a sobering insight into feminism's PR problem. When Agbeze believes in the goals of feminism, why does the label repel her? Perhaps because difficulty too often looks, from the outside, like obnoxiousness. Or perhaps the movement's internal battles turn people off.

*

In December 2018, the England Roses won the team prize at the BBC Sports Personality of the Year competition, as well as the award for greatest sporting moment. It was in recognition of the netball team's triumph at the Commonwealth Games, where Helen Housby scored in the final second, allowing them to beat the favourites Australia by 52–51.

Accepting the award, Agbeze was encouraged to make a speech by presenter Clare Balding. It was heartfelt. 'It's been a very long journey. Billie Jean King mentioned that you stand on the shoulders of those who went before you, and we're very tall girls – we've been standing on a lot of shoulders.' The England team had never won a Commonwealth gold medal before that game, and had never beaten Australia in a major tournament.

Watching Ama and her teammates on that stage, I felt . . . pride. For a moment, I had a glimpse of what makes men's football such a phenomenon. Sport can be a vessel for a national story, an outlet for patriotism, a way for people to invest a part of themselves in the unpredictable narratives generated by sporting competitions. By rejecting it – or feeling that it had rejected me – I was missing out. Looking at these tall, strong women in their ball-gowns, I felt something like a deep inhale, an expansion in my idea of what a woman can be. How often had I seen a team of women being celebrated like this, for *using* their bodies rather than parading them, for working together and winning? I thought about the number of times I've heard a woman doing some thankless task and saying, 'I deserve a medal for this.' Too right. Women should get more medals.

*

While we're being optimistic, here's another happy moment. Out there on the Internet, there's a clip of a press conference involving Andy Murray, Britain's greatest tennis player. He's sitting at the table, microphones in front of him. He's just been beaten by an

American player, Sam Querrey, and a reporter wants a comment on what that means for the tournament.

'Andy, Sam is the first American player to reach a major semi-final since 2009. How would you describe—'

'Male player,' says Andy.

'I beg your pardon?' says the reporter.

'Male player, right?'

'Yes, first male player.' Off-camera, you hear a nervous laugh. 'That's for sure.' (Meaning: boy, is that guy manly.) Others in the room laugh too. Andy Murray's expression doesn't change. He doesn't attempt to make the man feel better about being called out, softening the confrontation with a smile.

When Murray announced he might have to retire because of a hip injury, I rewatched the clip again and again.

It's the reporter's nervous laugh that's important, because in that clip Andy Murray acted unusually. He embarrassed someone by pointing out their blind spot. He made that man feel bad for implying that there is 'tennis' and there is 'women's tennis'. He made himself less popular, in the room, in that moment, by puncturing the chummy atmosphere with a remark that could seem grumpy, or graceless. He did it in the knowledge that he has been criticised in the past for failing to smile enough, to perform happiness and gratitude for victory. He did it anyway. Being a feminist unavoidably involves being a killjoy, because it involves puncturing the cosy bubble of consensus. That's difficult, and it can make *you* seem difficult for doing it.

Murray's mother Judy, who supported him doggedly through his early career, retweeted the clip with the words: 'That's my boy' and a heart emoji.*

---

* The American women who reached the finals, who got forgotten that day? The Williams sisters. You might have heard of them.

In 2016, at the Olympic Games, it happened again. 'You're the first person ever to win two Olympic tennis gold medals,' BBC reporter John Inverdale said. 'That's an extraordinary feat isn't it?'

Murray, deadpan, returned the serve. 'Well, to defend the singles title. I think Venus and Serena have won about four each.'

I love Andy Murray for those moments, all six foot-plus of his Scottish grumpiness, because he took on some of the burden that women have to carry in calling out sexism. Discomfiting and embarrassing other people is emotionally draining; it's picking a difficult path over the easy one. I've done it plenty of times, and felt wearied by it, but as a woman I have a personal stake in reducing sexism. To see a man do it – to show affinity with us, rather than the cosy embrace of his male peers – is strangely moving.

It turned out that other women (and quite a few men) felt the same. When Murray tearfully announced he might have to retire, he was hailed as the quiet feminist of tennis. This was the man who appointed a female coach, Amélie Mauresmo, and defended her consistently against suggestions she wasn't up to it. He watched women's games himself. He supported equal pay, without the usual cracks about women needing to play more sets. He said it would be interesting to play against Serena Williams, and didn't immediately claim that he'd win.

Moments like that make my heart sing. Slowly, but slowly, our idea of normal is changing. On 17 May 2019, the Manchester City manager Pep Guardiola was asked by a (male) sports journalist about the chances of his side winning the FA Cup as well as the league and the Carabao Cup. 'Tomorrow you've got the prospect of winning the first ever domestic treble in this country,' the reporter said.

'Men's,' said Guardiola, without missing a beat.

The reporter ploughed on: 'How much does that excite you?'

Guardiola sighed. 'The first time in men's football. The women have done it.'*

*

Lily Parr first surprised the community around her with her ability with a ball: that hoofing kick, her dashing sprints, her Woodbine-smoking gumption. When the FA effectively destroyed women's professional football in 1921, she was denied the career she deserved. The sport staggered on for a few years, but another new rule – stipulating that players could not join a side more than fifteen miles from their home town – broke up the superstar squad fielded by the Dick, Kerr Ladies. There was one final tour, where the team arrived to find that Canada, too, had banned women's football and half their matches were cancelled. Then they discovered that the teams lined up to play them in the US were men's sides. They won four of their nine matches, and Lily scored several goals. But in 1923, the women played only three matches. Three years later, Alfred Frankland left the company, and the team lost its ground, and its name. It became Preston Ladies.

Tim Tate has some sympathy for the FA. There were irregularities in the Dick, Kerr Ladies books, he believes: the size of the crowds and the resulting profits from ticket receipts, once expenses were deducted, simply do not match. Possibly Alfred Frankland was pocketing the money; or perhaps he reinvested it in his team. As for the players, it is not surprising that they didn't put up a fight. Their presence in the factories had always been conditional on men's absence, and the success of the women's game was partly down to the wartime suspension of the men's league. Most would have expected to leave the team when they got married, anyway: by 1921, several of Lily Parr's original comrades had gone. It was 1971 before women

* Arsenal Ladies won the domestic treble, plus the women's Champions League title, in 2007.

were again allowed to play on men's pitches, and it was 1993 before the FA took over administration of women's football.

But there was a consolation for Lily Parr. Within days of starting her new job at the Whittingham hospital, she met a woman called Mary, and fell in love. They moved in together. Lily was named captain of Preston Ladies in 1946, and played her final game on 12 August 1950, at the age of forty-five. She scored.

Lily Parr died in 1978, of cancer. That year, a talented girl called Theresa Bennett was chosen to play for a local boys' team, and she challenged the FA in the courts to let her join it. Lord Denning, in the Royal Courts of Justice, denied her request. 'Women have many other qualities superior to those of men, but they have not got the strength or stamina to run, to kick or tackle and so forth,' he said. 'The law would be an ass and an idiot if it tried to make girls into boys so they could join in all-boys' games.' Since then, the rules on children's teams have been relaxed, but mixed adult teams are still banned by the Football Association. 'We don't know what women's football would look like if it had that history of investment and professionalism that the men's game had,' Anna Kessel says. 'It's really strange that even in primary school, [some] girls are not allowed to play football or rugby. This is harking back to 1921.'

What should the future look like? More men taking an interest in women's sport, investing it with the seriousness associated with masculinity. Women in male-dominated sports being taken seriously, not belittled by colleagues and harassed by fans. More coverage of women's sporting triumphs, and more televised games. More newspaper photos of women using their bodies, not just showing them off. More mums taking their sons to the football, and dads taking their daughters to the rugby. The end of golf-based office bromances. Crèches at gyms. Women doing exercise not to tame their bodies – another item on an endless To Do list – but because they enjoy spending time in the open air, with their friends, having fun. The future should see Lily Parr and Ama Agbeze getting every ounce of recognition that they deserve.

Perhaps you're thinking: I don't care about sport. Well, neither did I. But now I realise that's partly because sport didn't seem to have a place for me. If we open up sport to women, it sends a message that wanting leisure time is not being selfish or unreasonable. It might also clean out those festering pockets of sexism in football stands, rugby clubs and video-game voice chat. It is also a matter of simple justice. Women need time and space to play – particularly when we work so hard. And on that note, come with me to London, in the sweltering summer of 1976, and meet a woman who has had enough.

5. WORK

Patriarchy has not disappeared, it's changed form. In the new form, women earn the bacon, and cook it too.

Arlie Russell Hochschild, 1989

It was a hot day, the kind where tempers boil over. 'It had been the hottest, driest summer that London could remember,' wrote Joe Rogaly a year later. 'In the parks, and on Hampstead Heath, people swam and took happy snapshots of one another as if they were by the seaside.'

It was August 1976, and all those happy snapshots made it the busiest time of the year in the Grunwick film-processing laboratory in North London. In the days before digital cameras, people took their negatives to a chemist to be developed. From there, they were sent off to places like Grunwick. A few days later, the pictures would arrive back in a folded envelope, so you could discover how many you'd unwittingly taken with a thumb over the lens.

In the mail-order room, it was sweltering. There were no windows to the outside, and the air-conditioning unit was broken. Unhappiness simmered among the workers. Most were immigrants: Asians who had migrated to East Africa, and then on to London. Their manager, thirty-two-year-old Malcolm Alden, could not understand Gujarati, the language spoken by most of his employees. He also could not understand why everyone was working so slowly. It was, he discovered, a protest against the conditions at Grunwick: low wages, short holidays and abrupt sackings. Some of the young men at the lab, including a temporary worker called Sunil Desai, were angry. They had an answer to the insulting conditions. They wanted to join a trade union.

What happened next ignited an industrial dispute lasting for months, which attracted nationwide media attention. Twenty thousand people gathered in the streets around the lab. It was the first strike involving Commonwealth migrants to gain the wholehearted support of Britain's existing trade unions. It changed perceptions of Asian workers in Britain. It led to a backlash from the right, turbo-charging the rise of Thatcherism. The strike failed. And it wasn't led by Sunil Desai, or his angry young friends.

It was led by his mother.

*

Jayaben Desai was born in Dharmaj, a village in the Indian state of Gujarat, in 1933. At the age of twenty-two she married a factory owner called Suryakant and the family lived in Tanzania, East Africa after their first son was born. They travelled to Britain before the 1968 Commonwealth Immigrants Act made it harder for British passport holders from former colonies to enter.*

The couple both came from what Jack Dromey, the Labour MP who was then secretary of Brent Trades Council, describes as the 'mercantile and administrative classes'. They had been used to respect, but when they moved to England, respect was in short supply. As new immigrants, they were presumed to be cheap, disposable labour.

Jayaben Desai found this insulting. Her middle-class background, and her teenage experience of the Indian independence movement, reminded her every day of the gulf between the treatment of migrant workers and Britons. The reason she 'burned with injustice', Dromey told me, 'with those flaming eyes of hers, was they had had status, and then they arrived to a cold welcome in bleak north-west London, ending up in a bucket shop being treated in the way they were'. The academic Sundari Anitha, who has researched the Grunwick strike, agreed. 'She felt, and she perceived, mistreatment and lack of respect acutely, because it was new

---

* The government, which was worried that up to 200,000 Asians expelled from Africa would take up their legal right to live in Britain, rushed through the legislation.

to her. I think it's similar to when Gandhi was thrown off the train in South Africa: he was outraged because he was being racialised as a black person. And so it was new for them to be racialised in that way.'

Over the years, the Grunwick workforce had changed from a racial mix – white women, black Caribbean women, Irish women – to being dominated by South Asian immigrants. That affected how they were treated, as did their sex: more than 60 per cent of the Grunwick strikers were female. 'Women are constructed as nimble-fingered workers, and that construction relies on particular ideas about gender, stereotypes about passivity, docility and capacity for hard work, and that assumption that they will be easily exploitable,' Sundari Anitha told me. 'Certain jobs are constructed as women's jobs, which devalues those jobs.' Marginalised by their race *and* their sex, Grunwick's women felt they were at the bottom of the pile. As one of Desai's fellow strikers told the writer and activist Amrit Wilson in 1978: 'Imagine how humiliating it was for us, particularly for older women, to be working and to overhear the employer saying to a young English girl, "You don't want to come and work here, love, we won't be able to pay the sort of wages that'll keep you here," while we had to work there because we were trapped.'

In the mail room, the women were made to ask the manager if they needed the loo. 'If you were going to the toilet and it took too long, then he would ask why, what you were up to,' striker Lakshmi Patel told the BBC in 2019. Jayaben Desai counselled another woman not to be intimidated by this practice. 'Why do you feel ashamed, when he has no shame making you ask loudly?' she told her colleague. 'Learn how to say it in English, "I want to go to the ladies," and then just say it without any hesitation.'

Today, delivery drivers and warehouse packers report the same restrictions. Toilets are a feminist issue, because women need more loos than men. It's both a mechanical issue – we can't unzip and go – and also because women might need to pump breast milk or change sanitary pads or tampons. God forbid, we might need to wash our Mooncups in the sink. In jobs which require travel, like bus driving or haulage, women can't urinate on the hoof like men can (but, let's be honest, shouldn't). Incontinence is far more common in women, and is a particular issue after childbirth. Restricting toilet access is always petty and denigrating but it has an extra force when used against women.*

The toilet situation was not the only slight endured by Desai and her colleagues. The lab owner, an Anglo-Indian man called George Ward, kept a list of workers in descending order of productivity. The lowest ranked were often laid off, and the very existence of the list was a reminder of the insecurity of their employment. Overtime was compulsory and sometimes ran until 10 p.m. It would often be announced just before the end of the working day, making it difficult for mothers to collect their children from school. 'The women were treated particularly badly in the company,' Desai told a women's rally at Alexandra Palace in 1977. 'Pregnant women were not allowed to go to the antenatal clinic and women were refused time off to take their sick children to the doctor . . . We were insulted if we did not work harder. All this and more was suffered in silence by the Asian women of Grunwick.'

Sunil Desai, then a student, worked alongside his forty-three-year-old mother in the mail room. It was a Friday – 20 August – and so there was extra pressure to send out the processed photographs before the weekend. Earlier that day, another student called Devshi Bhudia had resisted what he saw as an unreasonable demand to sort thirteen crates of outgoing mail by the end of the day. After his dismissal, three other male workers walked out with him. Then Sunil got in trouble too: he was tickled by another student, and began to

---

* Don't get me started on loos. Is there anything more quietly radicalising than being trapped in an endless queue and watching men waltz straight by into the gents? Having a full bladder makes me 13 per cent more annoyed by sexism, it turns out.

laugh. The manager, Malcolm Alden, told him and his friend to 'stop chattering like monkeys, this is not a zoo'.

As she was preparing to leave, Jayaben Desai ended up in an argument with Alden over whether she would work overtime. His dismissive words to her son had also annoyed her. 'I addressed everybody,' Desai told Lord Justice Scarman's 1977 inquiry into the dispute. She asked Alden why he did not employ any white girls in the department. Perhaps, she implied, Grunwick relied on migrant women and students because they weren't seen as breadwinners, and so could be underpaid and casually laid off without making the management feel guilty.

Then she said something which has entered Grunwick's mythology: 'You said earlier that this is not a zoo. Well, what you are running here is not a factory, it is a zoo. In a zoo there are many types of animal. Some are monkeys who dance to your tune; others are lions who can bite your head off. We are the lions, Mr Manager.'*

Having delivered the speech, Jayaben and Sunil were escorted out.

*

By Monday, there were pickets outside the gates at Grunwick: a familiar sight in the 1970s, as strikers gathered to discourage colleagues from entering a workplace. More staff walked out at 3 p.m., and there was a scuffle around the corner as people from a nearby plant joined the unofficial strike. There was a problem, though. None of the people there was a member of a trade union. As they were recent immigrants, this was not surprising: the big trade unions were dominated by traditional occupations like manufacturing, and their idea of the 'working class' was often white, British and male.

---

* Joe Rogaly's book on the dispute, published in 1977, does not carry the famous exchange, but it does record that on the following Monday, the sacked workers gathered by the factory gates with a placard which read: 'Grunwicks [sic] is a zoo'.

But it also meant that the Grunwick workers had legally left their jobs and were entitled to nothing.

And so Sunil Desai, his friends and his mother decided that they needed to join a trade union. I don't want to get too misty-eyed here. It is difficult now to imagine the power the unions once wielded: in the 1926 General Strike 1.5 million Britons went on strike in support of coal miners, according to the National Archives. In 1970, 10 million working days were lost through strike action.

At the time of the Grunwick walkout, many unions were extraordinarily powerful, and they did not always use that power fairly or responsibly. 'Closed shops' – workplaces where only union members could be employed – led to dodgy hiring practices, such as family members getting preferential treatment, or particular ethnic groups being silently excluded. When I first started working on a daily newspaper, the older journalists would regale me with stories of the print unions, whose grip on Fleet Street was smashed by Rupert Murdoch's decision to print a paper without them. The printers had a macho, hard-drinking culture and they resisted technological advances which would reduce their numbers and power. Not all journalists were sorry to see them go.

It feels banal to say it, but one of the inevitable issues with trade unions is that they protect the livelihoods of their members – against everyone else. In the first half of the twentieth century, that membership was overwhelmingly white and male. And so women and minorities often struggled to get the backing of the biggest force then agitating for better pay and conditions.

Eight years before Grunwick, women went on strike at the Ford plant in Dagenham because their sewing jobs were classed as 'unskilled' while equivalent male roles were deemed 'more skilled'. Their jobs had been given a lower grade precisely to avoid upsetting (male) workers in other parts of the plant.

The Dagenham women initially received little support from the union leadership. When the Labour cabinet minister Barbara Castle invited them in for tea, she discovered that – quite aside from the controversial grading system – women at the plant 'automatically got 85 per cent of the men's rate'. As Castle wrote in her memoir *Fighting All the Way*, the strike confirmed her belief 'that equal pay was an issue that the Labour government could not ignore much longer'. She faced fierce resistance from fellow left-wingers. Men's wages were being held down to control inflation, so how could women ask for more money? It was a hard slog to pass the Equal Pay Act two years later. The 1970 Act made it illegal to pay women less for the same work. However, subtler forms of discrimination persist. Female-dominated fields tend to pay less than male-dominated ones, no matter the skill level required. Why? Because 'women's work' is done by women. Therefore, goes the unspoken reasoning, it must be easier.

Barbara Castle's struggle is worth remembering today because there is an easy, unquestioned assumption that all liberation movements – anti-racism, LGBT rights, feminism and disability activism – are pulling in the same direction. A rising tide of tolerance lifts all boats – that's the line. But gains for one group *do* sometimes come at the expense of another. That argument is difficult to make, but making it is vital. It is the difference between a happy-clappy self-help movement and a real political struggle. The idea of competing rights is a crucial part of the abortion debate, for example. How far can women control their bodies, even at the expense of a potential person growing inside them?

Fighting a patriarchal bogeyman – a white, rich, heterosexual, cisgender bogeyman, cackling and catcalling, probably wearing a monocle – is straightforward. Feminism is now most difficult when it clashes with another oppression. Take the insistence by some activists that there is no conflict between the rights of trans women and biological females in, say, elite sports. There clearly is, because male puberty confers similar advantages to doping – greater strength, speed and oxygen capacity – which are not entirely negated by suppressing testosterone production. A compromise is needed, separating trans women's legal right to change their gender from rules which need to take their biological sex into account. Or take the thorny question of religious fundamentalism, which often restricts women's opportunities and behaviour. Should ultra-orthodox Jewish and hard-line Islamic schools be allowed to teach pupils that homosexuality is wrong? Modern liberation movements are often lazy, assuming that a simple solution can be found, where no one feels discriminated against – or hand-waving away the conflict by implying that only one group deserves a hearing. If only.

There is also the question of whose needs get addressed *first*. 'The language of priorities is the religion of socialism,' said Aneurin Bevan, the Labour politician who helped found the NHS. The language of priorities ought to be the religion of feminism, too. There are times when Difficult Women need to put themselves first. The history of feminism is a history of women being assured their cause is valid – but told to wait their turn. It happened to the suffragettes, who were told that Irish Home Rule and universal male suffrage had to come first, and it happened to the munitionettes, ordered back into their homes to make space for returning soldiers.

That tendency is driven by an unspoken belief that sexism is somehow not a *proper* oppression, like racism or homophobia – oppressions that can also be suffered by men. And it's influenced by our ideas about womanhood itself. In a contest with any other minority, women are expected to pipe down and budge up, to be self-less and accommodating. It is difficult to insist, as the suffragettes did, that fighting sexism has to come first. But sometimes it is necessary. In the end, the Ford women's jobs were only reclassified as more skilled after another strike. Their struggle upset the working-class men they saw every day. They could not let that stop them.

I mention all this because women and ethnic minorities have often failed to find solidarity from the trade union movement, which was set up to mobilise the working class. Migrant women face a

combined dose of discrimination: they are not just oppressed as
migrants or as women, but as *both* at the same time. Tackling this
requires what the US legal scholar Kimberlé Williams Crenshaw
calls 'intersectionality'.

Crenshaw described a case from 1976, the same year the Grunwick strike began. An African American woman called Emma
DeGraffenreid sued General Motors for employment discrimination
on the grounds of race *and* gender. The company hired black men for
some types of jobs – principally on the factory floor – and white
women for others, such as typing. Black women were considered
suitable for neither. Where were the opportunities for them? A system which treated racial and sex-based discrimination as two
separate categories provided black women with no way to sue over
this. 'While a black applicant might get hired to work on the floor of
the factory if he were male; if she were a black female she would not
be considered,' wrote Crenshaw in the *Washington Post* in 2015.
'Similarly, a woman might be hired as a secretary if she were white,
but wouldn't have a chance at that job if she were black. Neither the
black jobs nor the women's jobs were appropriate for black women,
since they were neither male nor white.'

Intersectionality does not mean – as modern feminists sometimes use it – that sexism is a less interesting or important oppression
than others. It does not mean that women, implicitly, should get to
the back of the queue. Intersectionality means that any consider-
ation of sexism interacts with race, class, sexuality and disability to
create unique forms of discrimination. In the case of Grunwick, Jayaben Desai – as an Asian woman – faced a double expectation that
she would be quiet, docile and uncomplaining. She resisted it.

Similar situations to the one described by Crenshaw arose in
Britain, as migrant women realised how differently they were
treated both from their husbands and their white female colleagues.
In 1972, there was a strike by 380 hosiery workers in Mansfield.
'A white woman would never be suspended if her work was bad or if

she behaved in an "undisciplined" way. An Asian woman would often be suspended for two to three days,' wrote Bennie Bunsee in the feminist magazine *Spare Rib* in 1974. 'White women workers were on an average wage – most of the Asian women worked on a piece-rate basis [paid for each piece of work]. This meant that they had to work much harder to ensure sufficient wages.' Asian women were given documents outlining their rates written in English, which they could not understand, and were told to sign them immediately. Their union ignored their suggestion of getting an interpreter. As the relationship between management and workers soured, one woman was told she could no longer wear a sari to work for 'health and safety reasons'. That strike ended when a factory committee, including eleven Asian workers, was set up. The migrant women were granted access to better jobs and white and Asian women agreed to discuss their pay rates together. However, wrote Bunsee, the 'strike had raised many issues, not least of which was the dignity of the Asians themselves as a people. A familiar slogan of the workers was "we will not go back like dogs".'

In May 1974, workers at the Imperial Typewriters factory in Leicester walked out. The company had increased its turnover from the late 1960s onwards by employing migrants, with a particular focus on women. The strikers protested about a dozen infuriating pinpricks, which added up to an obvious lack of respect: they got fewer tea breaks and were not allowed to visit a doctor in working hours, for example. The management decided to close the factory rather than resolve the problem.

At Imperial Typewriters, 'the power of the women came not only from their being half of the strike force, but from their position as mothers and housewives in the community', wrote Ron Ramdin in *The Making of the Black Working Class in Britain*. 'In the past, Asian women fully supported the industrial demands of their menfolk. Given low wages, they had no choice. The alternative was

scabbing.* This strike was unique in that the women had the collective power to make their demand for equal pay a priority. They
were the latest section of the working class to fall into factory
production.'

In the 1970s, as women moved out of the house and into factories
and offices, they gained the ability to organise collectively for better
conditions. But their employment was constantly depicted as a threat
to the existing (male) workforce. The radical potential of working
women's collective power was repressed by setting them against
their husbands, sons and brothers. It was divide and rule.

*

After walking out, Sunil Desai called Jack Dromey, who put him in
touch with the Apex union. To their credit, despite the unorthodox
walkout Apex backed the Grunwick workers, which meant they
could get strike pay and legal advice. By 31 August, 137 of the 490
people at the lab were on strike, receiving £8 a week (which later
rose to £30) from their union. But Grunwick's managers insisted
that the strikers had no right to walk out, and that joining a union
afterwards was meaningless. George Ward, the owner, resisted all
pleas to give the strikers back their jobs.

Unlike in Dagenham, there was immediate solidarity for the
Grunwick workers from the wider movement. The local postal union
'blacked' the mail to the laboratory – refusing to deliver its post. But
it soon bowed to pressure from the government and resumed deliv-
eries. 'We thought we had won,' Jack Dromey told me. 'And when
postal blacking was called off, it was a devastating blow.' George
Ward had launched a legal challenge against the postal union's act of
solidarity with his workers, backed by the leader of the opposition,
Margaret Thatcher.

* 'Scabbing' is continuing to work when others are on strike.

A meeting was called at the Brent Trades and Labour Hall. Standing on the podium, all four foot eleven of her, Jayaben Desai held the audience spellbound. 'She would always say to me, "Mr Jack, my English, it is not good,"' Jack Dromey told me. 'But I've never come across anyone who had that way with words: inspirational, Shakespearean, it was utterly remarkable.' Desai invoked Gandhi – whose long campaign of non-violent resistance to British rule galvanised India – to prevent her fellow strikers falling into despair. 'You could see this audience, predominantly women,' says Dromey. 'You could just see their shoulders come up.'

When the postal blacking was called off in November 1976, the strikers knew that they were in for a long, bitter winter. They sent delegations to more than a thousand workplaces around the country: women in saris arrived at steel mills and engineering factories and car plants and dockyards. That, said Dromey, brought home 'to the big battalions of the working class, which was predominantly white-led at the time, that there was a world of work about which they knew absolutely nothing'.

This is when the legend of Jayaben Desai, leader of 'the strikers in saris', was born. She was aware of how different she looked from the accepted image of a union militant – red face, jowls, moustache – and she exploited it. Black and white newspaper photographs don't do her justice: colour footage shows a diminutive figure in a bright blue hat and pink sari, illuminated against ranks of policemen in identical navy uniforms. A factory manager once tried to intimidate her. 'You can't win with that sari on,' he said. 'Why don't you change into a miniskirt?'* Desai's reply took inspiration from Indira Gandhi, then prime minister of India: 'I'll tell you something, manager. Mrs Gandhi wears a sari and she runs a country of 600 million people. You can't even run a little factory.'

---

* Let's pause a moment and consider whether we think that man would have respected a woman in a miniskirt more. OK, that's long enough.

Like Annie Kenney in her mill-girl clogs and shawl, Desai both embraced and subverted the stereotypes projected on to her. She was no submissive Asian woman; she was undoubtedly a matriarch. 'Some of the stories I heard back, from Sheffield Steel Mills, for example,' said Dromey. 'That Mrs Desai, said the convenor, *bloody hellfire*. I said: *I know what you mean.*' Pictures from the picket line show younger men in extravagant collars and shoulder-length hair, with the women in thick checked coats over their floor-length saris and shalwar kameez. 'End slave labour' read one placard. 'Greedy Rude Ugly Nasty WICKed' read another.

In footage from the BBC, a reporter asks Jayaben, 'How long will you stay here?'

She looks at him, totally nonplussed, and replies in lightly accented English. 'Until we have finished this dispute.'

A year, he asks?

'Any time.'

Five years?

'Ten years.'

She smiles at him with calm finality.

By the next summer, June 1977, more supporters were descending on the laboratory every day. By 11 July – a Friday – there were 20,000 people at the gates. The protesters tried to stop a bus taking non-striking workers inside. Public sympathy for the strikers started to fade as television reports began to show busloads of pickets (including miners brought in by their union leader Arthur Scargill) and riot police in full gear. 'Policemen's helmets started flying,' observed one reporter at the time. There were 500 arrests over the two years the strike lasted.

In the late 1960s, fearing that voters would become fed up with trade union militancy, Barbara Castle had tried to moderate the unions with a White Paper called 'In Place of Strife', which called for measures such as ballots before strike action. However, Castle's abrasive personality and obvious ambition – she was definitely a

Difficult Woman – alienated key colleagues. She was dismissed out of hand by many in the trade union movement because of her sex. In her autobiography, the chapter describing this period is called 'In Place of Popularity'. The unions resisted rule changes. Her plan sank, and her star fell. For the rest of the decade, the Conservatives would treat the trade unions as an enemy to be defeated.

With the Tories on the attack, the Labour prime minister, Jim Callaghan, found the unrest embarrassing. He commissioned a judge to settle the Grunwick dispute. We should be thankful for this decision, because Lord Justice Scarman took extensive evidence from both strikers and management, capturing voices which would otherwise be lost. Jayaben Desai testified at length, telling the commission that the overtime demands were particularly distressing 'because it was a lonely place and ladies were scared to go [home] alone'. Scarman recommended that the union should be recognised, and the sacked workers reinstated. George Ward, who had been born in New Delhi, protested that he was an immigrant himself.* He ignored the report.

The way Jayaben Desai's reasonable demands were woven into a story of dangerous union militancy was a foretaste of the next decade. She was experiencing the beginning of a wider backlash. We now know that police used 'excessive violence' against striking miners at Orgreave in 1984. According to an independent investigation, there was 'a false narrative from police exaggerating violence by miners, perjury by officers giving evidence to prosecute the arrested men, and an apparent cover-up of that perjury by senior officers'. The South Yorkshire chief constable at the time, Peter Wright, was also involved in the campaign to blame the 1989 Hillsborough disaster on unruly, drunken fans rather than policing failures.

---

* Again, this shows the importance of a structural rather than personal analysis. Why should the immigrant background of Grunwick's owner automatically make him immune to exploiting other migrants?

The police were no more friends to the Grunwick strikers than they were to the suffragettes. Both sets of women were seen as disruptive agents, threats to public order, enemies of the state. Suspicion of the strikers was amplified by the right-wing press and an emerging network of right-wing ideologues. 'Often the dispute has been described as a dispute of the militant left,' said Dromey. 'Actually, in political terms, the most significant thing about it was the emergence of the militant right.' Keith Joseph, a leading Thatcherite thinker, warned that it would represent 'all our tomorrows' if the union won.

Two factors ended the strike at Grunwick. The TUC lost its nerve, withdrawing support under pressure from the Labour government. Its general secretary Len Murray argued that the public would never have supported the actions demanded by the strikers – cutting off not just Grunwick's post, but its water and electricity supplies. After various legal battles, the House of Lords upheld George Ward's right not to recognise a trade union at the factory. The strikers in saris had proved that women and migrants were a neglected and exploited part of the workforce, but they had lost their own battle. The Grunwick strike committee announced on 14 July 1978 that the strike was over.

The next year, Margaret Thatcher's Conservatives won the general election on a manifesto promising to limit union power. 'We cannot go on, year after year, tearing ourselves apart in increasingly bitter and calamitous industrial disputes,' it said. 'Too often trade unions are dominated by a handful of extremists who do not reflect the common-sense views of most union members.'

Jayaben Desai, who said she walked out because she had 'self-respect', still had it. But she had little else to show for two years on the picket lines.

*

Ayesha Hazarika heard the story of Grunwick in the dying days of Gordon Brown's government. The Labour Party was exhausted after more than a decade running Britain, and from dealing with the financial crisis. The department Hazarika joined was dispirited and worn out.

Her new boss was Harriet Harman – Jack Dromey's wife, although it would be fairer to describe Jack Dromey as Harriet Harman's husband. Harman was deputy leader of the Labour Party – although not deputy prime minister, as her predecessor John Prescott had been. She was also minister for women and equalities, and it was in this role that she wanted Hazarika's help.

The younger woman had worked on equalities in government already, under trade minister Patricia Hewitt in 2003. 'It was always given to people as a consolation prize,' Hazarika told me. 'Nobody cared about the post that much, and Harriet came along and she absolutely loved it. This was her complete political mission.'

Hazarika wasn't a teenage politics obsessive. She studied law at Hull University and worked in the music industry. She also dabbled in stand-up comedy, to which she has since returned. Hazarika attributes her unusual route into politics to her background: her parents moved to Glasgow from Assam in India, and they had an idea of what 'good immigrants' did. 'You put your head down, you don't really get involved in politics,' is how Hazarika describes it. Glasgow's tradition of left-wing firebrands – think former nightclub owner Tommy Sheridan or trilby-wearing provocateur George Galloway – further convinced her parents that politics was not for people like them. 'My mum always said to me, "You could never be involved in politics, it's for white, working-class men." So it didn't even occur to me that a lot of women would have been involved in the trade union movement, let alone a woman of colour.'

The way Hazarika describes it, the Equalities Office was a 'Cinderella department', overlooked and underestimated. Under anyone but Harriet Harman, it might well have emitted a lot of hot air, a handful of right-on press releases, and little else. But Harman is the Labour Party's most recent Difficult Woman. Elected at the age of thirty-two when five months pregnant in 1982, she has spent her career as an unashamed champion of women's issues. She married Jack Dromey after meeting him through the union disputes of the 1970s. 'Love across the barricades,' laughs Hazarika. In the New Labour era, she acquired a reputation as 'Britain's most ear-drillingly insistent feminist' (copyright: Quentin Letts of the *Daily Mail*).

Harman's career demonstrates one of the key qualities of a Difficult Woman: she persisted. Sacked from Tony Blair's first cabinet after a year, she was dismissed as 'batty Hattie'. But she gradually built a power base in the Labour Party, and her pet issues – such as the niche idea that childcare was an important policy area – moved to the mainstream. In the three decades between the Grunwick strike and her appointment as deputy Labour leader, the trade unions declined in power, but women's rights at work steadily advanced. In 1993, maternity leave was extended to all women, not just those who had worked for long qualifying periods. In 2003, male employees received paid paternity leave for the first time.

Harman also inspired a generation of women to enter the Labour Party, and to question its male-dominated power bases. The TUC, founded in 1868, only acquired its first female general secretary in 2013. Several unions have still never had a female leader. The big unions did not support Harman's deputy leadership bid, and she took out a personal loan to run for the position.

When I profiled Harman in 2017, the thirtysomething Labour MP Jess Phillips explained the debt her generation owed to her. 'It's like: my mum had to moan about the patriarchy, whereas I get to be funny about the patriarchy,' she told me. Harman's lonely battle had little space for fun. Today's feminists, with greater strength in numbers, can afford to laugh at sexism as well as fight it.

Crucially, Harman rejected the idea that women should see each other as competition. The US feminist Katha Pollitt called this 'Smurfette syndrome': just as there is only one female Smurf, we imagine there is only one slot for women at the top table. If *she* has it, then *I* can't: so I have to bring her down. You could also call it the 'Margaret Thatcher' approach: Thatcher appointed only one woman to her cabinet in her whole time as prime minister.* She argued that women were being held back by their own lack of ambition, and that feminism amounted to a demand for special treatment. 'I did not get here by being some strident female,' she told an audience in Glasgow before the 1979 election. 'I do not like strident females. I like people with ability who do not run the feminist ticket too hard. I reckon if you get anywhere it is because of your ability as a person and not because of your sex.'

Deep breath. Point one, Mrs T: you absolutely *were* a strident female. In 1948, you were rejected for a job at ICI because the interviewers found you 'headstrong, obstinate and dangerously self-opinionated'. You did not want to stay at home and bake cookies any more than Hillary Clinton did. 'Of course, to be a mother and a housewife is a vocation of a very high kind. But I simply felt that it was not the whole of my vocation,' you conceded in your 1995 memoir. 'I needed a career because, quite simply, that was the sort of person I was.'

Point two: as well as your own ambition, you benefited from advantages that other women around you did not have. Perhaps most importantly, you had a husband who supported your career, rather than expecting you to sacrifice everything for him. That caused *huge* comment at the time, and even now, large sections of the men's rights movement would still describe Denis as a pussy-whipped 'beta'. 'If marriage is either a takeover or a merger, then my parents enjoyed the latter,' wrote your daughter Carol. You also had a full-time nanny, in whose bedroom the children slept. They were later sent to boarding school. You were able to work

---

* It was her friend Janet Young, who became the Conservative Leader of the House of Lords. She blocked lowering the age of consent for gay men, and the repeal of Section 28.

like a man, making the most of your 'ability as a person', unhindered by the second shift of caring responsibilities that fell on other women.

Point three: you benefited from advantages won for you by strident females. The suffragettes and suffragists who ensured that women had the vote. The campaigners who fought for women to enter the universities, without whom you couldn't have gone to Oxford. The campaigners who ensured that when Denis's first wife left him for another man, the couple were granted a divorce. Those who agitated for the 1919 Sex Disqualification (Removal) Act, which allowed women to qualify as lawyers – something you did before your election to Parliament.

Point four: your actions show that you knew many colleagues and voters would take you less seriously as a woman, and you tried to anticipate their concerns. You took lessons to lower your voice, so you sounded less 'shrill' and more authoritative – more like a man – in the House of Commons chamber. You might have reckoned that 'if you get anywhere it is because of your ability as a person and not because of your sex', but many talented women have never been able to achieve their full potential because of the barriers in their way.* Sorry, Mrs T, but you were dead wrong.

By contrast, Harriet Harman always insisted that she was not an exception. That made her enemies in the male-dominated trade unions and Labour movement, so she built a fortress inside the Equalities Office instead. Labour's 2005 manifesto had promised to narrow the gender pay gap, and to review inequality across all disadvantaged groups. The power players in Gordon Brown's Downing Street saw this as a 'tidying up exercise', according to Ayesha Hazarika. But Harman had other ideas. She told her 'beaten down' civil servants that she wanted to do something really big, and when they

---

* People still ask me regularly if Thatcher is a 'feminist icon'. My answer is that she's not *my* feminist icon.

said that Number 10 wouldn't let them, she told them pointedly: 'You answer to me, not to Number 10.'

Then Harman summoned all the individual equalities commissions for race, disability and so on to her offices in Admiralty House in Whitehall, and told them to give her their top three requests. 'When they came to see us,' said Hazarika, they had internalised the message of 'don't be too ambitious, don't do anything radical, don't try and rock the boat in any way. So they all came out with the weakest, weakest things ever.'

So Harman, Hazarika and their team decided they would have to bulldoze through their own, more radical demands. First was pay transparency: getting businesses to reveal what they paid their male and female workers, and the gap between the two. By now it was 2007, and Downing Street was preparing for an election (which, in the end, was 'bottled' by Brown). So there was huge resistance at the top of Labour to doing anything which would upset business leaders. A commission was set up – usually a good way to bury any potential radicalism under mounds of paper and months of deliberation. Harman bypassed it, announcing that a simple hourly figure would be used to calculate the pay gap. Her solution wasn't perfect, but it would shine a light on the problem.

It certainly did. It took a decade for Harman's plans to be put into action, but in April 2018, companies with more than 250 employees had to reveal their pay gap. Early data from 10,000 businesses and public sector organisations revealed that women's median hourly rate was 9.7 per cent less than men's. At the BBC, six male presenters – Huw Edwards, Nicky Campbell, John Humphrys, Jon Sopel, Nick Robinson and Jeremy Vine – took pay cuts. The China editor Carrie Gracie, who quit after discovering men in equivalent roles were being paid more, received an apology and back pay. She donated the money to the Fawcett Society, the charity organisation named in honour of the suffragist Millicent Fawcett.

Once again: information is power. The data proved women were underpaid, and it gave them a weapon to use in future negotiations. Hopefully, this transparency will also smash the long-standing myth that women aren't assertive enough at work, and that's why they are paid less than men. A 2016 study by the Cass Business School, which looked at 4,600 workers, found that the problem was not 'reticent female syndrome' but straightforward discrimination. Full-time women workers were as likely as men to ask for a pay rise. Men were just 25 per cent more likely to get one.*

Both Harman and Hazarika felt that it was easier to be difficult with data on your side. This is why the fight was so important. 'That went right up to the wire,' said Hazarika. 'Harriet had to pull a bit of a Barbara Castle on it, go in and see Gordon [Brown] and kick off about it . . . We decided between us that this was the hill we had to die on.'

As ever, those in power came up with good reasons not to give feminists what they wanted. In this case, it was the possibility of an election, and the idea that equalities legislation would be used to paint Labour as an anti-business party, a champion of right-on griev-ances. Hazarika says that the Number 10 advisers desperately tried to get Harman to drop her demand for pay transparency. 'You've always been about the greater good of the party,' Harman was told. 'Why would you risk your entire reputation?' As a devout Labour loyalist, she nearly folded. 'I was like: you can't, this is your legacy,' says Hazarika. 'And she absolutely stood firm.'

The Equality Act, as it became, did not just usher in pay trans-parency. It also extended anti-discrimination legislation to cover age, and permitted political parties to keep using all-women short-lists for MPs. This was also fiercely resisted by Number 10, and Hazarika recalled getting a call from a special adviser there

---

* The study also found that part-time workers were less likely to ask. And guess which sex dominates part-time work? Women. Once again, equal pay is a more diffi-cult concept than it looks.

shouting at her about it. 'And I remember Harriet saying to me: unfurrow your brow, because this is what life is like. We're not going to get anywhere if we seek permission, and weep. We have to be really difficult and really unreasonable.'

The Act's most radical provision – which has never been pursued – is the 'public sector equality duty', which tried to return class to the political discussion. Any decisions taken by national or local government should pay 'due regard to the desirability of exercising [power] in a way that is designed to reduce the inequalities of outcome which result from socio-economic disadvantage'. In other words, would they help or hurt economic inequality? It was described by the *Guardian*'s Polly Toynbee as 'socialism in one clause'. But it has never been enacted.

Like the Equal Pay Act before it, the Equality Act only just squeaked through in the last days of a Labour government. It received royal assent on 8 April 2010. Two days earlier, Gordon Brown had gone to Buckingham Palace and asked for a general election. It was an election he would lose, ushering in a Conservative government led by David Cameron and George Osborne, supported by Nick Clegg of the Liberal Democrats. They would bring in a regime of 'austerity' which fell hardest on women, because women rely more heavily on public services. The coalition government could do this because they did not have to analyse the effects of their Budgets by gender, nor pay 'due regard' to reducing inequality.

Harriet Harman's revolution remains unfinished.

*

'At some point, you have to be badly behaved,' says Ayesha Hazarika now. 'You have to kick off. You have to threaten to either go public, to name and shame, or resign, or cause a stink, or a scandal happens.' Being difficult gives you leverage – but it is also exhausting.

During her time working for Harman, Hazarika says that she and the Civil Service team turned from being 'tiny wee

mice' – worried about upsetting the men in Number 10 – into confident, demanding, *effective* operators. Although the two women came
from the party's soft left (and have both been criticised for their
lack of support for Jeremy Corbyn's leadership), at the time they
were seen as 'crazy, sort of socialist, feminist, ridiculous people'
and banned from using the word 'class' in official documents and
speeches because it was deemed too frightening.

This is another way feminists get screwed over by history.
Women like Barbara Castle and Harriet Harman fought great battles to enact legislation which now seems like common sense. So
they get little credit. The mainstream tradition of the party, which
once regarded their views as madly fringe, instead rewrites them
as pushing on an open door. Men get to be radicals. Women are bat-
tleaxes and harridans when they are pushing for change, then
irrelevant old biddies, or soft-focus saints, once they've achieved it.
In terms of achieving her political agenda, Harriet Harman has had
incredible success. And yet the current fashion in Labour is to deride
her as an irrelevant 'Blairite', while praising the backbench career of
Jeremy Corbyn, which has no significant legislation to show for it.

Jayaben Desai nearly suffered a similar neglect. 'I'm sure there
are tons of really active Asian women in the trade union movement,
but we don't really hear about them,' says Hazarika. 'I thought, if it
would be unusual *now* for a strong woman of colour to be involved in
these type of disputes, I couldn't even believe that a woman back all
those years was involved, particularly at a time when Enoch Powell
had quite recently mobilised the trade union movement to march.'

Hazarika believes that George Ward, the Grunwick owner,
employed South Asian women because he believed they would be
submissive, with a strong work ethic, and would 'give him no trouble
at all'. Desai's protest, then, smashed expectations of both her ethnic
background and her gender.

Like I said earlier, let's not indulge moist-eyed paeans for 1970s
trade unions without acknowledging their imperfections. But

equally, let's not ignore the fact that their decline is part of a wider pattern in Western politics: a move from collectivism to individualism. This has spread to both the feminist and LGBT movements, which now often focus on personal decisions rather than class-based actions. It darkly amuses me that two of the wokest media brands, Vice and BuzzFeed, have strongly resisted their employees forming unions.

Meanwhile, one of the #MeToo movement's greatest villains should be the incredibly dull Conservative politician Chris Grayling. He might not have masturbated into a pot plant or demanded massages off aspiring actresses, but he did terrible damage to victims of workplace sexual harassment by introducing an upfront fee to begin an employment tribunal.* In the three years after the policy was enacted in 2013, the number of tribunal claims fell by 79 per cent. The Supreme Court later ruled that the fees of between £390 and £1,200 were unlawful. The government refunded everyone who had paid them, but it could not undo the injustice of all the cases which were simply never brought.

Trade unions also gave many workers a political education, teaching them that the relationship between managers and workers is an ongoing negotiation rather than a natural law. Unions encouraged workers to see that they were stronger together and could reject low wages and poor conditions. Perhaps we have become complacent about some of the victories won for workers in the last fifty years, as progress once again erases the struggle that preceded it. Since 1999, Britain has a minimum wage (although it is still too low to live on). Our membership of the European Union has bolstered domestic laws on flexible working, health and safety and pregnancy discrimination. We might need to fight to keep these after Brexit: when politicians talk about cutting 'red tape' and 'bureaucracy', it's

---

* For legal reasons I would like to clarify that I claim no insight into whether or not Chris Grayling has masturbated into a pot plant.

worth asking what they mean. It is undoubtedly more efficient for employers to sack women who get pregnant. It's vital for feminism that they are legally prevented from doing so.

The majority of union members today are women: 54.6 per cent in 2017, up from 45 per cent in 1995. 'The average British trade union member is a fortysomething, degree-educated, white woman working in the professions,' wrote Claire Mullaly of the TUC in May 2018. So the decline of the unions since Grunwick has a feminist dimension.

*

Jayaben Desai was undoubtedly a Difficult Woman. The strikers in saris defied stereotypes about the passivity and domesticity of South Asian migrants, even as Desai played up to them in the press when it suited her cause. She was an inspiration, marshalling her troops long after they had been advised to give up. She was unyielding in her belief that the workers in that laboratory deserved better than they got.

It's easy to boil down Grunwick to a simple, saccharine story about the moment when trade unions finally embraced the concerns of migrant women. The truth is more complicated. It is notable that the most high-profile accounts of the dispute were written by white men, and that few of the other strikers apart from Jayaben Desai achieved any public recognition.* When I talked to Sundari Anitha, she warned me about the 'whole cult around Jayaben'. There was a risk, she said, 'when you forefront the exceptionalism of one person, you might inadvertently reinforce the idea that what they did was unusual and extraordinary in a way that it wasn't common for other South Asian women to do that'. She has a point. But I still find something inspiring about the tiny figure of Jayaben Desai, a thick coat

---

* Sometimes by choice: I tried to contact several other Grunwick strikers, and received no response.

over her pink sari, placard in hand. Like our other Difficult Women, she expanded our idea of what a woman could be.

In their book *Striking Women*, Sundari Anitha and Ruth Pearson express concern that 'the celebration of the strike increasingly resembles a kind of political nostalgia, a longing backward glance to the muscular activism of mass picketing, confrontation of the police and a centrifugal drawing together of all the progressive elements in the labour movement and the wider left'.

They compare Grunwick with a strike by women of South Asian descent at the airline catering firm Gate Gourmet in 2005. 'In stark contrast to the concerted support for the Grunwick workers, trade union solidarity for these women was conspicuous by its absence,' they write. This was partly a legacy of Margaret Thatcher's anti-union reforms. Baggage handlers wanted to take action in solidarity with the women, but it was illegal under anti-strike laws passed in 1980.

There was, however, one common thread between Grunwick and Gate Gourmet: the idea of migrant workers as 'naive' in their demands and approach to strike action. Sundari Anitha told me that the Gate Gourmet workers, who found agency workers in their place, walked out immediately: they had a 'long history of industrial militancy, they were used to trade unions, they were just disappointed in *that* trade union's lack of initiative'. Yet that was represented as not understanding how trade unions worked. 'Later on, when prison officers took an unballoted action, the media represented that as very principled: look, they don't care if they lose their jobs, because it's an unballoted action, what a principled stand they've taken,' she said. Some things change; some things stay the same.

After the strike, George Ward's factory prospered, although changes in technology ended the fashion for paper photos and it closed in 2011. He died in April 2012.

Jayaben Desai's health was not good after two bitter winters on the picket line. But she was able to return to the industry for which she had trained, sewing, and became a teacher at Harrow College. At the age of sixty, she passed her driving test – and encouraged other migrant women to do the same, reckoning that it would increase their freedom. 'Some Gujarati men still refuse to honour her because they disapprove of forceful, independent women,' wrote Graham Taylor in an updated version of his book *Grunwick* in 2015. 'She remains to this day a prophet not fully honoured in her own community.'

When Jayaben died in 2010, her family scattered her ashes near the sources of the Indus and the Ganges rivers, and in Rotherhithe, on the Thames. As a Hindu, she had believed that humans are united by the rivers which all flow into the ocean. In 2016, forty years after the Grunwick strike began, she was one of seven women named on the BBC *Woman's Hour* power list. The night before the announcement, there was a reception at Buckingham Palace hosted by the Duchess of Cornwall. Sunil – now known as Shiv – Desai and some of the other strikers went along. 'I'm not a great royalist, personally,' says Jack Dromey, with some understatement. 'But I just thought it absolutely wonderful that George Ward is in the proverbial dustbin of history, and all these years on, Jayaben Desai remains a legend.'

6. SAFETY

The home is by far the most dangerous place for women.
Helena Kennedy, *Eve Was Framed*

'Erin Pizzey? I thought she was dead!' says one stalwart of the Second Wave when I mention the name. A pause. 'But then, I suppose people say that about me.'

Jayaben Desai still does not have the recognition she deserves. And neither does Erin Pizzey – for very different reasons. She ought to be a feminist hero. In 1971, she founded the first women's refuge in Britain, with no money and no official support beyond the use of a run-down council semi with four rooms, a galley kitchen and an outside loo. The house in Chiswick, West London, helped hundreds of women escape abusive partners and rebuild their lives. As well as a place to stay, it was a community centre where women could get help with claiming benefits, starting divorce proceedings, or quitting drink and drugs.

Alongside equal pay, the refuge movement is one of the greatest achievements of the Second Wave. By 2017, there were 276 refuges in England, with 3,798 beds.* Pizzey's work in Chiswick led to the creation of Refuge, which is now the largest charity of its kind in England. It has an annual income of £13.3 million and employs more than 200 people.

As well as providing practical support, the refuge movement changed the language we use to describe violence inside the home – and with it, social attitudes to 'domestic violence'. For centuries, it had been assumed that since marriage was a form of ownership, a man could 'discipline' or 'correct' his wife however he saw fit. If he

* Even so, according to the charity Women's Aid, more than 10,000 women had to be turned away in 2016–17.

killed her in the process . . . That was regrettable, but perhaps she provoked him. Maybe she nagged him, or flirted with other men, or withheld sex. He must have had his reasons.

This forgiving attitude did not run the other way. Until 1828, a woman who killed her husband was prosecuted not for murder but for 'petty treason', an offence designed to punish those who rebelled against their superiors in law. Servants who killed their masters were also guilty of petty treason, as was a layperson who killed a priest. The punishment was burning at the stake, although a woman would usually be strangled to death before her body was burned. The practice continued until the 1790s.

The crime of petty treason itself was abolished by the Offences Against the Person Act 1828, which also made assault cases easier to try in court. But as late as the end of the nineteenth century, judges continued to argue over the right of men to inflict 'moderate chastisement' on their wives. Did this mean beating them or simply confining them to their homes? Even though 'wife-beating' was criminalised, its existence was still silently accepted. Why should the law interfere in a couple's private relationship? Today, this legacy shapes our attitude to domestic violence, and our response to it. There is a particular legal and social history of excusing it and ignoring it.

The Second Wave aimed to break that silence. In 1973, the Labour MP Jack Ashley told the House of Commons he wanted 'to draw the attention of the House to a subject cocooned in prejudice and buried in fear – the problem of wives who are victims of domestic violence'. It was a difficult subject to talk about, he said, because 'the general experience of these women is that no one wants to know . . . Too many men flippantly attribute it to "female provocation" or even "a perk of marriage". In fact the torment and misery of these wives is just another, but more savage, aspect of sex discrimination.'

Ashley observed that there was a temptation by polite society to dismiss violence as a working-class failing; not something perpetrated by People Like Us. He told the story of a civil servant's wife who went blind from a haemorrhage of the retina caused by repeated beatings. 'So much for the myth of normal domestic disputes confined to inadequate homes,' Ashley said. When a Home Office minister glibly asserted that the problem was that women did not report this abuse, Ashley offered examples of complaints being dismissed. 'Even when I fled to a police station with my face covered with blood all they did was write a report down in a book,' one woman had told him.

During his speech, Jack Ashley credited one activist above all for uncovering the hidden misery of thousands of battered women. 'Already the Chiswick Aid Centre has received hundreds of applications from women in distress all over the country,' he said. 'The centre was established by Mrs Erin Pizzey, a compassionate and remarkable woman who first identified the problem, then promptly did something about it.'

As he made that speech, Pizzey was watching from the gallery, along with women from the refuge. The chamber was nearly empty – whereas, Ashley pointed out, a debate on cruelty to dogs would have packed it out. Looking down on him, Pizzey decided that for domestic violence to be taken seriously, she needed to be seriously loud. Over the course of the 1970s, she turned herself into a celebrity. The first of her many books on domestic violence, *Scream Quietly or the Neighbours Will Hear*, was turned into a TV documentary. She attracted fans like Boy George and the author Fay Weldon, and rich backers such as the *Observer* editor David Astor. The Chiswick refuge itself became famous: Roger Daltrey and Kenney Jones of the Who paid a visit in 1980.

But there's a reason why Pizzey has faded from memory, even as the refuge movement endures. From the start, her relationship to the Women's Liberation Movement – a loose collection of groups which held an annual conference starting in 1970 – was fractious. It quickly became poisonous. In *Sweet Freedom*, Anna Coote and Bea-trix Campbell noted that four years after the creation of Pizzey's lone outpost in Chiswick, the National Women's Conference recorded that twenty-eight groups had already set up a refuge, and another eighty-three were working on it. Thanks to Erin Pizzey, this new movement – and this old problem – could not be ignored. But in 1975, they wrote, Pizzey 'stormed out after a row and has gone her own way ever since'.

'She single-handedly did as much for the cause of women as any other woman alive,' wrote Deborah Ross in the *Independent* in 1997. 'A great battler with a great, Beryl Cook body, she moved mountains by seeming more mountainous herself. She was awarded umpteen prizes. She went on every chat show going. She was listed in *Who's Who*.' But by the time Ross met her, Pizzey was living in a hostel for the homeless in West London, having left behind, in order: a second husband, a career as a writer of bodice-ripping novels, and substan-tial debts to her Italian landlady. She was fifty-eight.

Four years later, Dina Rabinovitch of the *Guardian* found Pizzey poised to release a book on women's violence through the Internet, having failed to find a mainstream publisher. Rabinovitch was sur-prised that Pizzey was now so thoroughly outside the feminist mainstream. It came 'as a shock to someone of my generation – we grew up hearing about the work she did for other women'. She was left wondering 'if a man who'd done so much would be quite so alone'.

By 2009, the break was complete. Pizzey wrote for the *Daily Mail* that she had realised feminism was 'a lie' and that 'women and men are both capable of extraordinary cruelty. Indeed, the only thing a child really needs – two biological parents under one roof – was being undermined by the very ideology which claimed to speak up for women's rights. This country is now on the brink of serious moral collapse. We must stop demonising men and start healing the rift that feminism has created between men and women.'

Pizzey is now an advocate for the men's rights movement, serving as editor-at-large of the anti-feminist website A Voice for Men. The editor of the site, Paul Elam, once vowed that he would never deliver a guilty verdict as a juror in a rape trial, no matter what the evidence was, because the court system has been corrupted by our 'false rape culture'. He has also called feminists 'human garbage', adding: 'the idea of fucking your shit up gives me an erection'.

Men's rights activists, or MRAs, contend that women's violence against *men* is under-reported, and that women perpetrate abuse against men in more subtle ways than a fist to the face.* The real domestic-violence scandal, they argue, is the way that male victims are ignored. The real rape scandal, they believe, is that too many men are convicted of rape. Many see this as part of a broader picture: they reject the idea of patriarchy and point to the ways in which men get a raw deal. More men than women die by suicide; more men die in wars; more men work in dangerous occupations such as deep-sea fishing; more men are in prison. All of those facts are true, but they are not incompatible with feminism. The gendered division of labour, the idea that men must defend their honour or status with violence, the taboo on talking honestly about feelings of weakness and vulnerability . . . To me, these are mirror images of the harmful stereotypes and expectations imposed on women.†

So here's what puzzled me about Erin Pizzey. Her autobiography talks in heartbreaking detail about women who were beaten savagely by their partners. She knew several who went back to an

---

* There are also men's groups such as CALM which raise awareness of men's issues without the heavy overtones that these problems could be solved if only feminism were defeated.

† That said, here's a difficult question: if you believe in gender quotas for company boards, do you also believe in them for fisheries? According to EU research, 'women feel unwelcome in the seagoing fishing subsector, but have little interest in participating anyway. It is not surprising that very few women are involved (3 per cent of the workforce)'.

abusive partner – and were killed as a result. How does a woman go from founding England's first refuge for domestic-violence victims to hanging out with MRAs?

*

By her own admission, Erin Pizzey was deeply shaped by her childhood. She was born in China in 1939, and her family includes a twin sister, Rosaleen, and a brother called Daniel. Her father's career as a diplomat took the family around the world and she was raised in boarding schools – a relief, she says, compared with living with her 'dysfunctional and violent' parents. She also had an early insight into life under an all-consuming political ideology in communist China.

She now lives in a top-floor flat in Twickenham, West London. I thought she might be crabby and guarded, seeing me as an emissary of a political movement she now views as the enemy. The truth was more complicated. She was happy to set up an interview, via email and then phone, and invited me to her home.

I ordered her memoir, *This Way to the Revolution*, which depicts Pizzey as a plain-spoken housewife who didn't have any truck with the ideology-obsessed bluestockings she found in the Women's Liberation Movement. She wasn't interested in theory. She felt separated from the feminist movement by class, education and aspiration – what was so great about going to work in a job you merely tolerate? Reading it, I could feel the familiar grooves of the arguments about feminists versus 'ordinary women'. There has long been a tendency to depict feminism as an elite project, and it is true that university-educated women are more likely to describe themselves as feminists. I recognised something else, too: Pizzey's desire to define herself against the most absurd and extreme elements of the movement, the Maoists and the lesbian separatists. I recognised it because I've felt that urge too. It suits outsiders to define feminism by its extremes – they're easier to argue against, or to ignore – and so insiders feel continually pressed to reject them too. No one 'owns' feminism, and no single woman sets its rules. That is both liberating and troublesome. Unlike with a political party, there is no mechanism to kick people out of feminism. That boundlessness is difficult to negotiate.

In the 1970s, however, there were formal structures, which Pizzey duly rejected. In her telling, the Women's Liberation Movement was full of activists called things like Artemis and Gladiator, who wanted to smash the nuclear family and looked down on her for loving her husband.* She and her friends in the 'Goldhawk Road Group' refused to pay their subscription fees and stopped turning up to meetings. Instead, they resolved to help local women without any affiliation to the wider movement. The first refuge – known as the 'Big House' – was anarchic: it was supposed to hold thirty-six people, but Pizzey felt unable to turn anyone away. There were endless battles with the council, endless attempts to raise money, endless rows with whatever luckless bureaucrats were trying to formalise the situation. The council took her to court for overcrowding; she turned it into another publicity stunt, threatening to stage a sit-in with battered women in Downing Street.

From the start, Pizzey observed that women who 'escaped' struggled to live independently. 'I often used to joke that the first day a woman came into the refuge she was on a high because she was safe and so were her children,' she writes in her memoir. 'The second day she was busy getting their lives organised, but by the third day I would notice that the high had dissipated. That was the day she was most likely to think about going back to her partner.'

Within months of the refuge opening, several of its former residents had died. One, called Sonia, received a late-night phone call from her partner when the refuge's address was mistakenly included on her divorce papers. She went back to him, and later crashed her

* It is worth noting that other members of the WLM have rather different recollections. The ever-polite Tess Gill described Pizzey to me as a 'curious character'.

car head-on into a tree. She left behind two daughters. Another, Jenny – 'a big, laughing Afro-Caribbean woman with six children' – could not bear to leave her home, even though her husband repeatedly threatened to kill her. Soon after she left the refuge to go back there, he stabbed her to death. 'I put Jenny's picture up in the cubbyhole next to that of Sonia and wondered how many more faces of women I had loved would come to line those walls.'

*

When I made it up the stairs to Pizzey's flat, the first thing which greeted me was a poster reading: 'Margaret Thatcher, milk snatcher'. (She claims to have coined the phrase.) I knew from her memoir that she had a large multiracial family, and that her twenty-two-year-old grandson Keita killed himself in Wandsworth Prison in February 2000. A paranoid schizophrenic, he had been arrested for snatching a handbag. Pizzey wrote in the *Guardian* earlier that year that Keita was afraid of walking the streets – not just because of his illness, but also because he felt the reflected fear of others as they looked at a six-foot-tall mixed-race man.

Erin's daughter Cleo had been only fifteen when Keita was born; his father was one of several teenage boys who lived in Pizzey's happy but chaotic house in West London. Her memoir records that her husband, a BBC journalist, didn't react well to her journey from diligent housewife to activist. The woman who wrote that all a child needs is 'two biological parents under one roof' banished her own husband to the basement. He later left altogether.

This was an intriguing piece of the puzzle. Pizzey preached about feminism destroying the nuclear family, but her memoir tells a story straight out of *The Feminine Mystique*, in which Betty Friedan chronicled the boredom and ennui of middle-class American house-wives. Woman feels isolated at home, woman acquires new interests, woman decides motherhood alone is not fulfilling, woman outgrows the man she married. Yet far from being a tale of destruction, the story Pizzey tells in *This Way to the Revolution* is a fundamentally happy one. She turned out to be a natural organiser, lobbyist and refuge house-mother: I can't believe a life of suburban conformity would have suited her better.

In person, Pizzey was just as warm and welcoming as she was over email. Her stairlift whirred into action to take her down the few steps to the kitchen to fetch me a glass of water, and when she returned I dived straight into the controversy. My book is about women who advanced the cause of feminism, I said, but I'm guessing you wouldn't want to be a hero to feminists. 'Well, there wasn't any possibility,' she said. 'I was born in China, raised in the Middle East, and I was used to big communities . . . So when I was married, at home with the children, and my first husband was in television, I experienced what I could see right the way across women all round me, just the loneliness of isolation.' Her idea of the women's movement was 'sisterhood would be powerful, we would stop competing against each other, we would start co-operating with each other'.

But from the start, she didn't like women she met in the wider movement: they had pictures of Chairman Mao on the wall. 'They weren't housewives like us,' she recalled. 'They were highly politicised.' As she saw it, most feminists who worked in universities, politics or the media were Trotskyites, Marxists, Stalinists and Maoists. 'But I just kept saying to the Maoists, "How can you stand there and tell us that the Chinese Revolution is a huge success when women are being dragged off and [their foetuses] aborted?" And how can the Russian groups, the Trots and the Leninists, and all the rest of them, particularly the Stalinists, deny the fact that Stalin murdered millions and millions and millions of people? And there were no women ever in the Politburo. Oh, jolly good, you're allowed to drive tractors. But that isn't anything that we, as ordinary women, believe in.'

From the start, she thought that feminism was encouraging women to see themselves as victims. She also felt that political lesbianism – the idea that women should renounce sleeping with men, whatever their personal sexual orientation – was being used as a purity test. '[The lesbians] were the ones that were telling us that we were sleeping with the enemy and we just all – my little group – just looked at each other and thought, "Fuck this."'

Then there was the small matter of the Angry Brigade, a left-wing group which carried out two dozen small bomb attacks on targets such as banks, the homes of Conservative MPs and a BBC outside broadcast unit covering the 1970 Miss World pageant. Pizzey was sure that some of the radical feminists in the groups she attended were involved in a plot to bomb the clothing shop Biba. She went and told the police as much. Unsurprisingly, this did not endear her to the rest of the movement. 'They thought I was nuts anyway, because I wore make-up, and told terribly bad jokes, like saying, "Is it political to smell?" because we weren't allowed to wear deodorants.'

*

If I'm honest, I regarded Pizzey as a warning. The purity politics, the petty dictators, the navel-gazing – all this seemed very familiar. Except my peers were not the radical feminists of the 1970s but the Internet feminists of the 2010s. When Caitlin Moran's blockbuster *How to Be a Woman* was published in June 2011, I was an assistant editor on the *New Statesman*, a left-wing weekly magazine; when the paperback came out I had just been made deputy editor at the age of twenty-eight. It was a big promotion which surprised both me and the older men in the office, and it involved taking charge of the magazine's website just as Internet traffic soared across the British media.

The next few years were bloody: feminism's equivalent of a civil war. Fair and unfair criticisms blended into one giant screaming mass, fuelled by Twitter, and left everyone angry and hurt. Persistent themes emerged: X was too privileged, and her feminism was blinkered. Y had used a 'problematic' word or concept and needed to apologise. Z was a transphobe, a 'white feminist' or insufficiently 'intersectional', a word which was rarely heard a few years before, but was suddenly everywhere, with little regard to the original meaning as defined by US legal scholar Kimberlé Williams Crenshaw. Often, the criticisms were valid: early on, two black feminists asked me to have coffee with them, and explained that my commissioning blitz was leaving out women of colour. Scarred by a million Twitterspats, I became defensive, when I should have simply done them the courtesy of listening. At other times, though, the criticisms were driven by jealousy, or that heady mix of sadism and self-righteousness which characterises a moral crusade. One prominent black feminist tweeted that I was 'worse than the EDL', which suggested a lack of familiarity either with my work or that of the far-right, Islam-bashing thugs of the English Defence League.

With the benefit of hindsight, that period was so fraught because it was a gold rush. The beneficiaries of the post-Moran publishing boom were disproportionately white, middle class and university-educated. That wasn't their – our – fault, of course, and no one enjoys being a metaphorical punching bag. And as the civil war rolled on, criticism of a rigged system became interchangeable with personal rivalries.

All this has happened before. In 1976, a few years after Erin Pizzey founded her refuge in Chiswick, the American feminist Jo Freeman wrote an article called 'Trashing: the dark side of sisterhood' in *Ms* magazine. It generated an outpouring of letters from other women, who felt that they had also been subject to this practice. Trashing, explained Freeman, was not criticism or disagreement, which were a healthy and normal part of any movement. 'Trashing is a particularly vicious form of character assassination which amounts to psychological rape,' she wrote. 'It is manipulative, dishonest, and excessive. It is occasionally disguised by the rhetoric of honest conflict, or covered up by denying that any disapproval exists at all. But it is not done to expose disagreements or resolve differences. It is done to disparage and destroy.'

Freeman, like Pizzey, had her negative experiences in real-world collectives. The online feminism of the 2010s added a new dimension, because it was possible to be the target of a trashing by several hundred people at once, in real time. 'Even as online feminism has proved itself a real force for change, many of the most avid digital feminists will tell you that it's become toxic,' the American journalist Michelle Goldberg wrote in the *Nation* in 2014. 'Indeed, there's a nascent genre of essays by people who feel emotionally savaged by their involvement in it – not because of sexist trolls, but because of the slashing righteousness of other feminists.'

Online feminism became obsessed with language. A kind of priesthood had sprung up to adjudicate what terms could be used. Anger is a great engine of change, and activists are often dismissed by those who currently hold power as 'too radical' or 'too aggressive' in their demands. But outrage had become prized for its own sake, and online feminists had lost the ability to distinguish between genuine anger and mere spite. Worse, self-appointed 'allies' had gone full *Crucible* by performatively denouncing their peers to demonstrate their own righteousness. 'What's disgusting and disturbing to me is that I see some of the more intellectually dishonest arguments put forth by women of color being legitimized and performed by white feminists, who seem to be in some sort of competition to exhibit how intersectional they are,' the Jezebel blog founder Anna Holmes, who is black, told Michelle Goldberg. She found it 'dishonest' and 'patronising'.

I had talked to Goldberg for the piece, telling her that the Intersectionality Wars had affected how I wrote. 'Being more aware of a greater range of sensitivities is vital if you're not to blunder, blind, into areas about which you know very little and stomp all over them in your Privilege Boots,' I said. 'But equally well I know there is a group of people ready to mine anything I write for evidence to support their pre-existing views about me (while ignoring anything that runs counter to the narrative they've created).'

When the piece was published, I noticed that I wasn't quoted. Goldberg had done something vital: since so many of the criticisms levelled at prominent feminists were ostensibly about their tone-deafness on race, she had only quoted women of colour. The piece could not be dismissed as a privileged white lady moaning about meanies on the Internet. That allowed her to unpick the fact that, as Rutgers professor Brittney Cooper put it in the article, 'there's an actual injury . . . [but] I'm not sure that black women are benefiting from the toxicity'.

In other words, the grievance was real. White women *were* benefiting disproportionately from the new interest in feminism, and the feminist movement had often focused on the concerns of middle-class women over those at the bottom end of the income scale. But trashing was not, and is not, the answer.

My own trashing was a traumatic experience. I was accused of endangering lives, because my rhetoric was so hate-filled that people reading it would surely kill themselves. I was a racist. I was a transphobe. I was out of touch because I was middle-aged. (Funny: I was then twenty-nine.) My friends and I were the 'cunts of East-wick'. I was keeping a blacklist of writers and using my immense power to keep them out of British journalism. I had dropped my double-barrelled name to hide my aristocratic roots. (Painful: my divorce was still recent.) A caricature developed, a shadow Helen that stalked me around the Internet: absurdly posh, oblivious, ruth-lessly careerist and concerned only with fripperies. 'Go back to writing about how great your tits are,' wrote someone who clearly knew nothing about my writing but was at least well informed about my tits. When I ran a feminist panel event, it included both a woman of colour and a trans woman. Surely people could see I was trying to share my platform with more marginalised women? Instead, I was criticised for charging for tickets. 'I'm a working-class woman with children in London, am I going to give up a family meal (£5)?' wrote one tweeter.

I felt like giving up. How was I supposed to rent the hall without charging for tickets?* Everything I did just made it worse. My objections were 'white-women tears'. Defending myself was bullying. When I left Twitter for a few days, I was mentioned in an article in the *Evening Standard* about the phenomenon of the 'Twitter flounce'. Two of the writers I regularly commissioned were described as racist for using the phrase 'muchos love' in a tweet. It was not, perhaps, a coincidence that they had recently signed a 'six-figure deal' to write a book about feminism.

The most panic-inducing experience was the attempts to isolate me. Any contact with me was deemed to make other feminists unclean. When J. K. Rowling followed me on Twitter, someone told her that this hostile act had ruined the Harry Potter books for them. 'I hate you Helen Lewis,' read one blog. 'You are a piece of shit as well. And I hate you.' My existence itself, and my success, was a provocation. I was taking up a space that another, more worthy, woman could have held. A Daily Dot piece about my defence of Caitlin Moran (for an ill-advisedly flippant remark about the TV series *Girls*) noted that I was 'white, straight, and cisgendered, the top of the feminist food chain in terms of intersectionality'.†

It was, as Jo Freeman wrote, a 'character assassination'. Any good-faith – and deserved – criticism got lost in a sea of jealousy, resentment and retaliation. I was far from blameless: I began to hate my new enemies. I was not kind to them. I let my personal feelings cloud my professional judgement, and I defended my own and my friends' writing on partisan grounds rather than on its merits. The

---

* The next feminist event I ran, I offered to let people sponsor a ticket for someone who couldn't afford one. I got several donors, but no take-up on the free tickets.
† For the record, I wouldn't describe myself as either straight or cisgendered. 'Respect how people identify' seems to work only one way.

vitriol only abated when I blocked everyone involved and stopped replying to criticism. That said, I look forward to screenshots of these paragraphs circulating on social media to prove what an arsehole I am. Hello!

The trashing did not drive me out of feminism – and certainly not into the arms of the men's rights movement. But I can see how it could have done. Then again, the surprise shouldn't be that feminism has experienced so many divisions. The surprise should be that we are surprised. When humanity (led by men) has contested the allocation of scarce resources, or seen a clash between strong personalities, or come up with differing interpretations of a sacred truth, it has often treated itself to a cheeky war. A few mean blog posts suddenly don't seem so bad.

*

But Erin Pizzey didn't just fall out with feminism because she disliked other feminists. There was also a fundamental political disagreement: she thought that the mainstream women's movement treated men as the enemy. She thought that women's own capacity for violence was being understated. And she thought that some women were beaten up by their partners *because they wanted to be.* That's a crude way of putting it – she prefers to talk about an addiction to violence, and dysfunctional relationships in which both sides drive a vicious cycle. But if I state it like that, you can see why the rest of the movement – and her successors at Refuge – wanted so urgently to tidy her out of the way.

Pizzey's theory, elaborated in her book *Prone to Violence*, attempted to explain a phenomenon which baffles outsiders and horrifies campaigners tackling violence against women. Why do so many of them return to their abusers? When I spoke to Tess Gill, who knew Pizzey in the 1970s, she told me that she had given up working as a lawyer in domestic-violence cases. She found the stories 'so grim, and then I found that I was getting inured and not reacting emotionally when people described what they'd gone through . . . most of these women used to go back to their husbands, because they had nowhere, it was the only person that took any interest in them, [they had] low self-esteem, and the fact that he beat them didn't mean that they could manage to function without him. So it was a bit dispiriting.'

The first woman who walked through Pizzey's door, when she set up in a Chiswick community centre, had been badly beaten. 'She just took her jersey off, and [her partner] had battered the shit out of her,' Pizzey told me.

What happened to her, I asked.

'She never left him. And it's not going to be a huge surprise to you that the second person, woman, coming into the refuge was her daughter.'

Pizzey's own mother was violent, she says, and never left her father: 'They fought all over the world.' There was no obvious reason for their disagreements. Her father's job was well paid and they had servants, so it wasn't money worries or stress or exhaustion that led to the violence. But both their own families had been violent and dysfunctional. 'When the mothers came into the refuge, I had a questionnaire, and the questionnaire always asked how much they knew about their own backgrounds. So to me, it was always a learned pattern of behaviour.'

No other refuges existed at the time, and intimate-partner violence (IPV) was still seen by almost everyone, including the police, as a normal part of married life. 'Just a domestic' was the phrase many women report hearing as the officers got back into the car. There was no literature, no academic research, on its causes.

In this vacuum Pizzey developed her theory that some women, because of their upbringing, were addicted to violence. That explained why they kept going back. 'I lost women, and slowly, I came to the conclusion . . . You know, a woman would say to me, "I'm just like my mother." She'd say to me, "I love him," and there she is, with cigarettes put out all over and a smashed-in face. And I'd say, "How can you describe that as love?" and it wasn't love, it was addiction.'

It followed, then, that there were two types of women visiting the refuge. 'Most women who are innocent victims of their partner's violence will be able – particularly if they have children, because they want to put their children's needs first – will be able to leave, because they're not actually involved in addiction,' she told me. In *Prone to Violence*, she puts it like this: 'A battered person is the innocent victim of another person's violence; a violence-prone person is the victim of their own addiction to violence.'

*

I don't know if I winced when Pizzey used the phrase 'innocent victim' – but reading it back, I certainly do. The idea that good, responsible, strong women leave – and those who do not have only themselves to blame – is a shocking one. Women are most at risk of being killed when they leave their abuser. Some abusers deliberately seek out victims they can manipulate. Victims are often isolated from their family and friends, and their abuser – between bouts of violence – is the only person who shows them love. All this is more complicated than an addiction to being beaten, kicked or burned with cigarettes.

Nonetheless, Pizzey makes an important point. One of the reasons that domestic violence is difficult for outsiders to understand is that victims both love and fear their abusers, and often try to excuse, ignore or cover up their behaviour. That is why the police treat intimate partner violence differently from other crimes, and do not insist on a victim's consent or compliance before prosecuting.

The standard model of domestic abuse we now use focuses on power and control. It is not purely about physical violence. Since the Serious Crime Act of 2015, it has been illegal to demonstrate a pattern of coercive, controlling behaviour. That might mean sharing explicit photographs of a partner without their consent; restricting their access to money or friends; controlling what they wear; tracking their phone; or threatening to reveal private information. This allows police to prosecute perpetrators for incidents which are not *individually* criminal, but add up to a campaign of psychological terror.* 'You destroy someone's normal,' is how Luke Hart describes it. He should know. His father Lance waged a decades-long campaign of coercion against his mother Claire, as well as Luke's sister Charlotte and brother Ryan.

After Claire Hart finally left her husband in the summer of 2016, Lance tracked her down to the local leisure centre in Spalding, Lincolnshire and hid under a car with a shotgun. When she and nineteen-year-old Charlotte left the swimming pool, he shot them both. Then he killed himself. At the police station afterwards, Luke and Ryan saw posters about coercive control – and finally recognised that their father had been, in their words, a 'terrorist'. Both are now anti-domestic-violence advocates. 'People often shout you down with coercive control, saying, "It's not that bad, it's not that bad,"' Luke told me on the phone from the house he still shares with Ryan. 'People kept asking us for an example of what he did, but it wasn't one thing he did, it was every time the kettle wasn't filled up, he'd yell at us for hours. Every time he dropped a plate, he would yell at us, how we'd stacked it. Every time we dropped a plate, he'd yell at us.' He sighs. 'Every part of your life is the slow crushing of those prison bars.'

That has a strange effect. From the outside, a controlled household can look just like any other. Calm father, quiet mother, well-behaved children. 'Someone who's incredibly successful at

---

* Coercive control is a hard crime to prosecute (perhaps rightly so). In England and Wales, there were 7,034 arrests between January 2016 and July 2018, the BBC found, but only 1,157 cases ended with someone being charged. There is no gender breakdown of the arrests available.

coercive control, like our father: one, they're invisible their entire lives, and two, they can kill and then everyone says they're a nice person.' The police told Luke and Ryan not to read press coverage of the murders. When they did, they discovered that the articles were full of the phrases used when an outwardly respectable man commits an atrocity. You know the ones. He 'snapped'. He was 'driven' to do it. He was a 'loving husband'. It was 'out of character'.

But as Luke pointed out to me, his father didn't 'snap'. Lance Hart planned the killing: he lay in wait, under that car. Before setting off he wrote a rambling, self-justifying screed. The brothers refuse to call this a suicide note. To them, it's a 'murder note'. 'He was very self-righteous, constantly, about everything,' says Luke. 'He wanted to think he was a good person, but he wasn't at all. And what he wanted was us to control ourselves with him never having to intervene, and his murder note, for example, was full of self-righteousness. He even praised himself on being non-violent for his entire life.' And then he went out and killed two women.

Luke Hart is not surprised that so many spree killers and terrorist bombers turn out to have previous convictions for domestic abuse.* Both groups 'base their lives on self-righteous ideology'.

The model of coercive control explains why victims don't leave. They are robbed of their power and independence, often over months and years. They worry that their children will be taken away; they are deprived of the money they need to leave; they don't have any support networks because their partner has driven away their friends and families. Their self-worth has been eroded in a campaign of personal annihilation. This dynamic is not always gendered, but it happens in a society where men have traditionally controlled the

---

* The wife of Rachid Redouane, one of the London Bridge attackers, moved to a refuge after leaving him. The wife of Khalid Masood, who drove a car into pedestrians on Westminster Bridge in 2017, told a newspaper she left him because he was violent and controlling.

family finances and which assumes a man should be in charge at home. All that, plus sheer physical strength, makes it easier for men to coercively control women than the other way round.*

'To say there's fault on both sides is to forget that there's a power dynamic,' says Luke Hart when I tell him about Pizzey's theory about cycles of violence. 'Some women do kill men in domestic homicide. But often, when you dig deeper into the nuance, it's found that they were being abused for such a long period of time that *they* snapped or it was in self-defence . . . Our father killed our mother and sister, not out of defence, because we never were a threat to him. The only [threat] was that we would escape his control; he killed so that he forever maintained control. It's amazing that she misses that, I suppose, but to us, that's blindingly obvious, having grown up in that situation.'

When I asked Luke Hart for a favourite memory of his mother and sister, he struggled to think of one. 'All of our best moments were effectively spending our time with our dogs in the garden, whenever our father was at work or away, and we managed to steal those moments.'

The model of coercive control is backed by the research done since the 1970s – none of which Erin Pizzey could have seen when she founded the Chiswick refuge. Also, her use of 'innocent victims' does not imply that she believed that the other group of women – the violence addicts – should be left to die. On the contrary, those were the women she wanted to help most, using her unorthodox methods. Her refuge was run like a commune, but it had rules. Disruptive women and children were not to be indulged because of the trauma they had experienced. They could be voted out by other residents. Tough love:

* In June 2018, twenty-two-year-old Jordan Worth was jailed for seven and a half years after pouring boiling water over her boyfriend Alex Skeel. She had coercively controlled him. When the police arrived at their house, both insisted that Alex's injuries were self-inflicted. 'I was in love with Jordan and it took me a long time to have the courage to say she was abusing me,' he said later.

that was Pizzey's approach. She disagreed with refuges which allowed only three stays, on the basis that a 'revolving door' helped no one. In Pizzey's reckoning, women needed deep therapeutic interventions over months or years to break the cycle of violence.

However, you can see why her diagnosis was so appealing to the men's rights movement. MRAs feel it is unfair to assume the woman must be the 'victim' if a heterosexual couple's argument turns violent, because that status leads to sympathy (and government funding). If there is no overwhelming dynamic of male violence against women, just a mass of dysfunctional couples, then men are being wronged by the feminist fight against 'male violence'.

I raised this with Pizzey when she told me that she felt closer to the difficult cases. 'I learned very quickly, yes, she comes out of one violent relationship, the next thing you know, she's in another, and another, and another,' she said. 'So these are the women who I saw who were victims of their childhoods, and for many of them, as I said, out of our first hundred, sixty-two were as violent or more violent than the men they left.'

Define violent, I said. Because we hear all the time about women killed by men, while very few men are killed by women. Refuge and other charities say two women a week are killed by current or former partners.

'Of two women a week, one man is killed.'

By a woman? Or by a same-sex partner?

'By their partner.'

Those are not the statistics that I have seen, I said.

'You see, this is the problem. You have to look at evidence-based statistics, the feminist-based statistics aren't evidence-based.'

Where would be a good place to look at evidence-based ones?

'A lot of them are on my website. Looked there?'

I'll go and have a look, I said.

*

I went and looked. Pizzey's site is called Honest Ribbon, a reference
to the White Ribbon movement, which works with men to end violence against women. 'We are concerned by the current fad to define
the problem of domestic violence in terms of gender,' it says. 'As the
scientific evidence, presented to you on this site by the world's leading experts in domestic violence, shows with complete clarity,
violence in the home is not a gendered problem.' Who that 'we' refers
to is unclear, although another page clarifies that the site is hosted
by A Voice for Men. I couldn't find the statistics she referred to
anywhere.

That statement – 'violence in the home is not a gendered
problem' – is incorrect. Yes, the statistical evidence is messy,
because there is no such crime as 'domestic violence'. The term cov-
ers IPV, as well as behaviour that last year was child abuse but the
victim has now become an adult, and elder abuse. The latter is
almost certainly under-reported, and may well be less gendered,
because a middle-aged female carer is stronger and more powerful than a ninety-year-old of either sex. The next problem is
defining violence. A single slap is materially different to kicking
your partner down the stairs, but statistics struggle to capture
that nuance. Then there's the issue of self-defence; police regularly arrive at the homes of couples to find each side claiming the
other one started it.

I can see the temptation, faced with all this difficulty, to throw
your hands up. *Why talk about gender at all?* But treating domestic
abuse as a gendered problem gives us an insight into perpetrators'
mindsets – the self-justifying stories they tell themselves, and the
social conditions which reinforce their behaviour. And it helps to
explain why domestic violence often goes unnoticed and unre-
ported. I talked to David Challen, whose mother Sally killed his
father Richard after years of abuse. She was initially convicted of
murder, but this was reduced to manslaughter on appeal. Her lawyers had argued that provocation – a defence associated with men

who 'snap' and kill a nagging or faithless wife – should also apply to
women worn down by years of coercive control.

Like the Harts, David Challen told me that learning about coercive control was revelatory; suddenly his childhood made sense. 'I
knew there was a tangible term to put everything that I've seen
under one umbrella,' he said. Until then, it was hard to explain how
his parents' relationship was poisonous, because it fitted an old-
fashioned template of marriage: man in charge, submissive wife
trailing behind. He believes that we have to confront the gendered
nature of domestic violence to overcome men's defensiveness. 'Talking about male violence makes some men feel that you are not on
their team,' he says. 'The quiet majority of men are supportive of
you, but those men don't want to speak out as much, because that
risks their place in whatever circle they're in with their other men.
Their masculinity is at stake.'

Since Erin Pizzey wants the evidence-based statistics to get a
wider airing, here they are. The self-reported data from the 2018
British Crime Survey found that nearly twice as many women
reported being victims of domestic violence as men in the last year
(7.9 per cent of women in England and Wales, compared with 4.2 per
cent of men), although the gender of perpetrators, and their relationship to the victim, is not recorded. The twenty-eight police forces
which supplied data found that 75 per cent of victims of domestic
violence were female, while for specifically sexual offences, it was 96
per cent. 'The estimates do not take into account the context and
impact of the abusive behaviours experienced,' adds the Office for
National Statistics. 'Research suggests that when coercive and controlling behaviour is taken into account, the differences between the
experiences of male and female victims become more apparent.'

In domestic homicides, the pattern is stark. According to figures
compiled by the campaigner Karen Ingala Smith – with whom I
worked at a domestic-violence charity called Nia – there were 143
women killed in the UK in 2017 where a man was the primary

suspect. The phrase 'her partner has been charged with her murder' features again and again, with numbing force, in the media reports. In one case, the man involved had to use a second knife after the first one broke from the force of his attacks. In total, he stabbed his partner twenty times. Although 2017 was the year of terror attacks in London Bridge, the Manchester Arena and Westminster, the number of women killed by their current or former partners far exceeded the terrorism death toll.

As for male victims, NHS London estimates that around thirty men a year are killed in a domestic-abuse context: a third of these are killed by other men and a third 'by women against whom they have a documented history of abuse'. Once you discount cases where a long-term victim eventually turns on her abuser, ten times as many women are killed by men as the other way round.

This is uncomfortable, and it makes some men defensive, but it has to be faced. It is always important to acknowledge exceptions – there are men who develop breast cancer, for example, and they have many of the same inhibitions and worries as male domestic-violence victims. Seeking help might make them feel humiliated, unmanly, awkward. In services designed for women, they are literally the odd man out. These men need specialist support: there are now nine male refuges across Britain, and a national helpline.

At the same time, there is a good reason not to turn discussion of domestic abuse into a genderless soup of some people hurting some other people. That is because male violence profoundly shapes women's experience of the world. We take endless precautions when walking home. We fear getting taxis and minicabs. We walk through the underground car park with our keys gripped in our fist. We buy rape alarms. We reject the perfectly nice offers of a lift from perfectly nice men because . . . how can we know? If we get raped, we understand that the questions will start immediately. *Was she drinking? Did she lead him on?* All this is pretty ironic in a world where men are much more likely to be victims of

violence than women. But no one wonders if a man beaten up outside a pub was 'asking for it'. Should he have been out on his own?
What was he wearing?

Many rape and abuse survivors are 'difficult women'. They kept
sleeping with the guy who attacked them, they sell sex but still
believe they have the right to say No to a punter; they were drunk or
high when it happened. It is difficult to accept that many domestic-
violence victims don't leave. We all assume that we would, in their
situation. But a half-century of research, driven by the feminist
movement, suggests that we might not. David Challen said that he
was often asked by people why he didn't step in to protect his mum.
'I've actually had comments like "That's why we need people to man
up instead of becoming snowflakes,"' he told me. Throughout his
childhood, his father had belittled and controlled his mother, telling
her that she smelled, that she was ugly. Richard had once beaten up
Sally, early in their relationship, and she was always petrified to
stand up to him in case it happened again. David was twenty-three
when his father died. Richard's control and aggression was all he
knew.

The extent of male violence, and its effect on women's lives, is
now taken for granted by most feminists. Outside of the fringes of
the 'manosphere', few would disagree that something called
'domestic violence' exists, and that women are its primary victims. That is a problem in itself. When an idea hardens into
orthodoxy, campaigners lose the muscle memory built up when
making their case. That, in turn, opens up a space for opponents to
contest the facts.

Should the feminist movement talk more about male victims?
I'm conflicted. It's not the job of the feminist movement to be everyone's mum. For all her faults, Erin Pizzey created that first women's
refuge without permission, without money and without official support. Where is the comparable level of effort from the men's rights
movement to support the male victims they claim to champion?

When Luke and Ryan Hart launched their book *Operation Light-house*, they invited the actor Patrick Stewart to join them for a discussion. Why did Stewart go? Because his own father had been violent, and 'because domestic violence is a man's problem', he told *Guardian* reporter Anna Moore. 'We are the ones who are committing the offences, performing the cruel acts, controlling and denying. It's the men.' And yet, the reporter noticed, there were only five men in the audience.

In my experience, the people who raise the spectre of male victims in online debates – YouTube channels, online comments, blogs – are rarely doing so out of genuine concern for suffering men. Instead, they are engaging in a tactic called 'derailing', trying to stop a discussion which they don't believe should be taking place, perhaps because it paints men as 'the bad guys'.* Where men are prepared to engage with the subject, feminists can't become defensive, or hound them off our turf. Male victims cannot get airtime only in the context of feminism's alleged failings. But men do need to turn up.

I raised this with Erin Pizzey. She decried the extremism of the Marxist feminists and lesbian separatists, yet was prepared to overlook equally (to me) extreme statements from her new allies. I told Pizzey that I found a lot of what she said compelling, but then I felt uneasy when I saw her on A Voice for Men alongside Paul Elam. What about not convicting an alleged rapist under any circumstances? 'Do look at the context,' she said. What about when he said 'a feminist is a loathsome, vile piece of human garbage'? She started talking about the foundation of A Voice for Men, and how 'the aggression of a lot of those American women was very frightening'. But come on, you say feminists are anti-men. All this sounds anti-women. 'I actually did say to Paul, you know, from the very early

---

* At which point I have to say: men who beat up their partners are *absolutely* 'the bad guys'.

business, "Why are you doing this?" He said: "Well, it's the only way to get our voices heard." And he's happily married to a really nice woman.'

*

Talking to Pizzey made me think of Harriet Wistrich and Julie Bindel. A personal and professional couple, together they run Justice for Women, which campaigns on criminal-justice issues. In 1995, they helped free Emma Humphreys, jailed for killing her pimp at the age of seventeen.* Justice for Women has since helped women exploited into prostitution† have their soliciting convictions wiped from their records. Wistrich has acted for female immigrants held in Yarl's Wood detention centre; for women who had relationships with undercover police officers sent to infiltrate the green movement; and for the victims of the taxi driver John Worboys, who may have raped up to a hundred women, when he was given parole after just eight years in prison. Justice for Women got Sally Challen's murder conviction overturned. With Wistrich providing the legal muscle and Bindel the media firepower, they are a formidable force.

Like Pizzey, though, Bindel has found herself at odds with the rest of the feminist movement. She is on the unfashionable side of two of the most divisive and heated subjects in modern feminism: transgender issues and prostitution. She believes that the latter is violence against women, and sex-buyers should be prosecuted. The current generation of student activists take a more liberal position, stressing individual choice and agency. They argue that decriminalising both sellers *and* buyers would make the transaction safer.

On trans issues, Bindel has questioned the idea that we all have innate gender identity: that you can be a woman trapped in a man's

* Emma Humphreys died of an overdose in 1998; Bindel and Wistrich found her body.
† These women would not call themselves 'sex workers', because that implies selling sex is a job, an analysis they reject.

body, and vice versa. Having met her and worked with her, I would describe her as tough, mouthy and uncompromising, and I do not mean any of those adjectives as an insult. She sees her anti-snowflake persona as the result of her working-class, northern upbringing. Her vocabulary rejects the dainty linguistic tics of middle-class feminism. She regularly describes herself as a 'lezzer' and other praiseworthy women as 'top birds'. In 2011, she attacked Caitlin Moran's bestselling *How to Be a Woman* as 'fun feminism' which 'should be consigned to the rubbish bin, along with the Lib Dem Party'.

But unlike Erin Pizzey, Bindel has never broken with feminism altogether and gone her own way. Why did personal and political disagreements drive the one out of feminism but not the other? I called her to ask. Why hadn't she left feminism, even when the rest of feminism seemed to reject her? She had an answer that was both simple and complicated. 'I don't think that she was ever quite a feminist,' she said of Erin Pizzey. 'I have to say, before it sounds as if I'm being prescriptive and elitist, there is a set of aims and objectives and an ideological position of feminism.'

The difference between them, Bindel thought, was that Pizzey saw one injustice – and bravely tried to fight it. But she never tied that injustice to an overarching belief system. 'Being appalled at men beating women to within an inch of their lives, to the point where they have to escape because they'll be murdered otherwise with their children, and being a decent person to set up resources for them, is a great and good thing. But you don't have to be a feminist to do that.'

The late American feminist Andrea Dworkin once gave a useful definition of feminism: 'A political practice of fighting male supremacy on behalf of women as a class, including all the women you don't like, including all the women you don't want to be around, including all the women who used to be your best friends whom you don't want anything to do with any more. It doesn't matter who the individual women are.'

Bindel echoed that. She thought Pizzey did not accept the idea that there was a system of oppression called patriarchy, where men as a class oppressed women as a class. By contrast, Bindel had learned early in her life that 'for feminism you had to prioritise women, and always put women at the centre of your priorities and your activism, even if you couldn't stand them, even if they were fucking you over as individuals. And [even though] some men were much nicer than that.'

Hesitantly, I agreed. Personal relationships are always difficult; they cannot be the glue holding feminism together. There needs to be a sense of shared goals, a shared framework and a shared set of priorities. At the same time, though, we can afford to acknowledge the contributions of those who don't subscribe to our guiding philosophy. A history of feminism isn't the same as a history of feminists. Erin Pizzey's difficult relationship with feminism does not mean that she has to be written out of the story.

*

In 1976, the year after Erin Pizzey stormed out of the Women's Aid conference, the Domestic Violence Act was passed. It had been introduced as a Private Member's Bill by the Labour MP Jo Richardson, and allowed women to obtain a restraining order against a violent partner. 'Hitherto, it had generally been assumed that wife-battering was a private affair in which the forces of law and order should not intervene,' wrote Coote and Campbell. 'In many ways, Women's Aid has been the most productive of all campaigns within the Women's Liberation Movement.'

Refuge, the charity which grew out of the Chiswick house, now supports 6,000 British women and children every day. But the sector has new problems: council budgets have been steadily cut since 2010, reducing the money available to run women's services. Funds for translators and independent advocates have been stripped back, affecting immigrant and minority women in particular. The 'hostile environment' policy, intended to reduce illegal immigration, has made some victims reluctant to contact services, in case they are reported for overstaying their visas. In turn, this has helped abusers to control women through their migration status: for example, by holding their passport and refusing to allow them to renew a visa, or threatening to report them to the authorities. Because of these policies, there will be women right now who are still living with the man who will one day kill them.

Photographs of Pizzey's various refuges from the 1970s show overcrowded, anarchic spaces. That would be impossible in today's world of health-and-safety rules and headcounts and endless demands from funders to demonstrate 'key performance indicators'.

The professionalisation of the women's sector has had huge benefits, but something has been lost, too. Erin Pizzey's bohemian communities featured in documentaries, and she was regularly in the news, battling this council or that, making outrageous statements or writing things like *The Slut's Cookbook*. Now, refuges are hidden away for the very sound reason that this makes it harder for perpetrators to find them. An unfortunate side effect, however, is that their users can seem like an entirely different class of humans to 'ordinary' people. It reminds me a little of the way we talk about 'benefit claimants' in a way that doesn't recognise that millions of Britons claim benefits of one sort or another, including 9 million state pensioners. How many young feminists have ever seen a domestic-violence refuge, let alone volunteered in one?

Pizzey is also right that a small group of charities now 'own' the narrative around domestic violence. With the sector under perpetual threat of funding cuts, the temptation to rely on simple, powerful messages is obvious. The gendered nature of domestic-violence deaths is clear from the statistics. But under assault from men's rights activists and oblivious politicians, is the feminist movement overplaying a simple story of bad men beating up women? One think-tanker, who works in this area, told me off the record that she had grave concerns about the lack of interest in perpetrator programmes. How do we expect violent men to change their behaviour? The criminal justice system deprives them of their livelihoods, reputations and (sometimes) their freedom, and expects this to transform them magically into model citizens. Would she go on the record, I asked? She was nervous. No one wants to be seen as excusing male violence, or dismissing the experiences of thousands of brutalised women. I don't begrudge campaigners looking for the cleanest, sharpest methods to get their message across. But as a journalist, it's my job to prod and poke – and write the unvarnished truth.

As for Pizzey's theories about an 'addiction' to violence, I can see why they felt right to her. I was recently walking home from a fireworks display on Blackheath with my husband. A woman started screaming by the side of the road, and everyone in the crowd turned to look. When I went over, she was bent double, hyperventilating and screaming about how her boyfriend had been attacked. Along with a group of other women, I tried to calm her down. Someone called an ambulance. A man came over, who seemed to know her, and told us all to fuck off. Why were we getting involved? After a few minutes, she recovered her breath and let the man drag her off. The woman on the phone cancelled the ambulance.

I felt sick. Who knows what the real story was? But the man's aggression and her distress, followed by her meek compliance to his wishes, stays with me. Women *do* go back, and we need to understand why. And even the ones who do, even the ones who drink, even the ones who get into screaming matches with their partner in the street, even those who mistake control for affection, even the ones who don't look from the outside like 'innocent victims' – none of those women deserve to die.

The evidence shows that men suffer from violence in relationships, and this must be acknowledged. Otherwise, in the vacuum where that discussion should be, the snaking roots of something altogether nastier take hold. 'I can see why people looking in now would think, well look at all the money those women have got, Christ almighty,' says Bindel. 'In reality, everybody is massively struggling and domestic-violence victims and their kids are being put in one-room B&Bs, where they get stuck for years, so they go back to their violent husbands and they get killed.' Her message to men's rights activists worried about the lack of refuge provision is simple. 'Just do it already. Go out and set the fucker up.'

That's what Erin Pizzey did, for all that she fought and fell out with the women in the mainstream feminist movement. Today, the website for Refuge has a page called 'Our Story', which states that the charity 'opened the world's first safe house for women and children escaping domestic violence in Chiswick, West London, in 1971'. Pizzey's name does not appear.*

Towards the end of my conversation with Pizzey, I suggested that she had been airbrushed out of the history of the refuge movement, because she was too difficult, too unorthodox, too contrarian, too inconvenient to the dominant narrative. She agreed. 'I don't think anybody knows who I am any longer, it's just all gone,' she said, as the weak winter sun flooded her top-floor flat. 'That doesn't matter. I just quietly get on. I still do see anybody who wants to see me, and . . . that's OK.'

* I contacted Refuge while writing this chapter, and submitted questions to its chief executive Sandra Horley, but never got answers back from her.

7. LOVE

If feminism was reduced to one word, it would be this: no.

Lierre Keith

When Erin Pizzey rejected feminism, she was tidied away, turned into an obscure footnote to the history of the refuge movement. But even those who keep the faith can be written out if they prove too difficult.

On 11 August 2018, the *Times* columnist Matthew Parris wrote an article defending the right to make offensive jokes. In passing, he mentioned a lesbian pioneer: Maureen Colquhoun. The Labour MP had lost her seat in the 1979 election, at the same time as Parris (a Conservative) first gained his. 'A fierce firebrand of a feminist, her sometimes zany, always brave campaigns raised eyebrows, but Labour could live with individualists,' he wrote. 'Not lesbians, though. When she came out she was sunk, and deselected, and finished.' Colquhoun celebrated her ninetieth birthday the next day, he said: 'Maureen remembers when you couldn't be gay. Is the day coming when you cannot laugh at gays or mock our sometimes-silly excesses, or tell us to stop whingeing?'

Huh, I thought, reading the column. Somehow, I had imagined that the first 'openly' gay MP – a phrase that will probably soon sound hopelessly quaint – was Chris Smith, a member of the New Labour government which took office in 1997.* Who was this Maureen Colquhoun?

My mental Rolodex of British lesbian pioneers had relatively few entries. There were the Ladies of Llangollen, two eighteenth-century Welsh women whose diaries describe them in bed nursing each other's headaches with suspicious frequency. There was Anne

* Smith was the first MP to come out *voluntarily* while in office, in 1984.

Lister – 'Gentleman Jack' – the Georgian landowner whose diaries give an extraordinarily frank account of her life seducing heiresses. And there was Radclyffe Hall, author of 1928's *The Well of Loneliness*. But no Maureen Colquhoun. If women get written out of history, then that goes double for women who identify with other women, who socialise with other women, and who love other women. And that matters to *all* women. We are not worthy of notice only when our lives intersect with those of men.

Maureen Colquhoun deserves better. She arrived in Parliament as a forty-five-year-old mother, married to the journalist Keith Colquhoun, and quickly gained a reputation as a troublemaker. It was 1974 – three years after Erin Pizzey founded her first refuge, and four years after the Equal Pay Act. The Second Wave was in full swing, and Maureen was at the vanguard. She wanted to abolish women's prisons, decriminalise prostitution and further liberalise the abortion law. She asked to be called 'Ms' in the Commons chamber. She demanded crèche facilities at Labour Party conference. She joined the left-wing Tribune group, and found an unlikely ally in Dennis Skinner, already a thorn in the side of the Labour leadership. Skinner regarded homosexuality as 'strictly for the upper classes and most definitely public school', according to Colquhoun's memoir *A Woman in the House*. But he was kind to his new colleague, showing her round the vast warren of Westminster and demystifying its strange and pointless rituals.

Maureen felt that Parliament was a 'maleocracy', and being a feminist there was lonely. As a councillor in Shoreham, she had been blocked from taking up posts because she 'talked too much'. In Parliament, she faced exactly the same criticisms. She was shrill, strident, obsessed. Even her own side found her a bit much. 'Certainly I have found in my life that I have had an uncomfortable ability for upsetting equally my friends and my enemies,' she wrote in her memoir.

Parliament was then working on the Sex Discrimination Act,

which gained Royal Assent in October 1975. This groundbreaking legislation outlawed direct discrimination – employers who paid women less than men for the same job; landlords who refused to rent to women; mortgage companies who demanded a male guarantor for a woman's loan.* It also established the Equal Opportunities Commission to monitor and enforce these new rules, and to issue guidance to advertisers about how to avoid sexist stereotypes. Until the passing of the Sex Discrimination Act, job adverts would regularly be targeted at one sex or the other. You can probably guess who got targeted for senior management roles and who got secretarial work.† Reading the parliamentary records from this time is like a portal to another world. On 22 February 1977, 'Mr Greville Janner asked the Secretary of State for Employment whether he will now take steps to render unnecessary the obtaining of authorisation by women who wish to work at night.' Wait, there was a time when women needed special authorisation to work at night? Yes there was. In 1948, the International Labour Organisation had declared that 'women without distinction of age shall not be employed during the night in any public or private industrial undertaking' – unless it was a family business.‡

For many in Parliament, outlawing sex discrimination was radical enough. But not for Maureen Colquhoun. The Britain of the mid-1970s was full of public bodies such as the Electricity Council and the National Bus Company. Colquhoun had a modest proposal:

---

* Men's rights enthusiasts might be interested to know that while the first clause addressed 'sex discrimination against women', the second dealt with 'sex discrimination against men'.

† Enforcement of these rules has always been tough, however, as companies often use coded language. In 2016, an employment agency called Matching Models advertised for a personal assistant with 'a classic look, brown long hair with B-C cup'. I suppose they could have argued that some men fit this description.

‡ Two things: the distinction between paid and unpaid work: no one was stopping women getting out of bed to breastfeed. And look how a 'chivalrous' regulation intended to protect women could be used to exclude them from certain jobs.

those receiving public money should give half of their places to women. The House of Lords, which at the time had just forty-nine women out of 1,105 peers, should also have a 50/50 gender split. As she later asked the House: 'Would the minister not accept that Britain had been run by men for generations and could not be in a worse position than it was today?' Her bill would become The Balance of the Sexes Act.

*

When I read about Maureen Colquhoun, I was researching another Difficult Woman from the same era. Jackie Forster didn't come out of the closet; she exploded out of it. 'You are looking at a roaring lesbian!' she told a crowd assembled at Speakers' Corner in 1969. She was already a public figure, which made her announcement all the more extraordinary. As an actor, she had a small part in the *Dambusters* film; as a television reporter, she had covered the wedding of Grace Kelly and Prince Rainier of Monaco. When Forster stepped off the stage at Speakers' Corner, the photographer Jenny Potter saw that she was shaking. 'Now that, I thought,' Potter said later, 'is real courage.'

When she came out at Speakers' Corner, Forster was forty-three. She had been born Jacqueline Mackenzie in 1926 to Scottish parents, and in 1958, she married a fellow journalist called Peter Forster. The next year she had her first affair with a woman. In 1995, her archive was transferred to the Glasgow Women's Library, which is truly one of the nicest places in the world. I arrived there on a blustery spring morning, and within ten minutes I had been offered two cups of tea. As I unpacked the collection, a group of Pakistani–British women downstairs switched effortlessly between Urdu and Glaswegian as they held a workshop on the history of the Race Relations Act. Almost the first thing I unwrapped from its tissue paper was a contact sheet of Jackie at Speakers' Corner that day, standing out above the crowd, with blonde hair and a dark coat.

Think of the world into which she was born. In the year of Forster's birth, 1926, England had its last general strike; the jazz song 'Black Bottom' was a hit; the silent-film actor Rudolph Valentino died at thirty-one. The television was invented that year; it would be another two years before the jet engine followed.

Jackie spent the early years of her life in India, where her father was in the army. In 1932, she was dispatched to Wycombe Abbey, an all-girls boarding school, where she had the traditional 'pashes' on her fellow pupils. In the Glasgow archive, I found her abandoned attempt at writing a memoir, for which she had two suggested titles. *Can't Even Think Straight* speaks for itself. The second was initially more puzzling: *Metamorphosis*, with two authors credited, Jackie Mackenzie and Jackie Forster. But it made sense. Like meek Lady Constance Lytton inventing her wilder alter ego Deborah, Jackie felt that she lived part of her life smothering her true personality. 'Talk of Jackie and Hyde!' she wrote to one prospective publisher.

At first, Forster was reluctant to believe that she was a lesbian. The word, she told authors Suzanne Neild and Rosalind Pearson, 'in the Fifties, as I understood, was just a short back and sides woman with a waistcoat . . . and I never saw myself like that'.

The word came to be important to her, and it remains important to many women who want to stress the particular interaction of homophobia and misogyny. The journalist Sophie Wilkinson told me that she calls herself a 'lesbian' rather than a 'gay' or 'queer' woman. 'There is a specific word for me, that defines my unique experience, as a woman who experiences oppression as a woman, and oppression as an easily read lesbian,' she said. 'You can add all kinds of things to LGBT, but I don't think anyone walks down the street and gets "Oh, you fucking asexual." That's my lived experience, as someone who is easily read as a lesbian.'

Jackie Forster felt the same. 'I refused to be gay all along the line, because it was such a heavy male imprint,' she told the author

Veronica Groocock in 1995. 'It depresses me the amount of time lesbians are spending following the male gay patterns. I just wish they'd do some thinking about the *lesbian* identity.'

For her, being a lesbian didn't mean rejecting femininity – photos in the archive show that she posed like a glamourpuss, a slim cigarette often clasped in her fingers.* But her sexuality was linked to a wider rebellion against feminine norms. Spending time with other women convinced her to 'unlearn' her female socialisation, she told Groocock. 'And the relief, the release, was marvellous . . . All these fuzzy thoughts and things like, "You mustn't appear too bright because men won't like you" and "Don't talk too much" and "Be nice" – all that was such a terrible straightjacket on me.'

No one I spoke to who remembered Jackie Forster described her as 'nice'. Her status as a Difficult Woman was quickly established. The gay historian Keith Howes remembers turning up to work at *Gay News* as features editor in the 1970s. Forster had also applied for the job, and her disappointment translated into resentment. She was always icy to Howes, he says, and he remembers her 'banging on (no pun intended) about "the penis-power of *Gay News*"' at the opening of a gay disco. Nonetheless, he has no hesitation in recognising her achievements. 'She was an original . . . the right person at the right time.' Stephen Bourne, who interviewed her for several television specials in the 1990s, echoed this. Was she difficult, I asked him? 'Everybody who puts their neck on the line is,' he said.

Once she came out, Jackie needed all the difficulty she could muster. By her own admission, Forster initially enjoyed 'heterosex' and slept with her husband Peter before she married him. In 1958, she had a doomed affair with a female acquaintance and got a divorce, hoping to be with her. Arriving in America, she discovered

---

* The archive contains the evidence of a long argument with the publisher of a book which put her photograph on the cover, artificially tinted in lurid colours. She thought it made her look silly.

the woman had moved on. She considered suicide, then went back to sleeping with men.*

One of the men she 'made a pass at' was the husband of a woman called Barbara Todd. But instead of sleeping with him, she fell in love with Babs. 'About two weeks later we kissed on the mouth, and about three months later we went to bed for the first time,' she recalled. They tried out the New York lesbian scene, 'dressed as straights, of course, because nobody must know'. They found themselves being moved on by 'diesels' – butch lesbians.

Two years later, Todd moved to England with her children. At the time, there was no real lesbian scene, even in London – nowhere to meet other women with the same experiences as them. And nowhere for women to meet romantic partners. In one pub, they came out to a couple of tweedy-looking women who were always together – only to discover that the other women weren't lesbians. And they were *horrified* by the mistake. Forster recalls in her unpublished memoir that she and Todd wore the most femme clothes they could find for months, because they were terrified of being outed.

As they became more politically aware, the couple made a vow. 'We said (not so precisely) that as long as we lived, knowingly, we wouldn't let any other woman go through this idiot shit,' Jackie told an interviewer. 'Out of that tiny little comment, so *Sappho* happened.' A monthly magazine based in Soho, *Sappho* was named after the ancient Greek poet from the island of Lesbos (the source of the word 'lesbian'). Her verses survive in haunting fragments: one says simply, 'you burn me'.

But *Sappho* was more than a magazine. It was a community hub, a safe space, a notice board, a source of advice. It ran a club for closeted wives. It raised money for women dismissed from the army for being lesbians. It had a beautiful embroidered banner, in the

* The story comes from Angela Stewart-Park and Jules Cassidy, *We're Here: Conversations with Lesbian Women.*

suffragette colours of purple, green and white, which could be taken on marches. It held meetings on Tuesdays at the Victoria pub in Strathearn Place, London W2. It organised a conference for lesbian mothers and more than a hundred women showed up.* It was somewhere lesbians could talk openly about their lives. It was cheeky and political. One cover showed Margaret Thatcher posing with Queen Elizabeth II. The caption read: 'We're off to the Gates', a reference to the Gateways, a famous lesbian club which ran from the 1930s to 1985.

Babs and Jackie nurtured *Sappho* together. But the notoriety it brought them would lead to the end of their relationship. Because Babs was about to meet Maureen Colquhoun.

*

While Jackie wrote and campaigned, Babs had another job, working as a 'gopher' between feminist journalists and politicians. Her predecessor in the role had been sent packing by Colquhoun when it was discovered that she was briefing the Conservatives too. And so Babs Todd went to talk to this terrifying red-haired firebrand taking on her own party, pushing it further and faster than it wanted towards equality for women.

Maureen Colquhoun had an advantage when they met for tea in the Commons. She already knew who Babs was, and she knew that Babs was a lesbian. Colquhoun had quietly subscribed to *Arena Three*, the predecessor to *Sappho*, and was now a subscriber to *Sappho* too. 'Babs and Jackie were the two most famous out women in the British gay movement,' she writes in *A Woman in the House*. 'I noticed at our first tea meeting that Babs wore a lesbian–feminist badge . . . An oval of pottery with the double women's sign in pink. I liked her.'

---

* Later, the childless lesbians like Jackie took the women's children to the zoo to entertain them during meetings.

While they worked on Colquhoun's bill, which would become The Balance of the Sexes Act, the two 'totally fell in love with one another'. The Home Secretary Roy Jenkins – now remembered as a great liberalising force in British politics thanks to his support for decriminalising abortion and gay sex – had made it clear he would not support quotas for public bodies. The idea of the Sex Discrimination Bill – which was going through Parliament that year – was to treat everyone the same, he said – although women might benefit more as they were currently subject to more discrimination. Colquhoun's bill suggested promoting women *because they were women*. It was too much.

On 16 May 1975, when Maureen Colquhoun arrived in the Commons to propose her bill, she found an interminable debate about guard dogs filling the available parliamentary time. She hurriedly sent the word round that the Home Office was behind the lengthy debate, and her fellow backbenchers agreed that she should have time to make her speech.

It is a masterpiece. It would cause a stir if given in the House of Commons today, when a third of MPs are female, and there have been two women prime ministers. In 1975 there were just twenty-six female MPs out of 635. It must have felt like a thunderbolt. Maureen Colquhoun thanked her fellow MPs for ending the 'excruciatingly boring' debate on guard dogs. 'The idea behind my bill is not original,' she began. 'It is one that I had no hesitation in borrowing from [George] Bernard Shaw, who warned the suffragettes, after they got the vote, that unless a bill was introduced to make it compulsory for men and women to be on public bodies and boards in equal numbers they would never get very far.'

After expressing a desire not to score points off Roy Jenkins – a 'thoughtful and helpful man', she conceded – she attacked his use of the Sex Discrimination Bill to shut down other feminist campaigning. 'Surely that bill is not now to be used as a weapon against us when we try to promote our rights?' After all, it would not wipe out the centuries of *past* discrimination. 'We in Parliament, who believe in making life better for women and that they should be the legislators as well as the makers of cups of tea, believe that our aims must be translated into laws,' she added. 'Today there are more public jobs on boards, corporations, councils and commissions within the gift of ministers than at any other time in Britain's history. It is also significant that nearly all the 4,500 jobs that I have discovered are jobs for the boys . . . It is intolerable to women that in 1975 half of society is not properly represented on these committees. Women have simply been excluded.'

She ran through a few public bodies – the Sugar Board, five men and no women; the Covent Garden Market Authority, six men and no women. 'The National Bus Company has seven men, no women,' she added. 'Of course, women do not travel on buses. Neither, apparently, do they travel on trains, because the British Railways Board has twelve men, no women.'

It is hard to find direct comparisons for these figures now, because of the widespread privatisation of industry. However, the National Farmers' Union has a 'Sugar Board', with only one woman alongside eleven men. The board of the private bus company Stagecoach has two women and eight men. It's 8–3 to the boys at (publicly owned) Network Rail and 5–2 at (privatised) Virgin Trains. Still, raise a small cheer: four decades on, the Covent Garden Market Authority is close to Colquhoun's target, with three women and five men.

Colquhoun had identified a vast network of privilege and patronage controlled by men for the benefit of other men. 'Jobs for the boys' were exactly that. The British establishment was a scam, in which a cosy gang exchanged favours with each other, often paid for by public money. Colquhoun's bill threatened that 'maleocracy'. 'I often wonder what the early campaigners for women's rights, such as Millicent Fawcett and Emmeline Pankhurst, would think of women today,' she concluded. 'Most women are still content to be treated like children handed out a few presents from man's wealthy hoard . . . Two battles face women today. One is to hold on to what they have won and the other is to get a better share of what they have not yet won.'

This is truly radical feminism, because it makes demands on power, instead of suggesting that women's behaviour is the problem. It does not ask women to 'lean in', to stop saying sorry, to deepen their voices, to stop wearing make-up if they want to be taken seriously. I think of that stuff as feminism-lite. There is a lot of it sloshing around, and it's really self-help under a thin, sugary glaze of activism. If feminism doesn't frighten people with power, it is toothless.

Think of the current craze for 'woke-washing', where businesses plaster themselves with 'LGBT-friendly employer' kitemarks, hold training days about diversity and encourage people to put their pronouns in their email signatures. It's great, but it changes very little. Recently, I went into a tech company which had signs on the loos proclaiming that anyone who self-identified as a woman could use the ladies. 'Gender diversity is welcome here,' the sign added. A lovely thought. Except I was visiting the tech company to talk about the systematic sexist abuse of women on its platform. Talk is cheap, action is expensive: it's why the suffragette slogan was 'deeds not words'. My corporate dudes, come back to me when you've funded generous parental-leave packages, or ensured that those asking for flexible working hours aren't underpaid and overlooked for promotions. You can have your pink kite mark when half your board and senior management team are women, when your office has a free crèche, and when harassment claims are properly investigated rather than hushed up with non-disclosure agreements.

Maureen Colquhoun's demands were not cosmetic. They were truly radical. And they were doomed to failure. Replying for the government, Dr Shirley Summerskill pointed to the Equal Pay Act and Sex Discrimination Bill as evidence the government was already tackling structural sexism. Colquhoun's bill ran out of debating time, meaning it would get no further in Parliament.

It was a huge disappointment. But then Maureen looked up into the public gallery, and saw a familiar figure sitting a few seats away from her husband Keith, who had come to support her. It was Babs Todd, with her daughter Mairi.

*

Once Babs and Maureen had left their respective partners, they bundled up their children and moved in together. The invitation to their housewarming party carried a picture of two women kissing. It found its way to the *Daily Mail*'s diarist Nigel Dempster. One of their guests had been, effectively, blackmailed by another journalist with the threat of revealing her sexuality to the US Embassy, from which she was trying to obtain a visa. As a lesbian, she could have been refused permission to travel to America 'for reasons of deviancy'.

Once the story was printed, the pair became the most famous, or infamous, lesbians in Britain. One of Colquhoun's parliamentary colleagues, Millie Miller, complained to her that women MPs 'won't be able to have our hair short or wear trousers in public for fear of being labelled . . . Lesbian!' At the time, Colquhoun remembered, she was wearing a skirt, heels and a silk blouse. The straight Millie Miller had short hair and was wearing a trouser suit.

Colquhoun decided to embrace the publicity, and in 1975 she added Babs Todd to her *Who's Who* entry, under 'partner'. And the storm didn't deter her from activism. She once turned up at Westminster with a group of prostitutes, and in March 1979 she gave a speech calling for all laws related to prostitution to be abolished. She supported proportional representation, an electoral system which is friendlier to smaller parties. She tried to be 'nice' about winning over converts, but found it hard. 'Pussyfooting . . . was really not my style,' she noted in *A Woman in the House*.

What drove her out of the Commons, however, was another incendiary issue: race. In January 1977, Enoch Powell – who had once predicted 'rivers of blood' if Britain accepted more immigrants – gave a speech in Manchester attacking new laws against preaching racial hatred. A journalist from the Press Association phoned Colquhoun for her reaction, and she criticised Labour's own record on race, saying that the party used 'soft words and put no money into solving the problems of poor blacks and poor whites in inner cities . . . They prefer to attack Powell rather than attack the real problems of racial conflict.'

The Canadian academic turned politician Michael Ignatieff once complained that running for office involved entering 'a world of lunatic literalmindness' (see also: social media). Colquhoun's remarks were interpreted as an endorsement of Enoch Powell's race-baiting rhetoric. She clarified her meaning to her local party, who withdrew their complaint. She was no Powellite: while a local councillor, she was thrown off all the committees for suggesting that a tenth of council houses should be allocated to immigrant families. Her criticisms were (and still are) correct: the left's rhetoric against racism is not always matched by policies or financial commitments. It's yet more woke-washing. And left-wing politicians' strong feeling of being 'on the right side of history' over issues such as apartheid can blind them to their own failings. Think of Labour leader Jeremy Corbyn refusing to accept that he might have a blind spot on anti-Semitism, despite criticism from Jewish community organisations across the political spectrum.

But Colquhoun's enemies knew a chance when they saw one. They painted her as a crank. They attacked her for calling the Duke of Edinburgh a 'British joke' and asking for rail season tickets to drop their 'male' or 'female' stamps.* They reheated an old story

---

* Ironically, the fact that rail season tickets used to record your sex is what now sounds cranky.

about her punching a parking attendant. On 27 September 1977, the party's general management committee voted 23–18 to remove her as a Labour candidate. She appealed to the national executive committee, which backed her, but then her own constituency party turned against her too. Its chairman Norman Ashby said: 'She was elected as a working wife and mother . . . this business has blackened her image irredeemably.'

The local party eventually folded, but Colquhoun was exhausted and demoralised. In the general election of May 1979, she was defeated by the Conservative candidate. She left the House. Margaret Thatcher, newly installed as Britain's first woman prime minister, would have one fewer 'strident female' to face on the opposition benches. 'Being a lesbian has ruined my political career,' Colquhoun told *Woman's Own* in 1977.

*

After Babs left her, Jackie Forster felt more attracted to women than ever – socially as well as sexually. 'I never thought they'd care because I was this horrible, bossy person,' she said. She tried dating, but realised that one-night stands were unsatisfying, like . . . heterosexuality. 'In the last year, I've had sex for its own sake, and it was just like having it with a man and so isolated at the end of it because there was no emotional thing taking over,' she told the interviewers in *We're Here*. 'It was very mechanical.' Later, she found a new partner, Lace; a page of her typed notes in the archive carries a scratchy handwritten addition: '4th lesbian affair. Lace. Greatest love of life.'

She campaigned for lesbians to gain access to the still relatively new technology of in vitro fertilisation (IVF). If women began to realise that they were gay *before* marrying men, rather than afterwards, the next generation would need medical assistance to become mothers. Jackie also wanted to make the case that lesbians could be mothers as a point of principle. At the time, it was routine that women who left their husbands for a woman lost custody of their children. 'The husband only had to say to the judge, "My wife is now living with another woman," or "has had a lesbian relationship", and that was it,' Tess Gill told me. Adoption and fostering were not an option: lesbian couples told Forster that they had been turned down flat by local councils.

This being the 1970s, the feminist answer was firmly DIY. In May 1974, *Sappho* ran an appeal, asking members of the Campaign for Homosexual Equality to volunteer as sperm donors. It was a time when feminists didn't wait for official permission. Then Jackie Forster found a helpful doctor called David Sopher, who ran a private fertility clinic in Belgravia. By the time the scheme was revealed, in 1978, ten of his patients had given birth to children.

The donors called when the sperm was ready, but were not told who it was going to, 'to prevent tension in the lesbian relationship or intrusion by the father'. They were, however, told when one of their donations resulted in a baby, and whether it was a boy or a girl. 'They celebrated on the town either way,' writes Jackie.

She had wanted the scheme to remain secret until the children were older, but an undercover reporter from the London *Evening News* broke the story on 5 January 1978. The headline read: 'DOCTOR STRANGELOVE'. It was an 'extraordinary and disturbing case' according to reporter Joanna Patyna. One leading gynaecologist claimed that such children would grow up with an 'identity problem' generated by an upbringing that was 'a medically abnormal mode of conduct'. The director of the National Children's Bureau, Dr Mia Kellmer Pringle, added: 'I am very uneasy for the sake of the children . . . There is evidence that some boys brought up without a father figure have difficulty in establishing normal heterosexual relationships.'*

The next day, the newspaper became even more excited as it

* There is no such evidence.

revealed that one of the IVF babies was living not with two women – but three. 'Some people prefer to call us a community,' one of the women told the paper. 'But we consider ourselves a family. I suppose we're extra-unconventional.' Jackie Forster and Dr Sopher must have known that helping three women in a relationship was even more provocative than helping a 'respectable' lesbian couple. They did it anyway.

There followed a two-week media frenzy which preoccupied everyone at *Sappho*. But just like Marie Stopes's libel trial, when people heard about the allegedly terrible and immoral things which some women were getting up to, many were intrigued rather than repulsed. 'The enormous publicity prompted a flood of requests for AID [donor insemination] from lesbians and single straight women way beyond our ability to cope,' wrote Jackie in her unpublished memoir, *Metamorphosis*. Straight feminists 'zapped' – held demonstrations outside – the *Evening News* offices in solidarity with their lesbian sisters, burning copies of the paper and spraying graffiti on its vans.

*

Why aren't Maureen Colquhoun, Jackie Forster and Babs Todd better known? When the Labour leader Jeremy Corbyn wrote a piece celebrating the progress of gay rights, he noted: 'Where we once only had my constituency neighbour Chris Smith in Islington South, we now have over forty Members of Parliament who are out.' Maureen Colquhoun did not get a mention.

The erasure of lesbians has troubled generations of feminist historians. 'If old women are rarely visible in the media, old lesbians have totally ceased to exist,' wrote Suzanne Neild and Rosalind Pearson in 1992. 'The image of lesbians shaped for us by the media is generally a sexual one, otherwise there is no reason for us to be acknowledged. Obviously, in the media's eyes, old women have no sexuality, every old woman automatically becomes a "granny".' The two authors compiled *Women Like Us* to show the real lives of older lesbians, to stop them slipping from the record. 'If we do not safeguard and value our history, then we risk generation after generation believing that they are the first to do this, to feel that struggle against our oppression.'

What form does that oppression take? The extent of violent homophobia against gay men is obvious, yet there has always been violence against lesbians, too. The black South African artist and activist Zanele Muholi, born in a township in the port city of Durban, is one of its most arresting chroniclers.* The women in Muholi's photographs include survivors of 'corrective rape', a phrase which gained wider recognition after the 2008 murder of the South African football player Eudy Simelane in a township on the outskirts of Johannesburg. Simelane was found in a ditch; she had been raped, beaten and stabbed to death. She was thirty-one years old. Her attackers had shouted: 'We will teach you, you are not a man, we will show you, you are a woman!' Four men were put on trial; two were convicted. This is the fear of lesbianism in its most raw form, a fear both of women's sexuality and their gender non-conformity.

'Some policemen in the township mock you, saying: "How can you be raped by a man if you are not attracted to them?" They ask you to explain how the rape felt. It is humiliating,' Thando Sibiya, a lesbian from Soweto, told the BBC's Pumza Fihlani in 2011, in the wake of another such murder. Another activist, Lesego Tlhwale from African gay rights group Behind the Mask, told Fihlani that butch women were a particular target. Some men 'are threatened by these kinds of lesbians in particular', she said. 'They say they are stealing their girlfriends. It is a warped sense of entitlement and a need to protect their manhood.'

Here in Britain, lesbians are also a target for men with a 'warped sense of entitlement'. The journalist Sophie Wilkinson told me that

---

* Muholi, who came out as lesbian during childhood, now uses the pronoun 'they'.

she and her girlfriend were harassed by a man in a McDonald's in Bethnal Green, East London, on a night out. 'A guy came down and sat next to us and said, right so you're the clever one and you're the pretty one, let's chat and come home with me,' she told me. 'When we said, no, we just want to eat our Chicken Selects, please leave us alone, he just refused. He was like, fuck you, you white slags, I know people in this area, I'm going to finish you.' The man went outside and returned with a drink, ready to throw it over them.

The man was never caught, and Wilkinson was unimpressed with how the police dealt with the case. 'The LGBT liaison couldn't understand that this was homophobic. Because misogyny doesn't fit within homophobia. But I know exactly what he meant by "white slags" – you're loose, you fuck each other, why won't you fuck me.' She said that she felt particularly responsible when she and her girlfriend got abuse, because she is the more visibly gender non-conforming. As a child, she asked to be called a boy's name for several years. She now wears minimal make-up and masculine clothes. When the couple were together, she said, it felt like 'I'm the one who's giving us away.'

A few months after I spoke to Wilkinson, another lesbian couple made the news after being attacked on a bus. A photo of the shocked, bloodied faces of Melania Geymonat and her partner Chris went viral in June 2019. A group of young men had harassed them, asking them to kiss, before physically attacking them. 'They surrounded us and started saying really aggressive stuff, things about sexual positions, lesbians and claiming we could kiss so they could watch us,' said Geymonat. 'They started throwing coins. The next thing I know Chris is in the middle of the bus and they are punching her. So I immediately went there by impulse and tried to pull her out of there and they started punching me. I was really bleeding.'

This is the reality of life as a lesbian – or any woman who rejects femininity. You are a target. You are seen as unnatural. You are treated as either a threat or an irrelevance. You are compared to images of lesbians in the media – the kind who pout and preen for the male gaze – and found wanting. Some men's sense of sexual entitlement is violently affronted by women who date other women – *um, where's the role for me in all this?* The grammar of porn has given them a way to reassert themselves, by seeing lesbian sexuality as entertainment. The radical idea that some women don't need a man is defanged by suggesting that they do, really: lesbianism only exists as a performance for the male gaze. It's back to the idea, challenged by Marie Stopes, that women exist as supporting characters rather than protagonists of their own lives.

Lesbian sex itself is mystified and marginalised. There's an urban myth in Britain that lesbianism was never criminalised, because Queen Victoria didn't believe it could exist. The truth is more interesting – and, from a feminist perspective, more depressing. The legal definition of sexual intercourse has largely revolved around penises. Under English law, rape is penetration with a penis. Adultery is defined as heterosexual penetration. And while sodomy was made a crime in 1533, and 'gross indecency' between men became a specific offence in 1885, politicians struggled to conceptualise what exactly lesbians could be doing with each other. In 1921, MPs debated adding a new clause to the 1885 Act: 'Any act of gross indecency between female persons shall be a misdemeanour and punishable in the same manner as any such act committed by male persons.' However, it was decided that merely acknowledging the existence of female homosexuality might tip women off that it was a fun thing to try.

So the confusion remained. As a man shouted at Jackie Forster at Speakers' Corner: 'What do you *do*, love?'

*

Maureen Colquhoun's memoir is vivid, funny and sobering. It left me wanting to talk directly to her. I asked around. One day, an email with a familiar surname appeared in my inbox: Clover Colquhoun,

Maureen's granddaughter. Would I like to speak to the couple? In 1992, Maureen and Babs had left London, and retired to the Lake District. She could give me the phone number for their home near Keswick.

I got through just before Christmas, with Maureen's daughter Mary bustling away in the background, getting ready for their big lunch. Both Maureen and Babs had been ill; Maureen apologised that she couldn't remember things – to whom she had first come out, for example. It was all so long ago and I had caught her 'at a time of life which isn't very good'.

Were you a difficult woman, I asked?

'I suppose you could say I was a very tiresome sort of woman! Well, just I was unrepentant. I was expected to be apologetic, and I wasn't: I was just pleased the whole thing was sorted, in my point of view.'

Apologetic about what?

'Apologetic about gayness.'

But you weren't.

'I was very pleased, actually.'

Maureen said she now believed that it was her sexuality which prompted the revolt against her; the Enoch Powell comments were just an excuse. As for regrets about her treatment, 'of course' she had some. 'But not overwhelmingly. I'm glad that I was able to fight it, strong enough to fight it, because you need to be pretty tough.'

She passed me over to Babs, who said: 'Hello, Helen, here's the other old lady.'

Babs remembered the early days of *Sappho* as a lonely time, because there were so few lesbians in the public eye. That climate of fear was stoked by newspaper reporting, such as the pieces which outed her and Maureen. 'My daughter, she must have been about fifteen, because she'll be going into her sixtieth year this year, and she's a doctor, she was incredibly supportive – and one day, she looked out of our windows – I lived in Hackney then, with the children, it was overlooking Victoria Park – and she saw some men in the bushes with telephoto lenses trained towards our windows.'

Homophobia against men often takes the form of fear, I said, whereas lesbianism is more often treated as a joke. Were you feared or mocked? 'Both, really: they were both fearful and mocking. I used to have children walking behind me, shouting "Lezzy" and things like that.' But her employer, the British Council, was supportive, and so were many of their straight friends. 'They knew we weren't a danger to young people or anything of the kind, which we were accused of, you see.'

Todd started to tell me that Maureen's daughter Mary was married, and had children of her own. I couldn't understand why she was so insistent about this, until I remembered the whole premise of 'Section 28', the legislation introduced by Margaret Thatcher's government in 1988. This banned the 'promotion' of homosexuality as a 'pretended family relationship'. It came amid suggestions that gay people were 'converting' (code for corrupting, or preying on) youngsters. It mattered that Todd and Colquhoun had children. They weren't outsiders to the straight world of nuclear families; they had come from it. 'It wasn't unusual for gay women to be married, because they didn't know they were gay when they got married!' Babs told me. 'It was the sort of thing that wasn't talked about.'

You and Maureen have certainly done your bit for feminism, I said. 'I hope so, because I think we've meant something to women who were very, very lonely and isolated.'

After I hung up, part of the conversation stayed with me. What did meeting Babs mean to you, I had asked Maureen? 'It's meant everything,' she said. 'It was a miracle we found each other.'

And then a surprise.

'We got married not long ago.'

Really?

'To prop up the legislation.'

Her daughter Mary was despatched to find out the date, which

Maureen couldn't remember. She knew it had been at Keswick register office, in the centre of the town.

Their wedding day turned out to be 6 May 2015. 'Oh,' I said, 'that's the same month I got married!' Me, for a second time, after a divorce. For Babs and Maureen, it meant official recognition forty years into their relationship, after they had already grown old together.

*

In the last hundred years, the campaign for lesbian, gay, bisexual and transgender rights has been phenomenally successful. But how well does the LGBT umbrella suit lesbians today? Maureen Colquhoun told me that she always believed in organising alongside men: 'I always felt quite strongly about that. After all, one didn't want more division in society, did one?' But others feel differently, not least because in LGBT terms, lesbians are a minority within a minority. Men dominate the movement by sheer weight of numbers, never mind their socialisation to be louder and more opinionated. From the 1980s onwards, gay men also had an obvious, terrible rallying point: the Aids crisis, and the homophobic backlash it provoked.

Jackie Forster was involved with the Campaign for Homosexual Equality, but grew disillusioned with it. 'I realised however forceful I was, or however much I was myself, the men, not consciously, forced a woman's role on me,' she told the authors of *We're Here*. 'I was not allowed to be, you know, a feminist woman in CHE, which seemed to be the big scene, because they simply didn't know what feminism was about.'

The recent success of the transgender movement – the T in LGBT – has posed new questions for lesbian activists. In some progressive online circles, lesbianism is now controversial because it is deemed 'exclusionary'. Women who refuse to consider trans women (the majority of whom still have penises) as sexual partners have been accused of bigotry. In 2014, the trans activist Julia Serano wrote: 'When the overwhelming majority of cis dykes date and fuck cis women, but are not open to, or are even turned off by, the idea of dating or fucking trans women, how is that not transphobic?'

Strangely, or not, there are few comparable attacks on straight men who are not attracted to women with penises, or on gay men who don't sleep with trans men with vaginas. The condemnation of 'exclusionary' lesbians goes back to that idea that women don't really have an active sexuality and specific desires of their own. We exist to enable other people's pleasure. 'The resistance of many lesbians to have sex with male-bodied people is framed as a matter of inequality rather than orientation, and therefore something to be corrected in the name of progress,' wrote the philosophy professor Kathleen Stock in 2019. 'Lesbian resistance is sometimes referred to as the "cotton ceiling", crassly riffing on the idea of a promotion ceiling for women at work, but substituting images of glass with that of underwear. Equally, sometimes those resisting are called "TERFs", because it is assumed that their resistance is a result of trans-exclusive radical feminism, rather than because they are homosexual.' Of course, many non-trans lesbians *do* consider trans women as potential sexual partners. But it is fine not to do so, either. Your vagina is not a democracy. No one else gets a vote on what you do with it.

Our changing attitudes to gender expression also challenge older ideas of 'butchness'. There are also many lesbian pioneers for whom rejecting femininity and sleeping with women were inextricably linked. They wore men's clothes, had mannish hairstyles, and perhaps even used men's names. Some passed as men to escape marriage and motherhood. We can't peer back in time and ask them if they identified as men, too, or just dressed and acted like them. So whose history do they belong to – lesbians, or the transgender movement? Take Anne Lister, who wore masculine clothes and was nicknamed Gentleman Jack by unkind locals. She wrote in 1820: 'I love and only love the fairer sex and thus beloved by them in turn, my heart revolts from any love but theirs.' In September 2018, a plaque commemorating her was installed at the Holy Trinity Church in York. It read: 'Gender-nonconforming entrepreneur. Celebrated marital commitment, without legal recognition, to Ann Walker in this church. Easter, 1834.' The word notably missing from the plaque was an important one: lesbian. Lister was also not referred to anywhere by female pronouns: 'she' or 'her'.

A local woman, Julie Furlong, started a petition describing the wording as 'lesbian erasure'. 'Anne Lister was, most definitely, gender non-conforming all her life,' it read. 'She was also, however, a lesbian. Don't let them erase this iconic woman from our history.' Following the protest, York Civic Trust agreed to rethink. The plaque now describes Lister as a 'lesbian and diarist [who] took sacrament here to seal her union with Ann Walker'.

The desire to 'claim' butch women as non-binary individuals or trans men persists. In her Netflix stand-up show *Nanette*, the Tasmanian comedian Hannah Gadsby, who has short hair and likes to wear suits, recounts getting a message from a stranger on Facebook urging her to come out as transgender. The thing was, 'I don't identify as transgender. I don't. I mean, I'm clearly "gender not normal", but ... I don't think even lesbian is the right identity fit for me, I really don't. I may as well come out now. I identify as ... tired.'

Why does this matter? It is deeply conservative to suggest that any sufficiently difficult woman from history – say, one who rebelled against the constraints of femininity by dressing and acting in a masculine way – must have really been a man. The implication is that 'real' women are feminine, and conformist. Our modern understanding of being transgender is very hard to apply retrospectively, given the limited life opportunities available to pre-modern women, the prejudice against butchness, and the repression of homosexuality. Transgender people have existed throughout history, but so have feminine men and butch women. Trying to squash historical lives into twenty-first-century categories is fraught with danger.

As for whether lesbianism is 'exclusionary', in the more radical 1970s, there was even a lively discussion in lesbian communities over whether dildos were – how shall I put this – cheating. 'I'm very anti-dildo,' confided Jackie Forster in 1992. 'Why do we want to ape men? That puzzles me.' She added that she could not understand 'queer politics', the idea that 'you can still define yourself as lesbian even if you sleep with gay guys and straight men – this, to me, is crazy . . . It does seem to me that is boxing us back into the "box" of sex, and we spent a long time in the 1970s getting out of that.'

When I read Forster's words, something clicked. Her statement that queer politics was turning 'lesbian' into a sexual identity rather than a political one illuminates a generational divide. The early lesbian activists had a greater demand than simply to love whomever they wanted. They wanted to reorientate their whole lives away from men, and towards women. Some of them went further. The American cultural critic Jill Johnston was uncompromising in her belief that *every* woman should renounce men. 'This book is for my mother, who should've been a lesbian,' reads the dedication to her 1973 book *Lesbian Nation*. 'And for my daughter, in hopes she will be.' Lesbian separatism was earnestly discussed in Britain, too. 'Men are the enemy,' read a 1981 pamphlet by Leeds Revolutionary Feminist Group, published by the Onlywomen Press. 'Heterosexual women are collaborators with the enemy. All the good work that our heterosexual feminist sisters do for women is undermined by the counter-revolutionary activity they engage in with men.'

Looking back, this seems extreme, even absurd. Too many women enjoy some sweet, sweet counter-revolutionary activity with men for lesbian separatism to succeed. But I find the desire to claim women-only spaces completely understandable. In the twentieth century, lesbians suffered a double marginalisation when fighting for their rights: gay men dominated the LGB movement, and lesbians were often shunned within the women's movement, where American feminist Betty Friedan fretted in 1969 about the 'lavender menace' putting nice, respectable ladies off the cause.* In response, a group of radical lesbians invaded the stage at the Second Congress to Unite Women in New York, distributing copies of their manifesto, 'The Woman-Identified Woman'. It begins: 'What is a lesbian? A lesbian is the rage of all women condensed to the point of explosion.' Friedan later apologised, but in 1980, the theorist Adrienne Rich was still struck by 'the virtual or total neglect of lesbian existence in a wide range of writings, including feminist scholarship'.†

Women who love women have also suffered another injustice: pornography has co-opted their identity as a fetish for straight men. Early in my career as a journalist, I had an editor who reacted furiously against the word 'lesbian' in headlines. Later, I met another male journalist with a similar dislike of the word. It took me years to work out their problem, but I think I understand it now. 'Lesbian', to them, was not a serious descriptive category of an activist movement. *It was a type of porn.* I might as well have been trying to publish stories about MILF rights.

In her unpublished memoir, Jackie recalled that the *Sappho* office in Soho was open to visitors. As well as lesbians and gay men, there were 'straight men in macs . . . Who were rapidly ushered out after buying a copy of *Sappho*, never to reappear. Presumably the prim, but genuine contents of the magazine went against the grain of their weirdo fantasies, so they renewed their patronage of the sex shop opposite.'

*

On that blustery day in the Glasgow Women's Library, I was packing up the boxes ahead of a long train ride back to London when

* Betty Friedan: undeniably a difficult woman.
† Rich attributed this to 'compulsory heterosexuality', arguing that we needed to examine heterosexuality as a political institution, rather than treat it merely as an innate sexual preference.

something fluttered out. It was a blank form. I turned it over in my hands. The nomination for an honour. 'If she had served any cause other than lesbian rights, she'd have been festooned with honours; she would have been Dame Jackie Forster,' said the academic Gill Hanscombe at the end of a 1997 documentary. Assertive, uncompromising, possessed of a healthy ego, desperate for the mainstream recognition she felt she was denied because of her sexuality ... *of course* she had wanted to be Dame Jackie.

I remembered what Stephen Bourne, who had known Jackie in the *Sappho* days, told me. He felt 'horrible', he said, that Forster had been forgotten. 'And I feel upset for not having thought about her.' He brought a sheaf of papers to my office: notes for his 1990s film about her; her obituary in the lesbian magazine *Diva*; a *Guardian* article about her speech at Speakers' Corner. The last cutting showed Jackie in a bar, cigarette in one hand, glass in the other, primed to recount an anecdote. Stephen Bourne was determined to do his bit to ensure that she didn't fall out of the history books.

Born the year that television was invented, Jackie Forster was ahead of her time. She died on 10 October 1998 at the age of 71. She did not live to see gay marriage legalised, lesbians allowed to serve in the armed forces, gay couples given equal adoption rights, the lesbian comedian Ellen DeGeneres host the Oscars, or the Scottish Conservatives elect a lesbian leader.*

But Maureen Colquhoun and Babs Todd did. In a trembling voice, Maureen Colquhoun read me a letter over the phone. It was from her local Labour Party. An apology. 'Nobody else has seen this letter,' she said. 'Apart from some of my friends.'

'I am writing on behalf of Northampton North Labour Party to express the party's appreciation of the very great contribution you made to the lives of many people in the constituency from 1974 to 79, when you served as our MP,' it began.

* Ruth Davidson, who had a child with her partner by IVF in 2018.

Some of the issues that you supported then, in particular in relation to sex workers and equalities, have since become more widely accepted. However, at the time, you were in the forefront of bringing these matters to public and political attention. You also had to endure media scrutiny over your personal life, and stood out courageously for public recognition of same-sex relationships, something which the Labour governments have subsequently legislated for, but which in the 1970s was still controversial. The Labour Party in Northampton appreciates the pioneering role you played and your total and lifelong commitment to our party. We understand that you continued in public service as a Labour councillor until two years ago, which is a remarkable record of service. The party here wishes you all the very best for yourself and your family.

How did you feel when you read that, all these years later, I asked? And Maureen Colquhoun – Maureen the firebrand, Maureen the troublemaker, Maureen who stood up against the 'maleocracy' in Parliament and the men hiding in the bushes outside her house – hesitated, but only for a moment.

'I felt like crying,' she said.

8. EDUCATION

Let us pick up our books and our pens, they are the most powerful weapons.

Malala Yousafzai

It's the sheep that makes the protest feel really insulting. On a cold winter afternoon in Edinburgh – is there any other kind? – a group of women were trying to get to their anatomy class. They wanted to become doctors. But there was a sheep on the loose.

The day was Friday 18 November 1870.* Queen Victoria was halfway through her reign. Earlier that year, married women in England and Wales gained the right to own property, Louis Pasteur established that disease was caused by germs, and Dante Gabriel Rossetti published a collection of poems rescued from the coffin of his wife and muse Elizabeth Siddal.

By 4.30 p.m. on a November day in Edinburgh, it's nearly dark, and the women would have been forgiven for being nervous as they walked to Surgeons' Hall, an elegant building in the city's Southside. A group of male medical students and local men were waiting for them outside the gates. Hundreds of spectators, sensing something was about to happen, were already milling around. There were no police present, either through incompetence or quiet sympathy with the protesting men.

As the women reached the hall, the gates remained closed. The young men inside were drinking whisky and smoking cigarettes, and they swore at the women. 'We waited quietly on the step to see if the rowdies were to have it all their own way,' wrote Sophia Jex-Blake in her memoir *Medical Women: A Thesis and A History*. Within a minute, one of their fellow students – Mr Sanderson – came out of the hall, opened the gates, and ushered them inside. It was a brave

* This was forty years to the day before the suffragettes' Black Friday.

thing to do. The jeers and howls continued, even as the women entered the anatomy classroom.

That's when the sheep got shoved inside the hall. Poor Mailie was named after the ewe in a poem by Robert Burns.* Seeing the animal, the university tutor Dr Handyside was withering. 'Let it remain,' he said. 'It has more sense than those who sent it here.'

After the class finished, the women refused to sneak out of the class by the back door. Several sympathetic male students surrounded them, and they made it home 'with no other injuries than those inflicted on our dresses by the mud hurled at us by our chivalrous foes', according to Jex-Blake. The next day, fellow students with big sticks kept back the crowd which had gathered to jeer. The intimidation continued for several days, until the 'rowdies' realised that their tactics were not working, and gave up.

What had provoked such outrage? Sophia and her fellow students wanted to become doctors, a profession which was then open only to men. Women could be nurses, of course, but that was a caring role – soothing and wiping – distinct from the masculine preserve of medical wisdom. Two years earlier, the University of London had become the first in the world to admit women as undergraduate students, although they were awarded a 'certificate of proficiency' rather than a degree. Something was shifting: women were staking a claim to higher education, and the middle-class professional jobs which lay beyond it.

The cool prose of Sophia Jex-Blake gives little sense of how fraught that Edinburgh day must have been. Her descriptions made me think of the spitting and jeering which greeted the first black students to attend white-only schools in the American South in the 1950s. In both cases, education was being desegregated – opened up to groups who had previously been excluded, or shunted

* Since she was owned by the department, Mailie was presumably destined for a future on the dissecting rather than dining table.

to second-class facilities. It is hard to imagine just how difficult it would be to learn in such a hostile environment.

Sophia and her fellow students became known as the 'Edinburgh Seven', or 'Septem contra Edinam' – Seven against Edinburgh. They were the first women to be full undergraduate students at any British university.

The story of the Edinburgh Seven is one of noble failure – and unexpected success. It began with a simple demand.

*

All she wanted, she said, was a 'fair field and no favour'. In an essay published in 1869, the twenty-nine-year-old Sophia Jex-Blake argued that women were naturally suited to a career in medicine, because of their traditional role in caring for the sick. The daughter of a prosperous lawyer, she had been educated first at home and then at private schools near her family's house in Hastings. She studied at Queen's College, London, where she developed what is often referred to as a 'passionate friendship' with the social reformer Octavia Hill, and stayed on to teach mathematics.*

Sophia features in Virginia Woolf's essay on women's rights, 'Three Guineas', as an example of the 'great Victorian fight between the victims of the patriarchal system and the patriarchs, of the daughters against the fathers'. Her father gave her £40 a year and refused to let her take a salary from her tutoring. Woolf imagines the conversation between them, as Sophia's father says it would be 'quite beneath' her to expect payment for her work. She replies: 'Why should I not take it? You as a man did your work and received your payment, and no one thought it any degradation, but a fair exchange.' She points out that her brother Tom earns a living as a lawyer, after all. Ah, replies her father, but Tom has to support a wife

---

* In later life, Jex-Blake's partner was fellow doctor Margaret Todd, whose biography of her was published in 1918.

and family. 'How entirely different is my darling's case! You want for nothing, and know that (humanly speaking) you will want for nothing.' Her father expected her to be financially reliant on him, and then on her husband. This was not the generous gesture it might seem: his generosity was conditional on her compliance.

But Sophia was stubborn, and decided to disappoint her father rather than submit to his benevolent dictatorship. On a trip to America, she visited a children's hospital in Boston and met the pioneering doctor Lucy Ellen Sewall, who was resident physician at the New England Hospital for Women and Children. This was the life she wanted.

There was a problem. To work as a doctor, she needed to qualify in medicine at a recognised university. The Medical Act of 1858 had been designed to discourage quacks and charlatans, but it had an unfortunate side effect: it gave the sole power to certify doctors to British medical schools, which were uniformly opposed to admitting female students. And so, wrote Jex-Blake, the Act 'made an almost insurmountable barrier to the admission of women to the authorised practice of medicine'.

That didn't stop them trying. In 1860, Elizabeth Garrett Anderson found a loophole after being rejected by all the regular colleges. She studied instead at the Worshipful Society of Apothecaries, a livery company in London, whose founding charter promised to examine any candidate who completed its course. Garrett Anderson had to take (expensive) private tuition, because she was not admitted to all the classes, and struggled to find a hospital placement. When she finally got one at Middlesex Hospital, she took an oral exam alongside the male students and did 'too well', according to Sophia Jex-Blake, 'thus arousing their manly wrath, which showed itself in a request that she should be required to leave the hospital'.

Garrett Anderson gained a licence to practise. She was one of seven candidates examined by the Society of Apothecaries in 1865, and she obtained a higher mark than any of the six men. But it was a short-lived triumph. A rule was promptly passed banning medical students from receiving any part of their education privately. Women were locked out of the profession again.

This illustrates a common theme in the history of sexism. Insist that women are unable to accomplish something; when one of them nonetheless accomplishes it, change the rules. The Olympics used to have mixed-sex skeet-shooting, until a twenty-four-year-old Chinese woman, Zhang Shan, won gold in 1992. She was unable to defend her title: at the next games, four years later, the shooting programme was segregated, and skeet shooting became men-only. In 2016, there were nine shooting events for men and six for women. After a woman, Kathrine Switzer, illicitly completed the (men-only) Boston Marathon in 1967 – in defiance of those who said the distance was dangerous for women – the Amateur Athletic Union banned women from competing in all events alongside men.

With the loophole used by Elizabeth Garrett Anderson closed to her, Sophia Jex-Blake needed to gain admission to a university. The rules excluding women had to be challenged. She chose Edinburgh, because the city was considered to be forward-thinking, but her initial application was rejected. In the spring of 1869, she placed an advert in the *Scotsman* newspaper, asking for other women to join her.

Four replied, and they all submitted their application in the summer. Another two joined later, completing the Edinburgh Seven. This time, the university allowed them to matriculate. They could formally attend the university and study for degrees, with the proviso that lecturers did not have to teach them alongside the men. That meant separate lectures, which they had to arrange themselves – and, naturally, higher fees. It was very far from the 'fair field and no favour' Jex-Blake had requested.

At Edinburgh, the seven women faced a range of reactions which will be familiar to anyone who has campaigned for women's rights.

Some (male) professors were sympathetic, and offered their help. A few were outwardly hostile: one told her that he 'could not imagine any decent woman wishing to study medicine – as for any lady, that was out of the question'. The majority, however, were simply apathetic. 'They did not wish arbitrarily to stretch their power to exclude women from education, and yet they were alarmed at what seemed to them the magnitude and novelty of the change proposed,' wrote Jex-Blake.

This is the group which often causes campaigners the most trouble: think back to Millicent Fawcett being told that the militant suffragettes were off-putting, by a man who had done nothing to advance women's suffrage himself. Or Tess Gill being told that ordering a drink from the bar was *'de minimis'* – not important enough to bother a court. When Sophia started her campaign, Dr John Brown, the brother of one of the Edinburgh lecturers, wrote to the *Scotsman* saying that women should be 'as free to study and to practise medicine as men are', although 'we may differ as to the degree of urgency'.

Apathy is often a front for conservatism. If nothing changes, the status quo prevails, which suits those who *like* the status quo. The question of priorities is also used against feminists, implying that whatever they are currently doing is not the *real* issue. The *real* issue is something else (usually something that your opponent has probably done nothing about themselves). One of the most memorable moments in my own development as a feminist was reading Deborah Cameron's work on language. It showed me just how deep sexism is woven into the words we use, whether it's gendered descriptions such as 'shrill' or 'bossy', or the fact that it took until the 1970s for women to get an honorific – Ms – which didn't indicate their marital status. Individually, these examples can look trivial, but together, they quietly shape our entire construction of reality. Cameron was delighted to arrive at Oxford University and discover its 'gender-free language' policy, but less delighted to discover she was one of 'only two and a half women in her department'.*

Here's the paragraph that stayed with me, though. 'I would never take the line that language is "trivial" or a "distraction" from more important issues,' she writes in *On Language and Sexual Politics*. 'There probably are more important issues, but political struggle invariably takes place on many fronts at once. No feminist fairy with a magic wand ever comes up and says: "OK, you can have non-sexist language or equal pay; now which is it to be?"'

This is why feminists have to be difficult. We face challenges from well-meaning allies, irritating nitpickers *and* outright opponents. The response to each must be different, but none of them should distract us. John Brown, who was able to qualify as a doctor in the late nineteenth century, might not have felt the urgency to change the system. But Sophia Jex-Blake, who could not, did feel it. She also sensed that apathy would curdle to antipathy if she carried on. She was right.

*

Why was it so important for women to qualify as doctors? It was August 2018. I had arrived in Edinburgh at festival time, so the area around Surgeons' Hall was festooned with posters for theatre shows promising 'an interactive exploration of #MeToo', and similar horrors. The nice man in the museum reception explained that I couldn't go inside the hall that day, as it is still a working part of the university, but that there was a plaque outside. He directed me instead to the pathology museum, which had a display devoted to Scotland's pioneering female surgeons.

Now: first tip. Never visit a pathology museum directly after lunch. Fascinating though the insides of human beings are, they are best seen on an empty (non-ulcerated, non-cancerous) stomach.

---

* I presume one of the women was part-time, rather than just a very opinionated torso.

I bitterly regretted my chicken burger as I contemplated a huge, hairy bezoar extracted from some luckless sod.* The case devoted to battlefield injuries wasn't much better.

Eventually, I found the surgery display, and there was the trenchant face of Sophia Jex-Blake staring back at me. I learned that in 1895 Lilian Lindsay became the first qualified female dentist in Britain, after graduating from Edinburgh University.

Jex-Blake and her contemporaries weren't just interested in being doctors; they wanted to improve women's health. They set up clinics staffed by, and catering for, women. As Caroline Criado Perez's book *Invisible Women* has shown, there is a 'gender data gap' which is particularly obvious, and dangerous, in medicine.

For decades, new drugs were regularly not tested on women, because of their 'unpredictable' hormones. Doctors had no idea how diseases presented differently in men and women. The latter are much less likely to have the classic 'crushing in the chest' symptoms of a heart attack, for example, and are more likely to die as a result. Studies show that men's pain is taken more seriously – it must be bad to make a stoic man go to the doctor, after all. In medicine, as with sex, women have historically been treated as men-with-a-difference.

Of course, there are male doctors who care deeply about sex differences and how they might shape drug prescription and diagnosis. But it's hard to see what you're not seeing: if an experience isn't part of your daily life, why would you 'get' its importance? Here's an example: in 2014, the first Apple health app for the iPhone allowed users to track the most incredible range of metrics, including their intake of a mineral called molybdenum. But it didn't allow users to track their menstrual cycles. Now – the number of people in the world who care about their molybdenum levels is probably lower than the number of people who care about knowing whether they

---

* Don't know what a bezoar is? Trust me, don't google it. You're happier this way.

might start bleeding through their white trousers. In fact, that's definitely true, because when third-party developers launched period trackers, they were a huge success. The most famous, Clue, reached a million monthly users in 2015, two years after launching.*

On my way out of the pathology museum, I stopped to look at a small skeleton hanging by the exit. It dates back to 1800 and belonged, according to the caption, to a woman with osteomalacia, a softening of the bones caused by vitamin D deficiency. The starkness with which the caption set out the known facts was like a punch to the stomach. The bone disorder affected the woman's pelvis, and she became pregnant six times, losing every baby. 'During her seventh pregnancy, doctors confined her to bed,' it noted. She consulted the surgeon John Bell, who made an incision into her womb to deliver the baby. 'The child survived, but unfortunately she [i.e. the mother] died twenty minutes later from blood loss.' The skeleton was sold to the medical college in 1825.

I looked up again at the tiny, childlike figure. Who was having sex with this woman, despite knowing that pregnancy could kill her? Did she feel obliged to keep trying for a baby because of the society she lived in? When the doctors advised her to stay in bed during her seventh pregnancy, did they not realise – or not care – that the miscarriages were her body's way of saying 'I can't do this'? Did they choose the baby's life over hers?

And then, the eternal question of women's history. Thanks to Edinburgh University's record-keeping, I know that the surgeon who operated on her was called John Bell. His contribution to medicine is written into eternity. But . . . what was *her* name?

I walked out into the August sunshine thinking: this is it, this is

---

* I'm a total evangelist for these apps. If you're a hypochondriac, it's useful to know that this is the time of the month your breasts *always* hurt, your gall bladder always gives you gip, or you always get a migraine. It also puts you in touch with your internal biochemistry in a way that is strangely humbling. Why am I so grumpy today? Oh.

the lesson. Medicine cannot be something that is done to women. It has to be done by them, too.

*

In her memoir, Jex-Blake speculates that the women's success turned the other students against them, just as Elizabeth Garrett Anderson's top marks had made her unpopular. One of the Edinburgh Seven, Edith Pechey, came third overall in chemistry. She should have won a scholarship, but it was instead given to the next best student, because he was a man. 'The so-called experiment was not going to fail of itself, as they had confidently hoped,' wrote Jex-Blake. Many other universities were coming to the same conclusion. Women were capable of intense study, smashing all the confident assertions about their limited intellectual capacity. So what was the new excuse for keeping them out of higher education?

The idea that women are innately stupid certainly had a good run. From the Reformation onwards, as schooling moved out of the control of the church, the subject of how much education women could bear had been a perennial talking point. In the seventeenth century, Bathsua Makin, who ran a school for girls in Tottenham, argued that some men 'desire to keep [women] ignorant to be tyrannised over'. Others made less revolutionary arguments for female education. Even Mary Wollstonecraft, in her early work *Thoughts on the Education of Daughters*, argued that women could better support their husbands if they had mastered writing and arithmetic. That argument won broad support. Higher education, however, was out of the question: it was the passport to solid, middle-class jobs which were exclusively held by men.

One of the opponents of greater female education was Queen Victoria. According to the Scottish poet Sir Theodore Martin in 1901, 'the Queen is most anxious to enlist everyone who can speak or write to join in checking this mad, wicked folly of "woman's rights" with all its attendant hours, on which her poor feeble sex is bent, forgetting every sense of womanly feeling and propriety'. At the time, this example of the poor, feeble sex had amassed an empire which covered a quarter of the earth's land mass. Like Elizabeth I, who told her troops she had 'the body of a weak and feeble woman, but the heart and stomach of a king', or that strident female-hater Margaret Thatcher, Victoria was a powerful woman who saw herself as an exception. It made her less difficult – less threatening to the status quo.

By the 1850s, excellent schools for wealthy girls, such as Cheltenham Ladies College, had been founded. In 1863, Emily Davies – a friend of both Elizabeth Garrett Anderson and her younger sister, the suffragist Millicent Garrett Fawcett – successfully argued that girls should enter the 'Cambridge Junior Locals', the exams taken by boys at sixteen. Davies thought that it would be harder to refuse young women entry to universities if they had the same qualifications as their male peers.* The achievements of Garrett Fawcett, Garrett Anderson and Davies are formidable. Between these three old friends, they helped topple the barriers to women accessing education, medicine and the vote.

Sophia Jex-Blake benefited from all this work, but she also felt the sting of the backlash against it. It wasn't only Queen Victoria who objected to 'women's rights'. By the winter term of 1870, some of the male students were openly hostile, 'shutting doors in our faces, ostentatiously crowding into the seats we usually occupied, bursting into horse-laughs and howls when we approached'. Fireworks were attached to her door. Her nameplate was repeatedly defaced. She received obscene anonymous letters. Men accosted her in the backstreets of Edinburgh, shouting 'anatomical terms which we could not fail to understand'. A petition against the women being allowed into the infirmary for practical experience gained 500 signatures. Jex-Blake suggests that some professors egged the men on,

* Davies would go on to co-found Girton College at Cambridge.

loudly suggesting that it was a wonder that nothing was thrown at the women. The presidents of the college of physicians and surgeons refused to attend a prize-giving if any female students were given awards. The ceremonies were abandoned, but the prize lists – with the women's impressive results – were still made public.

Her fellow students were not all opposed, however: twenty-three presented a petition asking for the women to study at the infirmary alongside them. A committee of professors and other worthies, including Charles Darwin, raised funds to pay their fees. The editor of the *Scotsman*, Alexander Russel, was also on their side.

It didn't matter. In the summer of 1871, the university's senate ruled that its lecturers could not teach the women alongside the men. In the autumn, it banned any more women from matriculating. At every turn, the university blocked women from studying, provoking one professor to tell Jex-Blake that he 'did not much approve' of female medical students, but he approved even less of the senate treating them so unfairly when they had already matriculated. He would give up his class of men and teach them instead, he said. But the authorities still resisted the women's presence, and after two more years of legal wrangling, it was ruled that the Seven should never have been admitted to the university. The women were ordered to pay £848 6s 8d in costs.

When she read the decision, Elizabeth Garrett Anderson wrote to *The Times*, urging the Seven to qualify abroad. Sophia Jex-Blake disagreed, insisting that the battle must be fought (and won) in Britain. She applied to St Andrews, which had no male medical students, to finish her course. She was rejected. She applied to Durham, and was rejected. She took unofficial lectures with sympathetic tutors at Edinburgh, and by the spring of 1874 – when she was thirty-four – she had learned everything that the university system could teach her.

Jex-Blake concludes the first section of her memoir by suggesting that if the university had simply admitted the Edinburgh Seven to mixed classes without a fuss, there would have been no uprising by the students, no riot, and no sheep in Surgeons' Hall. Then she does a little discrimination of her own. 'I have little doubt that this will ultimately be the usual arrangement as civilisation advances,' she writes of mixed-sex education. 'But I am equally certain that boys of a low social class, of small mental calibre, and no moral training are utterly unfit to be admitted to a mixed class, and I confess that I was most painfully surprised in Edinburgh to find how large a number there are of medical students who come under this description.'

Eek. In all the praise for Jex-Blake that I have read, there was no mention of how she appealed to middle-class sensibilities – portraying herself as a lady, and the supportive students as gentlemen, set against the rude, swearing, drinking lower-class mob. By now, that doesn't surprise me. Sophia Jex-Blake has been anointed a pioneer. That carries with it the temptation to tidy away her snobbery. It is a difficult truth that feminism has often succeeded because middle-class women have found solidarity with middle-class men against shared opponents. Difficult Women either tend to get tidied up, like Sophia Jex-Blake, or tidied away, like Erin Pizzey.

The consolation is that the freedoms the Edinburgh Seven fought for were eventually available to all women. But when the reforms are nebulous and cultural rather than written into law, it's no wonder marginalised women can end up feeling left behind by their sharp-elbowed sisters.

In 1874, Jex-Blake helped to establish a medical school for women in London. She travelled to Switzerland to qualify there, and at the same time the House of Commons passed the Medical Act, opening up medical training to women. After having her qualification rubber-stamped in Dublin, Jex-Blake became the third woman ever to register as a doctor with the General Medical Council. One of her first acts was to set up a clinic for poor women. It had been a long road, but Dr Jex-Blake could feel satisfied by what she had achieved.

By the end of the nineteenth century, 16 per cent of university students were women.

That said, it took until 1948 – within my mother's lifetime – before all British universities started awarding degrees to women. (Cambridge was the last to concede.) In 1998, during the second year of Tony Blair's time as prime minister, it invited back 900 women who had studied at Cambridge before 1948 to receive, at last, their degrees.

The oldest woman who attended that day was ninety-seven. She would have been eleven when Sophia Jex-Blake died. In two lifetimes, British women have smashed the barriers holding them back from higher education. It is one of feminism's greatest successes. It must now be replicated around the world.

*

Kathmandu is an overwhelming city – full pavements, hectic roads, a persistent dust that lodges in the back of your throat. On my first afternoon in Nepal, I walked to Durbar Square, a UNESCO World Heritage site which was devastated by the 2015 earthquake. There, among the collapsed pagodas and market stalls full of statues and scarves, I was about to see a goddess.

'She must have a body like a banyan tree,' reads one of the thirty-two qualifications to become a *kumari*, or living embodiment of the Hindu goddess Durga. Her neck should be like a conch shell, her eyelashes like a cow's, and her voice as soft and clear as a duck's.* She must come from the caste containing gold- and silversmiths, be healthy and have all her baby teeth. Above all, she must be not only a virgin, but a prepubescent. The day the *kumari* gets her first period, the goddess leaves her body. She spends twelve days in a dark room, before being sent back into the world.

In Durbar Square, with the afternoon light fading, I went into

---

* I suspect this was written by someone who had never heard a duck.

the *kumari*'s palace just in time for her hourly appearance at the balcony. The current goddess was four years old, and she looked about as nonplussed as you would expect. Dressed in orange, Trishna Shakya had a third eye painted on her forehead. She waved imperiously at the assembled tourists before retreating back into the wood and lacquer building.

I had wanted to see the *kumari* because she lives a life of luxurious imprisonment.

When she is occasionally taken outside, her feet must not touch the ground; she is carried in a palanquin. Visitors come from around the country to worship her; tourists come from all over the world to gawp. But all that ends when puberty arrives. Then, she has to rejoin her family, and consider her future. For the first time, she can walk across the road by herself. 'When I had to step out of my house for the first time, I didn't know how to walk properly,' a former *kumari* called Chanira Bajracharya told the BBC in 2014. 'My mum and dad, they used to hold my hands and teach me how to walk.'

What family could bear to see their little girl taken away from them so young? Well, as it happens, thousands of families in Nepal have to agree to exactly that – although their daughters don't leave their homes for a life of pampered seclusion. Instead of *kumari*, they become *kamlari*. The best English translation is probably 'indentured servant', although you could also argue for the use of another word: slave.

The practice was outlawed in 2006, but news travels slowly in rural Nepal. An hour's drive outside Nepalganj, near the Indian border, I talked to Sangita Tharu, who became a *kamlari* at ten years old after her parents needed money for farmland. The landlord turned up when her parents were out in the fields.

'My aunt fed me lunch and I went away,' she told me.

What, without saying goodbye?

'Yes.'

She walked to a checkpoint an hour away, then took a bus to

Nepalganj. When she arrived at her new home at 5 p.m., there was another *kamlari* in the house already. Sangita had not even taken any clothes with her.

I had travelled to Nepal with a British charity, Room to Read, whose mission is to improve child literacy. They work across South East Asia and sub-Saharan Africa, targeting countries with relatively stable infrastructure and no bloody civil wars. They also target girls, because 150 years after Sophia Jex-Blake tried to enter a university, female education rates still trail male ones across the developing world. In 2013, half of women in Nepal were illiterate. The reasons are both cultural and economic. In places where school costs money, families are more likely to send their sons. Girls are expected to help out more at home, which can affect their schoolwork. Some become pregnant and drop out. Others cannot afford sanitary towels and miss classes every month. Families value their sons more highly – they can travel to India or the Gulf States to work – because job opportunities for women are more scarce.

But educated women have fewer children, and have them later, reducing poverty rates. They also educate their own children better. Even though most women in rural communities also help with harvesting and other tasks, the worldwide, systematic devaluing of domestic and caring labour – because it does not directly generate income – means that girls get a raw deal. The young women I spoke to in Nepal reported that their brothers were given the best toys; larger portions of food; and more free time.

That day in Kathmandu, the experience of seeing the *kumari* left me uncomfortable. After all, I had just gawped at a toddler taken away from her family and placed in religious seclusion. *Kumari* now get to study with private tutors, and take exams, but their isolation is real. The unceremonious way that the living goddesses become plain old women the minute they get their first period is also jarring, particularly in a country with other strong taboos around menstruation. In the mountains, girls are still exiled to huts when they have their periods. In January 2018, a twenty-one-year-old died in a remote village after lighting a fire to keep warm in Nepal's sub-zero winter. She died of smoke inhalation.

Restrictions on female education are common across the world, enforced by law, custom or unofficial quotas favouring men. In 2012, Malala Yousafzai, a fifteen-year-old from north-west Pakistan, was shot in the head by a Taliban gunman because she campaigned for girls to go to school. She now lives in England and still campaigns for girls' education. Until 2017, women in Saudi Arabia needed their male guardian's permission to enrol in university, and campuses are still strictly segregated by gender.* China's education ministry bans women from studying mining, navigation and tunnel engineering, claiming they cannot lift heavy loads and would struggle to escape a mine if there was trouble. A few days after my visit to Edinburgh, examiners at Tokyo Medical University in Japan admitted that they had deducted points from the test scores of female applicants for many years. They wanted to limit the numbers of women doctors, reasoning that it would harm the country's health service if it was staffed by too many people who might leave to have babies. They apparently hadn't considered that a) doctors' future lives were none of their business; and b) making it easier for mothers to stay in the profession was also possible. The next year, when the handicapping system was removed, female applicants outperformed male ones.

There are no such gender quotas for medical school in Britain, although some might argue there should be – as women now far out-number men. They became a majority in 1996, and by 2003 accounted for 60.9 per cent of British medical students. The figure has stayed steady ever since. In the US, it took until 2017 for women to overtake men, but there too they are now the majority.

This shift is interesting, because one of the arguments used to explain women's under-representation in science and engineering

---

* However, more women graduate there than men.

careers is that they are naturally less good at these disciplines. Yet the picture is mixed. Women are the majority of biology undergraduates (as well as law, languages and history), while men dominate computer science, engineering and mathematics. Why would women succeed at law and fall behind in engineering? Why would men excel in engineering and lag in history? Funnily enough, my own life offers one example of how a girl can be dissuaded from male-dominated subjects. In the aptitude tests I took in Year 11, I scored highest in maths. But I went to an all-girls school, and the teaching was stronger in humanities subjects. So I took English.*

The argument made in Sophia Jex-Blake's day that women were not naturally suited to medicine has now been convincingly demolished. But sexism and sexist structures still permeate the profession. Women are more likely to become GPs, a career associated with part-time work and fixed hours, rather than hospital doctors, who are often required to work antisocial shifts. By 2015, nearly 150 years after the Surgeons' Hall Riot, only 10 per cent of surgeons were female. 'There is a culture that basically discourages females to pursue this career,' Dr Maria Irene Bellini of Imperial College, London, told the *Guardian* in 2019. 'I strongly believe that you cannot be what you cannot see.'

In Britain, the feminist revolution in education has succeeded beyond its wildest dreams. Last year, 29,000 more women than men applied for undergraduate courses. Every year since 2013 there have been around 300,000 more female undergraduates in Britain than male ones, and around 80,000 more women on taught postgraduate degrees. However, men still have the edge in research degrees: 58,150 versus 54,285 in 2016, according to the Higher Education Statistics Agency. And men still earn more over their lifetimes. This fits with what we know about the gender pay gap, which has effectively

---

* In the alternate reality where I took maths, I am probably much richer. But this book wouldn't exist. Don't you dare say 'win-win, then'.

closed between full-time British workers in their twenties. When women can study like men, and work like men, they are treated (and paid) like men. But when childcare responsibilities bite, many women move into lower-paid or part-time work; they also leave (or do not apply for) more senior positions in academia. In 2016–17, there were more than 19,000 professors in Britain, according to the Advance HE charity. Fewer than 5,000 of them were women. Only twenty-five were black women.

All that must inform the conversation. But so must another diffi-cult fact. In Britain, there is another group whose achievements in school, and whose resulting lack of career opportunities, is causing worry to education specialists. What to do about them is a difficult question for the feminist movement. Because that group is boys.

*

'Every September, I get a bunch of wide-eyed buggy-tailed children who dare not say a word out of edgeways or put a foot wrong,' Ashley Clayton tells me. 'They have never had a male teacher and live in fear that I will shout at them . . . I also get called "Miss" a lot. I have no idea why – I'm six foot tall and sound like Darren Gough!'

Ashley Clayton is a white man. He's also a minority. He teaches in a primary school, a profession in which just 15 per cent of the workforce is male. He originally wanted to teach PE at secondary level, and spent several years unsuccessfully applying before he was invited to an interview for a primary school course. 'The reaction from my mum was quite cynical. "Well, Ashley, you're a man, you'll be the headteacher in no time."'

When I spoke to other male primary school teachers, they told similar stories. 'When I trained, I was treated as a minority,' Rob, a Year 6 teacher from London, tells me over email. 'Being a white middle-class man, that's not normally how it is! I got £200 as a bursary.'

In two of the three schools Rob has taught in, he was one of only two men, the other being the headteacher. 'Unfortunately in teach-ing, the management level is dominated by men,' he says. 'I know I will be promoted more easily as and when I want to do management stuff. You need to go in to head or deputy in your first ten years of teaching, otherwise people think you don't have the drive or what-ever. So taking a career break is tough. And although working part time is easy, promotion is locked off.' That makes it hard for women who take maternity leave in their thirties.

For reasons such as this, men outnumber women in education leadership roles, even though the overall workforce is dominated by women. And it's often women propping up that system. 'I would def-initely say that female staff members have a preference for working for male heads,' Simon Brereton, the head of a state school in the Midlands, told me. 'I have often heard the same actions being described in very negative and sexist terms for a female rather than a male head.'

Female doctors helped to change the perception of the female body from an object of curiosity into a shell for living, breathing independent humans. Having more male primary school teachers would be just as transformative. Boys could see men in caring roles, expanding their ideas of masculinity. They could see what they could be. 'One boy I taught, he never had any male role models around,' Rob, the Year 6 teacher, told me. 'I hate to say these things, because they sound so sweeping, but his mum said to me: it's great he's seen that a man could hold down a stable job. And that being geeky wasn't a bad thing.'

In schools, white working-class boys are falling behind other groups at GCSE. And where there are strong cultural scripts for what female nerdy excellence looks like – from Roald Dahl's Matilda to J. K. Rowling's Hermione – many boys feel that academic achieve-ment is uncool. 'Young men are significantly more likely than young women to be less engaged with school and have low skills and poor academic achievement,' reported the Organisation for Economic

Co-operation and Development, an international forum for sharing economic data, in 2017. 'They are also more likely to leave school early, often with no qualifications. Boys in OECD countries, for example, are eight percentage points more likely than girls to report that school is a waste of time.'

We are used to talking about the lack of women in certain fields – politics, finance, law – and why that is a problem. But the same stereotypes that say women aren't suited to running countries also suggest that men shouldn't do traditionally 'feminine' jobs. That has profound consequences, particularly in rich countries where manufacturing is in decline, while jobs in the service sector are more resilient. If it's 'unmanly' to work as a nail technician, or as a nurse, or in a care home, or in a primary school, then we are locking men out of large sectors of the economy.

Many men I know are cautious about feminism because they feel it is blaming them personally, somehow, for things which are not their fault. The underachievement of boys has fallen prey to the opposite problem: it is now used as a cudgel to attack feminism. So feminists need to have something to say about it. What happens when men and boys are the ones who need 'affirmative action'? In the *Financial Times* in December 2018, Simon Kuper and Emma Jacobs addressed the problem. Whether through biology or socialisation, boys are slower to learn to read, and have more difficulty concentrating, they reported. Where most of the world is built around a male default – a box into which women struggle to squeeze their lives and experiences – we have designed a school system around an ideal pupil who looks a lot like a 'good girl'.

Rob, the Year 6 teacher, says it has taken him six years to realise just how ingrained his ideas about boys and girls were. 'From the earliest age, it's locked in that boys are boisterous, cheeky – girls are princesses,' he adds. 'I'd pull up girls for stuff like talking in class, but with the boys I'd think: I don't want to get into this, alienate them, so I'll let it go. The girls get the idea: I must always be perfect. The boys think: I can get away with this.' Simon Brereton, the headmaster, told me that this latitude is often withdrawn as the children get older, leaving boys bemused. 'Interestingly, this special treatment tends to end around Year 5 where boys find themselves in lots of trouble for things that would have been made light of in the past.' No wonder boys struggle at school, if they are receiving such mixed messages about what is expected of them.

Jonathan, a Year 4 teacher at a state school in West London, was forthright about the biggest challenge he faced. 'Our big problem is white working-class boys in education at the moment,' he told me. 'It feels like we're in a process as a profession of talking about that openly, because it's so difficult . . . These are sweeping generalisations but it feels like among our white families, parents want to be their children's best friends and be led by their children. Among our black and Indian families, there's much more premium put on education, culturally, and recognising adults and teachers as figures of authority.'

Like several of the other teachers I spoke to, Jonathan suggested that boys feel peer pressure to be disruptive at school. 'There's a socialisation where it is seen as not cool to want to read or study hard. I feel like that's not the case in a lot of private schools, where it's cool to be head of the football team but also to read a lot of stuff. So I try to build a culture where it's cool to read. That is maybe controversial because you have to do things like celebrating children being good at writing, which can feel elitist and exclusive.'

He tried to build connections with the boys by talking about things they liked. Luis Lozano – who teaches at a Church of England school in Folkestone – told me that he did the same. In his case, it was by revealing that he moonlights as a professional wrestler. 'The character I play, Will Power! the South-East Sensation!, is a villain who usually cheats and winds up the crowd,' Luis said. 'For the most part the children get that it's all just an act. The wrestling has also helped me build up a connection with some of the more rowdier young boys.'

Simon Kuper's and Emma Jacobs's article suggested that the success of boys from the top private schools disguised the problems of the group as a whole. Jonathan, the Year 4 teacher, echoed this. 'There is also a complacency from white boys: this group have meandered into top places and professions, so we don't need to worry so much about this school thing.'

Sam Addenbrook, who works at a school in Cumbria, identified another problem faced by the boys he taught. In Barrow-in-Furness, the main employer has long been the shipyard. 'The town has relied on its work for hundreds of years and there has always been that sense of "My dad has worked in the shipyard since he was sixteen and so will I,"' he told me. 'Therefore a lack of effort sets in and an "it'll be alright if I fail, I'll go in the shipyard" attitude.'

However, traditionally male jobs like this are disappearing fast. If boys can't go to the shipyard, where will they go?

*

The complicated picture of education both in Britain and around the world is fascinating and challenging. It also tells us something important about one of the nerdiest and most intractable questions facing feminism: what does 'equality' look like?

Social conservatives like to prod at feminism by asking whether feminists believe in equality of *opportunity* or equality of *outcome*. What's the difference? Imagine you have ten jobs. Should half of them be filled by women? That would be equality of outcome. Or should you say that everyone is welcome to apply, but you accept that – because of variations in intelligence, skills and experience – the results might be uneven? That's equality of opportunity. Social conservatives, and the men's rights movement, often argue that where women lag behind, it's because of innate biological differences between the sexes. This argument crumbles on contact with the story of universities in the wake of Sophia Jex-Blake. Does the fact that there are more female students than male ones today prove that men were thickos all along? Curiously not. This is more often attributed to a feminist plot. When men were ahead, that was natural and unarguable. Now it's women, Something Must Be Done!

Personally, I would prefer to focus on equality of opportunity. Looking at outcomes is sometimes useful – think of those statistics offered by Maureen Colquhoun, showing the male dominance of everything from the railway-network boards to the Covent Garden Market Authority. But quotas cause backlash, and can encourage people to game the system rather than tackle the fundamental problems. Companies which wanted to increase the number of women on their boards, for example, have found an easy way to do it: appoint female non-executive directors, who buff the figures but have little real power. I get asked to go on television so much because political journalism is dominated by men, and producers are desperate to have more female faces on their programmes. But the reason I can say yes to late-night or early-morning shows is because I don't have children. So I'm a woman who doesn't have the challenge (finding last-minute childcare) which holds back women as a class. I'm a lucky outlier. That's why I think it's usually better to look at the start of the process than the end. Fix the inequality of opportunity, and the outcomes will improve.

That said, trying to work out what a truly 'equal opportunity' looks like is hard. Does the job description include qualifications or skills which are more difficult for some groups to acquire? For example, in academia, are recruiters asking for lots of research papers on top of teaching work, which can exclude those with caring responsibilities? Is your hiring panel diverse, to offset the fact that we recruit in our own image? ('Ah, he reminds me of myself at that age.') Are the recruitment criteria skewed towards People Like Us, privileging eloquent bullshitters?

Inequality of outcome is a signal that something might be unequal at the start of the process. There is good research to show that even 'objective' hiring practices are flawed. Candidates with 'foreign-sounding' names are unconsciously discriminated against. Female candidates in their thirties might be quietly junked because of worries they will take time out for maternity leave. People with disabilities sometimes don't get a chance to explain that they can do the job perfectly well with a few adjustments to working hours or practices.

And there's more. Being a minority is draining, and that affects male primary school teachers or male nannies in the same way as female astrophysicists and female CEOs. First, there are the casual expressions of prejudice. What kind of man wants to work with children, anyway? (Subtext: are you a paedophile?) Don't you want to be a 'real' – secondary school or university – teacher? (Subtext: this is demeaning work for a man.) Many male primary school teachers said it was odd to be treated as an exception. Several found it hard to fit in at work, or found themselves thrown off-balance by their female colleagues making sexist jokes *about men.* There might be a day – oh, imagine it – when we need to think about how to make men feel more comfortable in politics, or academia, or editing newspapers. Gender differences are really differences of power. That means they could be reversed.

In British schools today, boys need exactly what Sophia Jex-Blake was asking for: 'a fair field and no favour'. One hundred and fifty years ago, she walked through the gates of a university, risking insults, abuse and worse. We know that around the world other girls like Malala still face those risks. The ones I met in Nepal still have to fight to go to school – whether it's because they are menstruating, or because they are expected to cook and clean on top of their homework. Education offers empowerment – not the sappy, commercialised kind, but the real thing. It offers the dangerous, liberating power of knowledge. Everyone deserves that.

There's no shame in positive discrimination. Of course there should be bursaries to get men into primary school teaching, because seeing men in those settings sends an important message to both boys and girls about what men can do and be. Perhaps that financial help is a taste of the future, when more white men will find themselves receiving the kind of extra help previously reserved for women and minorities. Equal opportunities means just that. Equal.

In every struggle, wrote Sophia Jex-Blake, 'there is a period of extreme difficulty, when success seems well-nigh hopeless; but when once that success is attained, there is, I think, a tendency to forget how hard was the battle, and how strong the forces marshalled against the cause of progress'. Amen to that.

9. TIME

My grandmother didn't have the vote, my mother didn't have the pill, and I don't have the time.

Dutch comedian Hester Macrander

Why is it so difficult for feminists to organise collectively? When I was thinking about the other fights in this book, from divorce reform to the refuge movement, the words of the suffragette Hannah Mitchell kept coming back to me: 'No cause can be won between dinner and tea.' The suffragettes benefited from so many of their foot soldiers being young, single women. Caroline Norton had the time to campaign for child custody law reform, because her own children had been taken away. Tess Gill's generation met in each other's homes, letting their children play together while they plotted revolution. Sophia Jex-Blake, as a lesbian in the nineteenth century, never married or had children. Neither did Lily Parr fifty years later. The same force which radicalises so many women – the burden of unpaid caring labour – also hampers them from doing anything about it. There's an old joke that the trouble with socialism is that it takes up so many evenings. Feminism struggles because it's hard to juggle it around cleaning the oven. The rise of the Internet and social media created an explosion in feminist commentary because – at last – the cause *could* be fitted in between dinner and tea.

Underneath all the other struggles that women face as a class is this one: their lack of time. Across the world, they do more unpaid caring labour, and have fewer hours of leisure as a result. Just think how different the economy would look if housework, childcare and elderly care put money in women's pockets. We need to change our idea of what 'work' is. Work is not what creates value for an employer. It's what creates a society. It's what takes up your time.

The basic idea is an old one. In 1898, the American suffragist Charlotte Perkins Gilman became an overnight sensation with a book called *Women and Economics*. In it, she wrote that married women worked enough hours in the home to earn a decent living – if only they were paid for their time. But they were prevented from taking a job, because – well, they were needed at home. 'The working power of the mother has always been a prominent factor in human life,' she wrote. 'She is the worker par excellence, but her work is not such as to affect her economic status. Her living, all that she gets – food, clothing, ornaments, amusements, luxuries – these bear no relation to her power to produce wealth, to her services in the house, or to her motherhood. These things bear relation only to the man she marries, the man she depends on – to how much he has and how much he is willing to give her . . . The female of genus *Homo* is economically dependent on the male. He is her food supply.'

In Britain, a group called Wages for Housework took up this idea during the Second Wave. They argued that the whole foundation of capitalism was rotten, because it depended on women's unpaid labour in the home. 'The modern individual family is founded on the open or concealed domestic slavery of the wife,' Friedrich Engels had written in 1884. They were single-minded in their promotion of this idea. 'We are always the indispensable workforce,' wrote one of the movement's founders, Selma James, in 1975. 'At home, cleaning, washing and ironing; making, disciplining and bringing up babies; servicing men physically, sexually and emotionally.' That blunt language gives you an idea how uncompromising Wages for Housework activists were in their analysis and their prescription for change. Certainly, other parts of the Women's Lib movement found them a bit much. 'To many women in the Women's Movement, the Wages for Housework campaigners come over like Jehovah's Witnesses,' wrote *Guardian* journalist Jill Tweedie in May 1976. 'Open any door marked Liberation and behind it is a woman with a Wages for Housework badge on her bosom, ten thousand leaflets in her hand, a fanatical gleam in her eye and her foot wedged firmly in the jamb.'

In Britain, Selma James was the best-known Wages for

Housework activist. Born in 1930 to Jewish immigrants to the United States, the young Selma Deitch had married her first husband at eighteen – the only way to escape her family, she said – and was a mother within a year. She had already joined a radical left-wing group, and her class-, race- and sex-consciousness increased as she worked in New York factories. When she was packing marshmallows for a supermarket, one of the worst-paid jobs, there were plenty of black women around her. As she moved to wiring and soldering television sets, a little further up the hierarchy, she noticed that her co-workers were now white women. Just like Jayaben Desai, she had discovered the secret sorting mechanism of class, race and sex in the workplace.

She began to talk to the leader of her group, the Trinidadian historian C. L. R. James, who later became her second husband. She told him about the struggle of being a 'housewife' – a word she applied to every woman in America, whether she worked outside the home or not. He encouraged her to write about it, 'since he had never heard anything political about housewives before'.* She was shy, lacking confidence, so he told her to write down each idea as it came to her on a slip of paper, and collect them in a shoebox: 'After a while, you open the box, put all these sentences in order and you have a draft.' So that's what she did. When she was ready to write the article, she dropped her son off at a nursery and went to a friend's house to write. 'I knew that if I stayed home from work to put the draft together, I would end up cleaning the oven or doing some other major piece of housework.'

The resulting pamphlet, published in 1952, is called 'A Woman's Place'. It is a short, sharp document. A full decade before Betty Friedan's *The Feminine Mystique* diagnosed 'the problem that has no name' – the boredom of suburban housewives – Selma James identified the same disease in working-class New Yorkers. She noticed

* Selma James tells this story in her collected writings, *Sex, Race and Class*.

that the single girls around her felt more independent than ever before. They thought their marriages would be different. And yet they found themselves becoming 'the household drudges their mothers were'. They discovered their families could not survive on one income; they went to work. They expected their partners to share the housework, but 'any idea of sharing the work disappears when children come'. They felt isolated, trapped, dehumanised. Their jobs came with no pay, no fixed hours, and no end: 'the terrible thing that is always there when you are doing the housework is the feeling that you are never finished'.

It fascinates me that Friedan's book was so heavily attacked for focusing on the problems of white, middle-class women, while Selma James's work on immigrant and working-class women was merely ignored. Her life is a reminder of the great contribution of Marxism to the Women's Liberation Movement in the 1970s. She read *Das Kapital* at the age of forty, she told an interviewer, and the experience was transformative. 'By the time I had studied for six or eight months I understood that the crucial question was women. There it was in the book. Marx's theory of value is based on the concept of labour power, and obviously what women do is produce this basic capitalist commodity. I thought everyone knew that, and they had neglected to tell me.'

It's an odd quirk of history that most of today's younger feminists know little about Marxism – I don't – and yet we have inherited an intellectual tradition which is steeped in it. Marxist criticisms of power structures have been completely absorbed by the feminist movement, while the word itself seems like a relic of an earlier age. Take the idea that women's sexual behaviour is obsessively monitored – through virginity tests, punishments for adultery, the idea that a wife should submit to her husband – to maintain a system where property is passed down from father to son. That comes from the work of Marx's co-author Friedrich Engels.

The Marxist tradition championed Florynce Kennedy's phrase

'horizontal hostility', where infighting diminishes the ability of a group to challenge their shared oppression. And it gave us the concept of 'false consciousness', defined by the *Encyclopaedia Britannica* as 'the notion that members of the proletariat unwittingly misperceive their real position in society and systematically misunderstand their genuine interests'. There's definitely a feminist version of false consciousness. If you're trapped as a housewife, you begin to take pride in how shiny your taps are, castigate other women whose taps are not sufficiently shiny, and refuse to contemplate a world in which shiny taps are not the best measure of your worth as a human being. You do not question why, if shiny taps are so important, you're not being paid to clean them.

By 1972, after travelling around the Caribbean, Selma James had moved to England and was involved in the budding Women's Liberation Movement. That year, she published 'The Power of Women and the Subversion of the Community' with the Italian activist Mariarosa Dalla Costa.* It was timely: the Conservative government was trying to take away Family Allowance, which had been introduced in 1945. It was one of the few benefits paid to mothers which gave them some financial independence. 'We must destroy the concept that the State gives the poorest of us – the unsupported mother – charity,' she wrote in an article in July 1973. 'We are entitled to a great deal more than the pittance of Family Allowance . . . Women with waged work must receive money for their entire workweek, not only the part where the capitalist is breathing down their necks. To posit this perspective is the first strategic step for women to stop him from breathing at all.'

The women's movement fought off the plan to scrap Family Allowance. James represented the radical fringe, thundering about capitalists being prevented from breathing. By contrast, the idea of

---

* By this point in the book, it might not surprise you to learn that James and Dalla Costa later fell out. James blamed a split 'on race'.

supporting mothers through the benefits system looked merely pragmatic and moderate. To me, that shows the importance of Difficult Women such as Selma James. She acted as an outrider for the women's movement, expanding the intellectual space it took up.

I'm praising James in the full knowledge that our attitudes to feminism are very different, by the way. I'd guess she would find me bourgeois, overcautious, too much of a career woman, and too ready to compromise with power. In turn, I disagree with her group's analysis that sex with your partner constitutes 'housework'* and her assertion to interviewer Michelene Wandor that 'Lenin was marvellous'. That is not the adjective I'd use to describe one of the architects of the repressive, authoritarian regime in Soviet Russia.† James was a founder member of the International Jewish Anti-Zionist Network, which supports 'the ending of the Israeli colonization of historic Palestine'. (The majority of the world's Jews support the existence of the state of Israel, although many have criticisms of its government and its discriminatory policies towards Palestinians and Israeli Arabs.) She was the first spokeswoman for the English Collective of Prostitutes, which campaigns for full decriminalisation of sex work, in contrast to the Nordic model of decriminalising sellers and criminalising buyers. 'No criminalisation of clients,' reads the ECP's charter. 'Consenting sex between adults is not a crime.' While I understand how that position fits into the Wages for Housework analysis – that all heterosexual sex is work for women – I find the logic unbearably bleak. And I don't really understand why anti-capitalists are so keen to defend the existence of a market in sex.

---

* Yes, for some women sex does feel like another item on a vast and unending To Do list. But that doesn't have to be the case, and the answer is honesty with your partner, rather than doling out blow jobs in return for emptying the dishwasher.
† Out of curiosity, I emailed Erin Pizzey to ask if she had ever met Selma James. No, she said. A shame. I would have paid good money to hear them discussing the marvellousness (or not) of Lenin.

Selma James was intensely relaxed about the cult of personality which sprang up around her, despite her own criticisms of hierarchies. 'She knew how to do battle,' fellow feminist Bea Campbell told the *Guardian* in 2012. 'A small Trotskyist sect formed her, and she has remained schismatic ever since. Schismatic, sectarian, polarising: Selma got on women's nerves.'

So yes: Selma James was difficult. But her intellectual tradition uncovered and named the power relationships within our society. It gave feminism a class analysis. This is vital, because the opposite of 'feminist' is not 'man'. The women's movement doesn't hate *men*. It hates patriarchy – a system created and supported by all of us, where men and women are legally, financially and socially unequal.

Conventional wisdom suggests that James and her campaign are a mere footnote to the Women's Liberation Movement of the 1970s. She found them too white and too middle class; they found her too doctrinaire and monomaniacal. But she injected something into the feminist bloodstream which has stayed there ever since. Today, the discussion of unpaid work – which disproportionately falls on women – is central to our understanding of inequality. In the west, where populations are ageing rapidly, a social care crisis is looming. Who will look after the elderly if the state cannot afford to? The answer will be depressingly simple: mostly women. For no money. 'We like to think that the unpaid work women do is just about individual women caring for their individual family members to their own individual benefit,' writes Caroline Criado Perez in *Invisible Women*. 'It isn't. Women's unpaid work is work that society depends on, and it is work from which society as a whole benefits . . . The unpaid work that women do isn't simply a matter of "choice". It is built into the system we have created – and it could just as easily be built out of it.'

To find out why it hasn't been, it's instructive to look at the end of Jill Tweedie's 1976 piece, where the tone changes once she has rehearsed the usual criticisms of Selma James. 'If you find that you feel as deeply uneasy and dismayed as I did when I first heard the arguments for wages for housework, ask yourself why. My own answer? I do not want to think about the anger I actually feel about "women's work". I do not trust myself not to direct it at my husband and children in lieu of taking action.' Women love the people they care for – and they often have closer relationships with them than they do with other women.

*

Jill Tweedie's words haunted me as I thought about my own time, which is running out. In my mid-thirties, that internal debate about having a baby has taken on a new urgency. I'm running out of time. But then, I wonder: am I prepared to do the unpaid labour involved in having a baby? Is that how I want to spend my time?

There is something resolutely un-modern about having a baby, starting with the birth itself. Friends who were always, always online disappeared off for twenty-four hours straight, into the blankness, returning with a photo of a wriggling grub and an air of exhausted valour. WhatsApp chats would be punctuated with apologies for their busyness, their air of distraction, their worries that they had disappeared from the adult world of jobs and career goals and Brexit and Trump into a vale of soft play and YouTube videos of cartoon sharks. They didn't get a minute to themselves. They were always tired. They were surviving. They would be around more soon.

None of this means that my friends don't love their children, or that they regret their decisions. But there sometimes feels like a vast conspiracy to shield us from the reality of what caring labour involves, from its monotony and drudgery and relentless physicality. It is a conspiracy in which we all enthusiastically participate. The same women who would confess their exhaustion and boredom on WhatsApp maintained Instagram feeds full of smiles, visits to the zoo, and toddlers dancing to hip-hop. Those snapshots are not even half the story: they are a fraction of it.

This distorted view of motherhood accounts for the success of forums such as Mumsnet, where the standard question is this: 'Am I being unreasonable?' Shortened to AIBU, mothers ask: 'AIBU to ask what I can do for packed lunches for a kid who doesn't like sandwiches?', 'AIBU to ask him to pay maintenance when he's taking a "career break"?', 'AIBU to not want to take the baby to the toilet with me?', 'AIBU to be angry and distressed at the amount of harassment my fourteen-year-old daughter faces?'

Reading through the AIBU forum, I want to scream at 95 per cent of the posters: *No, you are not being unreasonable.* It's the world that's being unreasonable, expecting mothers to be selfless angels, perpetually on call for their children's desires, an uncomplaining frame to a picture of someone else. One of the great achievements of labour reformers in the wake of the Industrial Revolution was to limit the working day. Except they only limited the *paid* working day. Unpaid caring work doesn't come with fag breaks, or lunch hours, or overtime.

Among my generation, one in five women will reach the age of forty-five without children. For my mother's generation, it was just one in every nine. This feels like the logical result of encouraging girls to be ambitious, to be 'feisty', to 'reach for the stars' – and then telling women that actually, they're needed at home. No wonder we delay starting a family, or opt out altogether. I want to warn twenty-something women that the old bargain has not changed all that much. You can only have it all if you do it all.

Despite all the progress made by feminism in a handful of lifetimes, having children still divides the lives of men and women. For full-time workers in their twenties, there is now no gender pay gap. But the lines diverge in their thirties, never to meet again. More women drop into part-time work, which is less well-paid per hour, because it offers them flexibility to juggle the school run and nursery pick-ups. Some take a lower-paid job closer to home. Some put aside their dream of reaching the next rung of the ladder: becoming a headteacher, a manager, a professor. For all of them, time is not on their side.

Several male friends tried to convince me to give motherhood a whirl, invoking the wondrous experience of seeing life afresh through the eyes of a child. Oh yes, I wanted to spit back, and what price did *you* pay for this wonder? What work of yours went undone, what ambition unfulfilled, what freedom was restricted?

I had always assumed that one day, perhaps on my thirtieth birthday, the biological urge would overcome me. This would make the decision less difficult. All my reasonable objections would be swept away on an uncontrollable tide of hormonal desire. Only . . . it hasn't happened. The difficulty remains. The idea of having children is a matter of pluses and minuses, two tallies on a page. Gains: great Instagram content, a feeling of having fulfilled my genetic destiny, no longer having to face the pitying stares of people who feel a child-less life is a shrunken one. Losses: my time. *All that time.*

*

While we're on the subject, Brigid Schulte hates the phrase 'me time'. I can practically hear the grimace over the phone. 'Whoever talks about a guy going to play golf as "me time"?' she told me. 'It trivialises it.'

Reading Schulte's 2014 book, *Overwhelmed*, radicalised me on the subject of women's time. It looks like a business manual but it is quietly, even covertly, feminist. Schulte found her own life 'scat-tered, fragmented, and exhausting' and set out to investigate the structures of modern life which created that feeling. She found that parents are particularly screwed by the modern economy. Single parents – the majority of whom are women – are really, really screwed. Even so, she resisted making the book into a feminist rally-ing call. 'I'd never covered women's issues,' Schulte told me. 'I'd always tried to stay away from them as a journalist. I worried in case the newspaper world saw me as soft, or I'd get pigeonholed. I wanted to be a Serious Journalist.'

What changed her mind was meeting a time researcher called John Robinson. He told her that American women had thirty hours of leisure a week – more than in the 1960s – even though most were now also working outside the home too. 'It blew my – excuse my language – fucking mind,' she said. Did she really have all that leisure? She talked to her WASPy friends, who longed for 'Mormon sister-wives or a few Muslim harem mates'. She talked to Latina immigrants who worked two or three jobs, and asked them when they had downtime. 'Maybe at church. Or when I sleep,' one woman replied.

And then Schulte realised the problem. She felt 'as if leisure was something I needed to earn'. Until her To Do list was completed, she never felt as though she could switch off. And guess what? Her To Do list was *never* completed. This was not unusual, John Robinson told her. Although average working hours have held steady for decades, people consistently report *feeling* busier.

There are two pieces to this puzzle, and it's hard to keep them both in mind at the same time. The first is that women have, indisputably, less free time than men. The Office for National Statistics recorded that British women had 38.35 hours of leisure time a week in 2015, the most recent year for which figures are available. Men had forty-three. And the gap has grown over the last fifteen years.

Mothers, on average, have less leisure than fathers. 'In 2015, fathers whose youngest child was under five took around thirty hours of leisure time per week compared with 28.5 hours per week for mothers of similar-age children,' found the ONS.

The second is that we have deeply gendered attitudes to free time, which mean that women feel guilty about relaxing. When both parents are at home with the kids, one often acts as the 'supervisory parent' – ensuring that no one is chewing the washing-machine cable – while the other is merely present. Guess which way round that usually goes?

That isn't all men's fault. Schulte found that women were keen enforcers of other women's sacrifices. When she first wrote about feeling overwhelmed, she received 'angry, snippy emails – and many of them were from women'. Some advised her to breathe deeply at traffic lights, other suggested that she take a bath, or go to a spa. 'The spa break is like a pitstop in a Nascar race,' she told me. 'You drive in, they buff you up and change the tyres and throw you back out there. It's not even leisure, it's more like maintenance to keep you on the road.'

Her words reminded me of something a friend once said: that approved leisure activities for women fell into two categories: 'crafting and sex maintenance'. Either you can make something for your home, or you can trim, pluck, wax or exfoliate.* You don't deserve any aimless hours just sitting on the sofa, thinking about whether Jack could have fitted on to that door in *Titanic*. 'Time is a feminist issue,' said Schulte. 'Throughout history, women have never had access to time. Their time has always been chopped up and fragmented and dictated by others. Interrupted by caregiving. There was something unseemly, or selfish, if you were a woman and took time for yourself.' There's a passage from *Overwhelmed* I can quote from memory: 'Women's time has always been subjected to unpredictable interruptions, while men's ability to experience blocks of unbroken time has been protected. The "good" secretary and the "good" wife were the ones guarding it.' Something clicked. Of course! Free time is about saying no. It's about having boundaries. It's about not being interrupted. It's Dad reading the paper, undisturbed. It's Mum trying to do her nails while on hold to the doctor, while telling the kids off for fighting in the background.

The literature on women's time is now sizeable. The titles are often pleasingly sarcastic: *Women's Leisure, What Leisure?* remains a personal favourite. And much of it owes a debt to fieldwork carried

---

* Personally, I find visiting a spa about as relaxing as any other time you have to make small talk in your underwear.

out by a social scientist (and mother of young children) in the 1970s. Her name was Arlie Russell Hochschild, and she gave us a new and vital phrase for the problem facing women who juggle paid work and responsibilities at home. She called it 'the second shift'.

*

Arlie Hochschild was a young academic when she had her first child, David. 'I wanted to nurse the baby – and to continue to teach,' she writes in *The Second Shift*, first published in 1989. 'Several arrangements were possible, but my solution was a pre-industrial one.' She put David in the corner of the office, where he mostly napped, and put a fake name on her appointment list so she could lock the door and feed him every four hours. The arrangement worked, but she began to wonder: where were the children of the men around her? She envied the 'smooth choicelessness' of male colleagues whose wives stayed at home. Women, by contrast, got screwed either way: 'The housewife pays a cost by remaining outside the mainstream of social life. The career woman pays a cost by entering a clockwork of careers that permits little time or emotional energy to raise a family.'

Hochschild wanted to study couples at the hardest time in their lives, juggling jobs and the demands of small children. The 'family wage' was beginning to slip away for the middle class, disrupting the 'traditional' model of a heterosexual marriage which had sprung up after the Industrial Revolution, with a wage-earning man and a homemaking woman.* If Mum was at work all day, just like Dad, who picked up the kids from school? Who cooked dinner and washed the dishes? And who was deemed to be responsible for the smooth running of the household?

What Hochschild found was depressing – but also, in hindsight,

* As Hochschild herself noticed, this traditional ideal was never adhered to by large numbers of poor and ethnic-minority families, who needed two wages to survive.

predictable. Bedtime stories still needed to be read, and ironing still needed to be done, so many women were doing a 'second shift' of unpaid labour once their day job was over. The statistics were staggering: over a year, women worked an extra month of twenty-four-hour days compared with men. 'Just as there is a wage gap between men and women in the workplace, there is a "leisure gap" between them at home,' she wrote. Capitalism had played a fine trick on us all: suddenly, most housing was only affordable with two salaries, and in any case most women relished their new economic power. But the price was constant tiredness and feelings of guilt and overwork.

Hochschild studied fifty couples for her book – all straight, all with young kids – and saw the pattern described by Schulte first-hand. Women's time was not their own. 'One reason women took a deeper interest than men in the problems of juggling work with family life is that even when husbands happily shared the hours of work, their wives felt more responsible for the home,' she wrote. 'More women kept track of doctors' appointments, arranged play dates, and kept up with relatives. More mothers than fathers worried about the tail on a child's Halloween costume or a birthday present for a school friend. While at work they were more likely to check in by phone with the babysitter.'

In May 2017, the French comic artist Emma came up with a name for this phenomenon: the 'mental load'. In a comic strip, she showed a frazzled mother juggling cooking and childcare until a pot boiled over. In comes the woman's partner, who declares: 'But you should've asked! I would have helped!' The strip went viral because it captured something about the gendered division of labour: seeing what needs to be done is a task in itself. Straight men had a tendency to see their partners as the 'manager' of household chores. They weren't using up brain space on working out what needed to be done.

The type of unpaid work done at home is also gendered, something Arlie Hoschchild discovered in her research. Men tend to do the non-time-dependent jobs, like cleaning the garage or replacing light bulbs. Women tend to get stuck with the ones which commit you to a schedule, like cooking dinner.

Again, this isn't all men's fault. As I said in the chapter on sex, none of us are psychic. And many of us have been raised in households where gendered attitudes to labour were so ingrained they were invisible. Schulte calls this 'the water we swim in'. My husband grew up in a house where his dad cooked, and whenever I arrive home to a dinner coming out of the oven, I give thanks for this simple fact. By contrast, my own mum remembers her mother-in-law insisting that Dad needed to play cricket at the weekends, because he'd been at work all week. 'As if having four children isn't work,' Mum said.*

Hochschild felt that she was charting a society in transition, as the homemaker/breadwinner default was replaced by dual-earner couples. Women moving into the workplace found that their time was literally more valuable, and they gained more control over their finances.

They also moved to offices and other physical spaces which were designated as workplaces. That must have been transformative. Writing this book has meant sitting at my dining room table for hours. While I'm there, I always feel guilty about the undone housework. When my partner returns home, I feel as though I should cook dinner. After all, I've been 'home all day'. The house itself is coded feminine, and therefore any work that happens within it feels devalued. It makes me feel more sympathy with Selma James, writing her first pamphlet at a friend's house, knowing that if she stayed at home, she would clean the oven instead.

One of the knotty problems that Arlie Russell Hochschild confronted was the insistence by the couples that they *wanted* things to be the way they were, even if the second shift was obviously making

* She also worked as a teacher once I was old enough to go to nursery.

them unhappy. This is the Marxist idea of 'false consciousness' in action, although you could also call it 'making the best of a bad situation'. Why wallow in misery you can't escape? Hochschild studied one couple – a feminist called Nancy and a traditionalist called Evan – who had a four-year-old son, Joey. Unable to get Evan to help with the second shift, Nancy stopped asking and 'half-consciously expressed her frustration and rage by losing interest in sex and becoming overly absorbed with Joey'.

This is the flip side to that feminist mantra about the personal being political. The political becomes personal. Feminism helps many of us explain our half-formed feelings of anger towards people we otherwise love: like Jill Tweedie, determined not to think about her unpaid labour at home in case it poisoned her relationship with her family. In the brutal words of Andrea Dworkin, 'women live with those who oppress them, sleep with them, have their children – we are tangled, hopelessly it seems, in the gut of the machinery and way of life which is ruinous to us'. Being oppressed by The Man is bad enough. Being oppressed by the wonderful but oblivious man you share a bed with is even worse.

I'm always talking about this subject with friends who have children. Whatever their egalitarian ideals beforehand, they often felt crushed both by their hormones and social expectations. Slipping into traditional gender roles was the path of least resistance. 'Even when my husband picks up the kids from school, they give him notes to give to me,' one told me. Another found it was impossible to look after a baby while working in a different city to her partner. She quit her job and took a less outwardly prestigious one closer to home. A lesbian couple I know felt the pull of breadwinner/caregiver too: the birth mother slipped into the traditionally female role, simply because she was initially the one at home with the baby.

These expectations hurt men, too. Male friends who took shared parental leave said they felt like the odd one out at mother and baby groups. A six-foot-six friend struggled constantly with prams that were too low and washing-up gloves that were too small. Another, Willard, tweeted that there was a stark divide at baby-friendly screenings in his local cinema. 'My boy and I watched *Rampage* alone in a 300-seat auditorium,' he noted. Last year, I took my friend Max to the pub, and he took his ten-week-old son, who dozed happily in a sling. While I was at the bar, the mixed-sex group of thirtysomethings at the next table couldn't hold back their astonishment. They were seriously impressed. A man? Caring for a baby? *On his own?* 'Where's Mum?' said one guy, in astonishment. Then they saw me. 'There she is!'

I disclaimed all responsibility for the baby, cute though he undoubtedly is. The scene made me feel happy and sad. Those people were a hair away from acclaiming Max as their king and carrying him aloft through the streets of Camden. But treating him as a wonderful freak was still treating him like a freak. And if I really had been Mum, I'd have felt a little bit miffed that Dad gets praise for something that is taken completely for granted when women do it.

*

How did Hochschild feel about *The Second Shift*, three decades on? Now in her eighties, she sees it as one of the most important books of her career. 'One reviewer said that it was like a scream in the dark, and yeah, it seemed to touch a nerve,' she told me over the phone from rural Appalachia, where she is now researching 'blue-collar white men who are retreating from life'. *The Second Shift* spawned a cottage industry of further studies, which found that men were beginning to do more at home. There has been a definite change. By and large, she said, straight couples now see the second shift as something to be shared, even if it is not fairly divided in practice.

In America, the gender leisure gap has narrowed, for an intriguing reason: men spend longer at work and they spend longer commuting. That might reflect mothers taking part-time jobs or ones that are closer to home, but there could be another explanation too.

Brigid Schulte has a hunch that the long-hours culture in many professional jobs is itself a form of backlash. 'We talk about demanding jobs, but there was a time before smartphones when work hours started to ratchet up and it wasn't just technology,' she said. 'This is something we did that was a way to disadvantage women. I don't think it's a real secret that we started valuing long work hours after women entered the workforce, when they would have been in positions to rise into management. What do you do? You want to keep them out, so you keep ratcheting the standards up. So if you have all the caregiving responsibilities, you're not going to be able to stay late and go to that 8 p.m. meeting. All of a sudden you've created another barrier, so that women can't possibly compete.'

Not long after we spoke, Schulte's hunch was proved correct. 'Women did everything right, then work got greedy' ran the headline on a *New York Times* piece in April 2019. In the 'greedy' professions such as finance, law, management consultancy – jobs which require high levels of education and offer high pay in return – 'the returns to working long, inflexible hours have greatly increased'. This set-up isn't much fun for men: they are usually the ones who end up pulling eighty-hour weeks to prove their devotion to the company. In return, though, they get what researchers call an 'overwork premium'. In America, those who work more than fifty hours a week get paid more per hour than those on forty. That wasn't the case in 1990. Working overtime is now a status symbol.

This isn't a gender pay gap in the classic sense, because women who work very long hours in management jobs also get the overwork premium. There are just far fewer of them: one in five fathers work at least fifty hours a week, according to research by Youngjoo Cha at Indiana University, but only 6 per cent of mothers do. It's a stealthy move back towards the male-breadwinner/female-homemaker model of the 1950s, only this time high-flying mothers get to glimpse a few years of being able to work like men.

Equating success with working long, inflexible hours has

allowed existing power structures to reassert themselves. Just
as women got a chance to compete for the top jobs, the goalposts
moved. And as more women have entered the workforce, we have
added another handicap: we now expect parents to spend more
time with their children than a generation ago. 'The number of
hours that college-educated parents spend with their children has
doubled since the early 1980s, and they spend more of that time
interacting with them, playing and teaching,' wrote Claire Cain
Miller in the *NYT*. Again: you can have it all, if you do it all.

Where previous generations let their children roam freely
around the neighbourhood, we now expect 'helicopter parenting',
hovering continuously overhead. We harshly judge parents who
leave their children alone, even for a second. In 2016, the NSPCC in
Britain received 1,300 phone calls with questions or concerns about
potential child neglect, an increase of a third on the previous year.
But how do parents know if they are committing a crime? The law is
fuzzy. In Britain, there is no set age at which a child can first be left
alone at home.* In 2004, Tim Haines of Worcestershire was arrested
and prosecuted for 'wilful exposure of a child to risk of significant
harm' when he left his two-year-old daughter in the car for ten minutes to buy Calpol. His conviction was overturned on appeal and his
five children were removed from the child protection register. He
spoke out after a mother in the West Midlands was given a caution
for leaving her six-year-old son home alone for forty-five minutes to
take a driving lesson.

There are numerous examples from America which suggest that
accusations of 'child neglect' are sometimes used to punish parents
for behaviour that the previous generation would find totally unre-
markable. These amateur child-protection enthusiasts can seem
more motivated by patrolling women's lives than concern for their

---

* The NSPCC suggests that under-twelves should not be left alone for long periods,
and under-sixteens should not be left alone overnight.

kids. In 2011, for example, a novelist called Kim Brooks was arrested for leaving her son in the car for five minutes as she ran into a store to buy him some replacement iPad headphones. When she got back, he was totally fine, but a bystander had filmed him and given the footage to police. There was no law in Virginia against leaving children in a car, but she was charged with 'contributing to the delinquency of a minor'. She was astonished: she knew the terrible risks of leaving children alone for hours on a sweltering hot day. But surely this was nothing like that?

It turned out that her experience was part of a trend. The magazine *Mother Jones* found 'dozens' of cases when it searched the archives in 2014. A couple called Danielle and Sasha Meltiv were twice reported to the police for letting their ten-year-old son and six-year-old daughter walk home alone from a local park in Maryland. An Arizona single mother called Shanesha Taylor was charged with child abuse and sentenced to eighteen months' probation for leaving her two children in a car for forty-five minutes while she attended a job interview. She was jobless and had no childcare. In 2014, a woman called Debra Harrell had her nine-year-old daughter temporarily taken into foster care, after she left the girl in a park while working as a manager in McDonald's.* Society is asking the impossible of parents, mostly mothers, in such situations. They are expected to juggle finding and keeping insecure work with the new demands of intensive parenting. There is simply not enough time in the day.

And what about those good Samaritans who call the police on parents, out of ostensible concern for child welfare? A 2016 study published in *Collabra*, 'No Child Left Alone: Moral Judgments about Parents Affect Estimates of Risk to Children', sheds some light on their motivations. The researchers described scenarios where

---

* Both Taylor and Harrell are black. I wonder if working-class women, non-white women and single mothers face extra disapproval due to stereotypical depictions of those groups as lazy, feckless and so on.

children were left alone, and asked participants to rate how much danger they believed the children faced. In some scenarios, the lack of oversight was unintentional: the parent had been injured and could not retrieve their child. In others, it was deliberate: the parent was working, volunteering for a charity, meeting a lover, or relaxing. 'The less morally acceptable a parent's reason for leaving a child alone, the more danger people think the child is in,' the researchers wrote. Their study suggested that we assume 'parents who leave their children alone have done something morally wrong'. There was one exception: fathers got a pass for leaving their children to run into work. That was treated as leniently as an unintentional absence. Mothers got no such latitude.

Reflecting on these results in the *New York Times*, four years after her own arrest, Kim Brooks wrote: 'We're contemptuous of "lazy" poor mothers. We're contemptuous of "distracted" working mothers. We're contemptuous of "selfish" rich mothers. We're contemptuous of mothers who have no choice but to work, but also of mothers who don't need to work and still fail to fulfill an impossible ideal of selfless motherhood. You don't have to look very hard to see the common denominator.' When you're a mother, no matter how you are dividing your time . . . Well, you must be doing it wrong. Brooks managed to get a judge to drop the charges if she did a hundred hours of community service and undertook 'parental education'. The biggest effect of the case, she wrote, was on her son. He became convinced that someone was going to abduct him.

All this feels like part of a bigger pattern. If women's time is not their own, then neither are their bodies or their lives. We love to police women's behaviour – and the welfare of children gives us a convenient excuse to do so. The welfare of foetuses, too. That has big implications in the abortion debate, as we will see, but it happens in wanted pregnancies as well. Expectant mothers are endlessly ordered not to do this, eat that or go there, even though many of the conventional warnings are overstated. In 2007, government guidelines were updated to insist that pregnant women avoid alcohol entirely, even though there is no good scientific evidence to support this. Drinking carries some risks, and no one *needs* to do it, runs the logic. So ban it altogether.

The same goes for soft cheeses. Pregnant women are told to avoid them because of the risk of listeriosis. This is both a very rare disease – it killed only thirty-three people in Britain in 2017 – and one spread largely through poor food hygiene. At the time of writing, the most recent outbreak in Britain was caused by pre-packaged sandwiches. No one is telling us to avoid them. Pregnant women are an easy target for endless hectoring: what kind of selfish bitch loves Brie more than her unborn baby? Just like our perception of danger to children left briefly in cars, this is a moral crusade disguised as concern.

All this is maddening. We know that going out to work full-time has not made women neglect their children. Among some groups, family time has actually *increased* in the last few decades. Yet the goalposts for being a 'good mother' have moved, just as the metrics to decide a 'good worker' have changed to penalise women who tried to compete in the greedy professions. We have to insist that a Difficult Woman needs time to herself. Not just a room of her own, but an hour or two.

*

It is a rare man who would today admit he thinks housework is purely for women, or boast that he has never changed a nappy. But while attitudes have changed, structures have failed to keep up. Only 2 per cent of men take up shared parental leave, introduced in 2015, which offers men and same-sex partners the chance to split paid leave with a child's mother. Encouraging and supporting men who want to spend more time with their babies would benefit everyone. The Scandinavian model, where a portion of paid leave is available *only* to men, might encourage more to take time off.

Finally, I want to note one thing. For both Arlie Russell

Hoschchild and Brigid Schulte, their research interests were partly driven by their personal experience. Having women in fields like anthropology and social science makes a difference to what gets studied. 'I started the book from my own experience,' says Schulte, who describes her hectic life with her young son and daughter in *Overwhelmed*. 'But just because my experience is as a woman doesn't mean there isn't a lot universal about it.'

Hoschchild met her husband Adam, a journalist, when she was twenty and he was seventeen. Even then, she says, she was already thinking about how to share the load. When she got a job as an assistant professor in Santa Cruz, he moved to be with her. When they had their second child – identified in *The Second Shift* as the 'crunch' time for couples – Adam took on his share of the childcare. While she experienced the pressures of working motherhood, she had a partner who allowed her the space and time to investigate the subject. She found the space 'between dinner and tea' to take up a cause. 'It was deeply meaningful to me that he was up for that, you know?' she told me. 'And before his time, before other men were . . . he was looked down on for being this wonderful husband! It's a curious thing: my struggle wasn't with him, it was with the culture that made it hard for him to be an equal partner with me.'

This is important: the story of gendered time is not one of beastly oppressive men and poor downtrodden women. It's a story of cultural scripts which we all follow without thinking. For women entering the workforce in the twentieth century, there was a bump in status and in economic independence. For men taking on more at home, there is no financial reward. And yet many of them are doing it anyway, because they know that it's fair.

*

From the mid-2010s, thinkers from across the political spectrum began to advance the same idea. The libertarian right in Silicon Valley worried that artificial intelligence would destroy middle-class 'knowledge economy' jobs, like accounting, just as factory production lines had devastated working-class occupations in the twentieth century. The answer, some argued, was to pay everyone a fixed stipend just to stay alive. This would stop the unemployed masses revolting and overthrowing capitalism completely.

In Europe, leftwing activists began to question whether the relationship between labour and capital – the fundamental structure of the modern economy – was hopelessly unequal. The rich were getting richer. What did that concentration of wealth mean for the rest of us, and our ability to pay the bills? What could stop people from having to accept low-quality jobs that paid less than a living wage, under threat of poverty and starvation? How could we reduce the crushing bureaucracy of the benefits system, with its finicky requirements and cruel sanctions?

From the left, the right and the radical centre, the same answer came back: a universal basic income (UBI). In 2016, I visited Finland, where a pilot scheme was underway to give 2,000 unemployed people a monthly payment of 560 euros. It has also been tested in the Dutch city of Utrecht, the Scottish city of Glasgow and the Kenyan counties of Siaya and Bomet. The Canadian province of Manitoba tried a similar experiment, called Mincome, in the 1970s. In 2019, I interviewed the respected economist Robert Skidelsky, a biographer of John Maynard Keynes, who was investigating the idea for the Labour Party.

There are plenty of criticisms of UBI. Will voters accept the idea of 'money for nothing'? Yes, argue its supporters, if they are the ones getting it. Is it fair to give a single man the same level of state support as a disabled mother of three? Critics suggest that UBI advocates are really just arguing for a higher minimum level of state benefits. Can we afford it? The radical left would happily reduce military spending to pay for it. Voters might demur.

All these are valid points. But the interest in UBI across the political spectrum suggests that the downsides of modern capitalism are becoming more obvious. During the time that it has been the world's dominant economic model, absolute poverty has fallen and productivity has risen. But underneath that story is one of unpaid labour – predominantly done by women – which has cooked the books. As economists are fond of saying: when a man marries his housekeeper, GDP falls. What they mean is this: when you pay a cleaner, that counts as economic activity. When your mum picked up your socks, that didn't. Her work is unrewarded and taken for granted. There is more to the economy than the bits which are easy to count.

'The omission of unpaid services of housewives from national income computation distorts the picture,' wrote Paul Studenski in 1958's *The Income of Nations*. But the data for unpaid work was too difficult to measure, and so it was excluded. So as women increasingly entered the workforce in the 1970s – the period Arlie Russell Hoschchild wrote about in *The Second Shift* – it looked like productivity shot up. Women's work was now part of the paid economy. That was great news if you were, say, a tax collector – all that new money to collect! Less so if you were a mother trying to juggle a day job and all the housework. You were putting more money into the state's coffers, without necessarily getting any more help in return.

Of course, there's another phrase we could use for 'universal basic income'. It's this: *wages for housework*. Selma James's original demands made clear that 'housework' was not narrowly defined as cleaning or cooking, but all the unpaid work done to subsidise paid work. Did framing the problem as one that primarily affected women lead to it being dismissed? I think it did. Benefits aimed at women will always look like special treatment. UBI is just as provocative and impractical an idea as wages for housework – but if men get it too, then it automatically looks more serious.

As the idea of UBI picks up supporters around the world, Selma James has perhaps the most bittersweet feminist legacy of all. The problem she described is now part of mainstream economic discussion. It just had to be stripped of its feminist connotations to get there.

10. ABORTION

If you're so pro-life, do me a favour: don't lock arms and block medical clinics. If you're so pro-life . . . lock arms and block cemeteries.

Bill Hicks

I try to imagine the expression on the police officers' faces when Kitty O'Kane, Colette Devlin and Diana King turned up to be arrested. In 2016, the three women protested against Northern Ireland's ban on terminations by arriving at Derry police station and declaring that they had bought abortion pills on the Internet. Under the country's harsh laws, they risked life imprisonment.

The photos showed three unlikely rabble-rousers in warm coats, jumpers and jeans. Colette was holding up a sign that read: 'Women will always have abortions. Make sure they're safe and legal.' There had been a flurry of international media attention at the time, but it was surprisingly hard to discover what had happened next. The faces of the pro-choice movement tended to be younger and punkier, bloggers in slogan T-shirts. What had prompted three women born in the 1940s to fight for abortion rights? They seemed like unusual rebels.

Of course, I was being both ageist and sexist – as if no one past twenty-five can possibly be a radical. Difficult Women come in many guises. Rosa Parks, the most famous protester of the American civil rights movement, still gets depicted as a sweet middle-aged lady who somehow blundered into her iconic refusal to move to the back of a segregated bus. But in 1955, Parks was secretary of her local branch of the National Association for the Advancement of Colored People, had attended Communist Party meetings, and had investigated the gang rape of a local black woman. 'People always say that I didn't give up my seat because I was tired, but that isn't true,' she wrote in her autobiography *My Story*. 'I was not tired physically, or no more tired than I usually was at the end of a working day. I was not old, although some people have an image of me as being old then. I was forty-two. No, the only tired I was, was tired of giving in.' There was something about the faces of O'Kane, Devlin and King that suggested a similar stubbornness.

Our culture gazes too intensely at girls, seeing only their surface, then looks straight through women as they age. I had to get on a plane, I decided, and meet these unexpectedly Difficult Women.

*

First, a digression. Until the Brexit vote and the rows over a 'hard border' with the Republic of Ireland, most people in mainland Britain were blissfully unaware that the 1967 Abortion Act was never extended to the six counties of Northern Ireland. There were entrenched, blood-soaked disagreements between the Catholic nationalists who wanted a united Ireland, and the Protestants who were aligned with Britain, but both sprang from a Christian tradition which held that life began at conception.

Diana King told me that she remembered, in the 1960s, walking down the street in Belfast and seeing two men talking. One was Reverend Ian Paisley, a Protestant minister who became one of Northern Ireland's leading Unionist politicians. 'The smaller man in black was a priest,' she said. 'I could see from the collar, a white one, and I was like, "Yeah this is Paisley who doesn't have anything to do with the Catholic Church, hates it," and I found out later it was a meeting about abortion.' Kitty O'Kane told me that she was brought up to be a good Catholic, and that meant accepting that 'suffering is from God to test us ... That was what you had to say to yourself every time you failed an exam or every time you got pregnant. God must have done it on her; nothing to do with me, guv.' The political dominance of religious parties had deeply affected their country's laws and codes of behaviour. Understanding that fact made all three feel kinship with Muslim women who rebel against strict dress codes in Iran and Saudi Arabia. 'There's that kind of realisation,' said Kitty,

'Oh shucks, I haven't got all the answers. I can prance around in trousers now, but when I was growing up, you know, girls wore skirts.'

Diana smiled in agreement: 'It's amazing. I don't know if I *have* a skirt now.'

Elsewhere in the United Kingdom, the 1967 Abortion Act works by providing exemptions to a piece of law from a century earlier. The Offences Against the Person Act 1861 made it a criminal offence to administer, or even procure, 'any poison or other noxious thing', or to 'unlawfully use any instrument . . . To procure the miscarriage of any woman'. The maximum sentence for a woman who has an abortion is life imprisonment.

So, technically, abortion is illegal. But there are exceptions in England, Scotland and Wales. An abortion is legal before twenty-four weeks, or later if the mother's life is at risk or if the foetus has severe disabilities, as long as two doctors sign off the decision.* In Northern Ireland, however, the only exemption comes if the woman's life is at risk. There are no exceptions for rape, incest or fatal foetal abnormalities. Teenagers raped by their fathers, or women whose babies will never take a single independent breath, must carry their pregnancies to term.

The bulk of Northern Ireland's abortion law stands unchanged since before the invention of the telephone, television or aeroplane. 'The situation in Northern Ireland constitutes violence against women that may amount to torture or cruel, inhuman or degrading treatment,' said Ruth Halperin-Kaddari, who led a UN investigation in 2016. 'Denial of abortion and criminalisation of abortion amounts

---

* Supporters of this system say the involvement of two doctors acts as a safeguard. I'm more inclined to see it as a punitive bureaucratic hurdle designed to make accessing an abortion harder, particularly since anti-abortion politicians in the US use similar tactics – such as requiring an ultrasound, or mandatory counselling – to chip away at provision.

to discrimination against women because it is a denial of a service that only women need. And it puts women in horrific situations.'

But in a country where politics is shaped so deeply by a religious divide, changing the law has proved impossible. Once the Good Friday Agreement was signed on 10 April 1998, bringing an end to the armed conflict between Republicans and Unionists, abortion became a devolved matter. It would be decided by the new assembly at Stormont.

Politicians at Westminster presumably sighed in relief – if they thought about the issue at all. Abortion was now somebody else's problem to solve.

*

I was raised Catholic, and went to a Catholic school. Sex education was limited and vaguely apocalyptic, in the style of the coach's lecture in Tina Fey's film *Mean Girls*: 'Don't have sex, because then you will get pregnant, and then you will die.' We were told that abortion was evil. By some twist of fate, none of my class got pregnant – at least, as far as I know – and so I never saw the agonising clash of abstract morality and biological reality. I was also lucky enough to be part of a generation where teenage pregnancy was falling sharply. I never dared go to the doctor to discuss contraception, and so my first serious boyfriend and I practised the withdrawal method for the best part of a year. Amazingly, it worked. I'm either resolutely infertile or extremely lucky.

All this meant I never sorted out my personal feelings about abortion. To some extent, I still haven't. If I got pregnant now, with a mortgage and a stable relationship, would I accept it as something which was 'meant to be'? Or would I find that I don't feel any more inclined towards having a baby simply because I've finally received proof that I could?

Either way, I am grateful to have the choice. Restrictions on abortion are restrictions on women's freedom to decide their own destinies. In the introduction of her book *PRO*, the American feminist Katha Pollitt revealed that her mother had a termination in 1960, before it was legal in the US. 'What did it mean that my mother had to break the law to end a pregnancy?' she writes. 'It meant that America basically said to her, it's the twentieth century, so we're going to let you vote and go to college, and have a family and a job . . . but underneath all that normal, forward-looking, mid-twentieth-century middle-class New York life is the secret underground life of women, and that you must manage outside the law. If you are injured or die or are trapped by the police, you'll only have yourself to blame, because the real reason you are here on earth is to produce children, and you shirk that duty at your peril.'

Even for those who would never contemplate an abortion, the existence and legality of the procedure changes their relationship with their own bodies. Pollitt writes that *Roe* v. *Wade*, the landmark 1973 judgement which liberalised America's abortion laws, 'gave women a kind of existential freedom that is not always welcome – indeed is sometimes quite painful – but that has become part of what women are'. There's that difficult truth of feminism again: it can set you free, but that brings its own anxieties. I think Pollitt's observation applies to the idea of having children more generally. I've spent hours agonising over the question, where the Helen of previous generations would not have done. To be responsible for making yourself happy is, strangely, a kind of burden.

Recent campaigns have begun to spell out exactly what a ban on abortion means: forced pregnancies. That means no say in a biological process which radically reconfigures your body. During pregnancy, a woman's feet can grow a size, thanks to hormones designed to make labour easier. Breast tissue changes permanently. The pH levels in the vagina change, increasing the likelihood of thrush. The blood carries more clotting agents, putting women at greater risk of deep vein thrombosis. Childbirth itself is the most dangerous thing that women voluntarily go through, unless they are base jumpers or landmine-clearance experts. Around the world, 830 women die in labour every single day, according to the World Health Organisation. In fact, the risks of pregnancy and childbirth provide the figleaf for the legal existence of abortion in Britain. The 1967 Act allows two doctors to sign off a termination if they agree 'that the continuance of the pregnancy would involve risk to the life of the pregnant woman, greater than if the pregnancy were terminated'. In a country where abortion is legal, having an abortion is always less risky than carrying a pregnancy to term.

Until recently, there has been an unspoken consensus in Britain. Yes, the current laws are odd and antiquated. But don't try to fiddle with them, because it would be dangerous to reopen the debate. In 2015, Conservative backbencher Fiona Bruce attempted to clarify that sex-based terminations were illegal, citing the widespread abortion of female foetuses in countries such as China and India. Feminist MPs saw this as an attempt to chip away at abortion provision generally. The former GP Sarah Wollaston, then a Tory MP, noted that there was no evidence of sex-based abortions as a 'systematic practice' in Britain. Changing the law would raise suspicions of ethnic-minority women seeking an abortion. Their choice might be questioned, where a white woman's would not. And what woman, faced with prosecution, would confide in her doctor about being pressurised to seek a termination? It is a difficult principle to accept, but women deserve access to abortion even when we don't agree with their reasons for having one.

*

For an idea of why abortion rights matter to all women, look to America, where there is now a co-ordinated assault on provision. Several states are debating 'heartbeat laws' which prevent terminations once a heartbeat can be detected. That can be as early as the sixth week of pregnancy – two weeks after a missed period – which is before many women realise they are pregnant. Abortion clinics have been hit with bureaucratic hurdles which are designed to make it harder for them to operate. Protestors surround clinics, shouting at women who use them, offering leaflets about 'abortion regret' and the supposed health risks of the procedure. In Britain, MPs from across the parties are trying to institute 'exclusion zones' around clinics to prevent this happening. In free-speech-obsessed America, that is not an option.

The US religious right is also bringing forward so-called 'personhood laws', which chip away at *Roe* v. *Wade*. These laws aim to enshrine the idea that a foetus – whether minutes from birth or a recently fertilised egg – is a separate legal entity under the law. But the more the foetus is treated as a person, the less its mother is.

Under personhood laws, women have been prosecuted after taking legal prescription drugs during pregnancy – because of the supposed danger to the foetus. In one case, a woman was charged with murder after trying to kill herself while eight months pregnant. A drug addict was charged with foeticide for having a stillbirth. In New Jersey, a woman known as VM was reported for child abuse and had her baby taken away after refusing a C-section.* In July 2019 Marshae Jones, a twenty-seven-year-old woman in Alabama, was arrested after being shot in the stomach during an argument with a female friend. She had provoked the confrontation, police argued, and so was responsible for her baby's death. The possibilities of this argument being extended were obvious. What about the woman who went on a roller coaster and miscarried? Who crashed a car? Who ate Brie? There is no way to live in the world without exposing a foetus to risk.

The charges against Marshae Jones were dropped after an

---

* VM, who had post-traumatic stress disorder, was described in hospital records as 'combative', 'uncooperative', 'erratic', 'non-compliant', 'irrational' and 'inappropriate'. However, she was deemed capable of informed consent. She delivered the child vaginally – and healthily – and in August 2010 the Superior Court ruled in her favour and returned the child, who was then four years old.

outcry. But they were an alarming sign of women's vulnerability in this particular culture war. 'It's clear we still have a long way to go until laws strategically passed to punish women – especially women of color – are shameful relics of our past,' tweeted Cecile Richards, former president of Planned Parenthood.

It suits conservatives to frame abortion as a moral issue: they are protecting precious human life. I would find this argument more compelling if advanced by pacifists who believed in generous state funding of maternity services and a strong welfare safety net. From the US right, which will not support a ban on the sale of military assault rifles to the public, and which has stripped away healthcare provision from the poor, it is deeply hypocritical. If life begins at conception, why does their interest in protecting it end at birth?

The feminist case for abortion rights rests on women's right to bodily autonomy. The state can't seize your kidney, or demand that you become a sperm donor, or force you to live in a certain area or marry a designated person. So why should it have the power to make you stay pregnant against your will? And it works both ways: the state should also not have the power to sterilise 'undesirable' groups. In 1974, it was revealed that fourteen-year-old Mary Alice Relf and her twelve-year-old sister Minnie were among 100,000–150,000 people sterilised every year under government-funded programmes. The sisters, from a black family in the American South, were both mentally disabled, and when their mother took them to get birth control, she was instead given a piece of paper to sign with an 'X'. This was taken as consent to sterilise them surgically. Other women agreed to be sterilised under threat of losing their welfare benefit. In the wake of a court case, the US government agreed to stop funding such sterilisations and to seek truly informed consent. What happened to Mary and Minnie shows why some activists talk about 'reproductive justice' rather than 'reproductive rights'. The right to have children can be just as contested as the right to abortion.

In countries where abortion is completely illegal, the suffering caused to women is immense. Abortions still happen, of course, but they are far less safe. In El Salvador, women have been prosecuted for having a naturally occurring miscarriage. Since the law was tightened in 1998, around 600 women have been jailed on suspicion of deliberately ending a pregnancy. One of them, Maria Theresa Rivera, spoke to the *Independent* in May 2016 after spending five years in prison. 'It was horrible, horrible, in the jail. One of my fellow inmates got beaten. It was very crowded and there was not much water,' she told reporter Andrew Buncombe. 'There were 250 women in a dormitory designed for 100.' At the age of twenty-eight, Rivera had been living on the outskirts of San Salvador with her son Oscar. One night, she awoke with intense cramps and went to the outside toilet, where she delivered a foetus. She fainted. She had not even known she was pregnant.

At the hospital, Rivera was told that she had given birth, and police went to search her house, where they found the foetus. She was given forty years in prison – a sentence which was overturned only when a court ruled there was insufficient evidence that she had provoked the miscarriage herself. The *Independent* story noted that, at the time of writing, there were twenty-five women behind bars in El Salvador for the same crime, 'almost all of them single, poor and largely uneducated – women who do not have the opportunity to catch the two-hour flight to Miami and visit a private clinic'. This is the grim reality of restrictive abortion laws. They most affect those who cannot afford to travel to escape them. Rich women in El Salvador can travel abroad if they need a termination, but poor women cannot.

But we shouldn't be complacent, looking at El Salvador from the vantage point of First World, liberal Britain. After all, we don't have to look very far to find stories of similar injustice. In fact, we just need to look across the Irish Sea.

*

I arrived in Derry-Londonderry Airport on a drizzly Saturday after-noon. The city is the site of the Bloody Sunday massacre, where British soldiers fired on unarmed protesters in 1972. It now hosts both a 'peace flame' and a peace bridge, on which John Major and Tony Blair appealed to voters to stay in the European Union. The majority in Northern Ireland voted Remain in 2016.

If you get pregnant in Northern Ireland, you can get around its restrictive abortion laws by travelling to England or Scotland. Just as in El Salvador, the current law hurts poor women more. Until June 2017, Northern Irish women had to pay for their abortions; they were not available on the NHS. This infuriates me: women whose taxes funded the health service were denied access to it. That law changed because of a campaign by Labour MP Stella Creasy and others.

Even now, though, GPs in Northern Ireland can't make referrals for terminations, and women have to go through the British Pregnancy Advisory Service or Marie Stopes clinics to arrange the procedure. They also need to get time off work. They might have to arrange childcare – 55 per cent of British women who have an abortion have already given birth at least once. They might have to find a plausible explanation for their trips to tell socially conservative family and friends.

In practice, it's possible to buy abortion pills online. This is illegal, but it's cheaper than travelling, and it's (relatively) safe. I say relatively, because if you take the pills after twelve weeks the chances of heavy bleeding increase dramatically. Women on Waves, which provides abortion advice and carries out terminations in inter-national waters, suggests that if women take the pills in the second trimester, they should do so in or near a hospital waiting room. 'Realise that you will lose a lot of tissue and blood, but also a foetus (the size depends on the duration of the pregnancy), which can be recognised as such,' its website advises. 'It can be quite distressing to see. You are strongly discouraged to do an abortion after fifteen weeks by yourself because of the high complication risk and because it can be very traumatic.'

There is also the risk of a visit from the police. That's what drove Kitty, Colette and Diana to act. They had heard the story of a twenty-one-year-old woman whose housemates informed on her for buying pills, and who was given a suspended sentence in April 2016. The court heard that the woman could not afford to travel to the mainland. 'This was the first time that we'd heard of anybody going to court for what they do with their own body,' Kitty told me.* There had been other cases: a Northern Irish mother was accused of buying pills for her teenage daughter. A couple in their early twenties accepted cautions for the same offence.

In conversation, the women's very different personalities emerged. Colette was birdlike, blonde and voluble, her conversation punctuated by occasional emphatic swearwords. She had looked me up online, and was pleased to discover I was doing something on 'how we counter the baddies, the attacks on women'. Diana looked every inch the elegant, practical matriarch. Slim, with white hair and bright red trousers, she was the only one with children of her own (plus stepchildren, and a foster daughter). The local activist Goretti Horgan told me that Diana's response to being told that she might have to spend two years in prison was pragmatic: she could catch up on her reading.

Colette knew Diana from protests against the arms company Raytheon, which had supplied Israel with the weapons used to invade Lebanon and repress dissent in Gaza. In 2006, nine men – the Raytheon Nine – had stormed the company's offices in Derry. Three years later, nine women repeated the protest. Goretti Horgan was one, Diana King another. They ended up stuck between two doors in the building, and so turned the situation into an impromptu sit-in.

* Suicide and attempted suicide used to be a criminal offence, but that law was overturned in 1961.

They argued to the judge that although they were committing a criminal offence, it was to prevent a greater one: the creation of what Diana called 'killing machines', weapons which could be used on children.

Kitty was more obviously fiery, burning with activist zeal: she had met the other two as a result of the abortion campaign. There had been grand plans for far more women to be involved, but these fizzled out when the implications of the law became clear. A conviction or caution under the 1861 Offences Against the Person Act counts as an assault charge. It has to be declared on disclosure forms when working with children or vulnerable adults, and on visa waivers for countries such as America. How could a teacher or a young woman who wanted to travel the world risk so much, the three women reasoned? 'Younger people than us have their lives,' said Kitty. 'Even if you don't get fourteen years in jail, which is definitely considerable, you get a conviction, and then people have their whole lives with that.' Plus, she said, their protest had gained so much attention precisely because they were past childbearing age.* 'Older women have much less to lose,' added Diana.

It turned out the police officers hadn't looked surprised when the three women turned up, because they had had to make an appointment beforehand. 'We had to wait weeks, didn't we, before they let us,' said Diana. 'We were very sedate.'

The women and their solicitor arrived at Derry police station on 23 May 2016, and were taken to a special suite to check over their prepared confessions. 'I wish to report that I have obtained the same "9 week termination pills" that two women from Northern Ireland have already been charged with "procurement of",' read Colette Devlin's statement. 'I am doing this because I believe, like these two women, that I am not breaking any law by acquiring the exact same pills, with the same protocols and same regimen, that are widely

---

* Colette was born in June 1949, Kitty in September 1947, Diana in March 1945.

used throughout the NHS in Scotland, Wales and England to induce terminations . . . I believe that these charges are vindictive and are symptomatic of the general attitude against women in both parts of Ireland.'

Kitty's statement – which used her full name, Kathleen – echoed these sentiments: 'The right to determine our own reproductive life ought to be a matter for ourselves.' Colette also condemned the 'fundamentalist' nature of past and present Northern Ireland governments, which had prevented the extension of the 1967 Abortion Act to the six counties. 'To challenge this preposterous situation, we have decided to hand ourselves in,' it concluded, followed by a sentence that echoed the suffragettes and the US civil rights movement: 'I believe that I have a legal duty to uphold good law, but I have a moral duty to disobey bad law.'

Then, after posing for photographs and giving a television interview, the three women went off and had a whiskey.

*

When I started writing this book, women in the Republic of Ireland faced a similar choice to their sisters north of the border. In 1983, the country's Eighth Amendment to its constitution gave the lives of mother and foetus equal weight under the law. That phrasing is fascinating, because it sounds appealing – every potential human deserves a chance – but its practical effects were ugly. Pregnant women were refused cancer treatment, because of the risk to the foetus. Although abortion was allowed to save a woman's life, consultant obstetrician Louise Kenny told the *Irish Times* she had witnessed care being denied for fear of breaking the law. 'It is an outrageous lie to say that the Eighth has never changed medical management or adversely affected the outcome of a woman with cancer,' she told the paper in April 2018. 'The Eighth Amendment casts a shadow over the care of every woman of reproductive age with complex medical needs in this State.'

In 2012, a thirty-one-year-old dentist called Savita Halappanavar had the misfortune to start miscarrying at seventeen weeks pregnant. She arrived at University Hospital Galway with the foetus half-delivered, and the sac protruding from her uterus into her vagina. She asked for an abortion, and was refused one. Nothing could be done, doctors said, until the heartbeat had stopped. One of the nurses told her and her husband that Ireland was 'a Catholic country'.

Three days later, as Savita's condition worsened, the medical team eventually diagnosed her with sepsis – blood poisoning – and agreed to give her the abortion drug misoprostol. She delivered the foetus before the drug could be administered. At 1.09 a.m., four days later, she died of a heart attack caused by the blood poisoning. In her statement to the Northern Ireland police, Colette Devlin had described the decision to refuse treatment to Halappanavar as 'tantamount to murder'.

In the aftermath of Savita Halappanavar's death, senior church figures claimed that the pro-choice movement was 'politicising' the tragedy. There was no evidence, they said, that Ireland's abortion laws were to blame. However, prominent voices began to disagree. Staff in the hospital spoke about the uncertainty created by the law. One doctor referred to a 'sword of Damocles' hanging over him. A senior obstetrician, Professor Sir Sabaratnam Arulkumaran, was asked to carry out an inquiry. He found that Halappanavar had died from 'medical misadventure' and her husband later settled with the hospital for a six-figure sum. In 2013, the Irish parliament, the Dáil, passed an Act explicitly permitting abortions where the woman's life was in danger, including from risk of suicide. Normally, three doctors are required to sign this off, but in an emergency it can be just one.

Yet further reform was inchingly slow. Five years after Savita's death, a clearly exasperated Sabaratnam Arulkumaran testified in front of an Irish government committee. He was unequivocal: the Eighth Amendment killed Savita Halappanavar. 'It was very clear the things holding the hands of physicians was the legal issue. Anybody, any junior doctor, would have said this is a sepsis condition, we must terminate,' he said. 'She did have sepsis. However, if she had a termination in the first days as requested, she would not have had sepsis. If she had the termination when asked for it, the sepsis would not arise. We would never have heard of her and she would be alive today.' So much for the right to life. Ireland's abortion laws meant that Savita Halappanavar – a thirty-one-year-old woman with a partner, a job, a family, a life – died an unnecessary death. She died to save a foetus which could never have survived.

Other women began to speak out, including those whose pregnancies were not viable because of conditions such as anencephaly, where the foetus has a brain stem and little else. These women had to go through nine months and the pain and risks of labour knowing there would be no baby to take home at the end. The Irish comedy writer Graham Linehan, who now lives in London with his wife Helen, went public with the story of discovering their foetus had acrania, where the skull does not close over the brain. 'In Ireland, Helen would be a criminal to have undergone the termination,' Graham told the *Guardian* in 2015. 'She would have had to carry the child knowing it would die in great pain shortly after she had given birth to it. I have always been very proud to be Irish but I am embarrassed by Ireland's abortion laws. This is just something you can't be proud of. It's barbaric.'

Then there were the more ordinary, less dramatic cases. Women who couldn't afford another child. Women whose relationships weren't stable enough. Women who simply did not want to be pregnant. During the campaign Repeal the Eighth Amendment, Caoimhe Anglin ran a project called Everyday Stories, which combined personal testimonies with illustrations of the women telling them. 'Photos can carry a bit of a pre-judgement,' she told me over Skype in the run-up to the vote. 'If a father was reading it, we wanted him to be able to imagine his daughter.'

Anglin found out she was pregnant in October 2016. She was twenty-seven, lived in Dublin, worked in IT and had a boyfriend who mostly worked abroad. 'Rent in Ireland has been going up and up, it's absolute madness,' she said. 'So when I found out I was pregnant I was understandably quite concerned, because I could barely afford my rent as it was, let alone if I were to bring a child into the world.' She went to crisis pregnancy counselling and spent three or four days thinking over the decision, before concluding that she couldn't afford to have a child. Her boyfriend supported her, and they both decided to travel to Manchester for the termination. She spent the night before the journey driving round petrol stations in Dublin using their ATMs to withdraw the 440 euros to pay for the procedure.

The next day, the journey was 'horrible'. She was tired and nervous. She worried whether she was doing the right thing. 'I remember sitting in a cafe in Dublin airport and my boyfriend's there getting breakfast, and he's like, we should get sandwiches and tea and all that stuff, and I was just sitting at the table. He came back and it just struck him that I'm not allowed to eat. I didn't say anything. But I remember that look in his eyes of complete helplessness.' As well as the termination, the couple had to pay for flights and a hotel. The clinic advises women not to travel straight back in case of complications, and in case the airline refuses them boarding because they look unwell.

Given the length of the trip, Anglin needed a cover story to tell her family. She decided to say her boyfriend had treated her to a surprise trip to go shopping for vintage clothes. 'I was knackered. We went from the clinic, to the hotel, to lunch – because you have to eat pretty soon afterwards because you haven't eaten in twelve hours,' she told me. 'And then it was like, right, well I still have the painkillers, and while there's still anaesthetic, we need to go to these vintage shops so that we have selfies and a vintage top to bring home in case anyone asks me. I look back on that and I think: *Jesus Christ. What was I thinking?*'

Back in Ireland, Anglin felt silenced, as though she couldn't, and shouldn't, talk to anyone else about her experience. For three months, she told no one except her best friend. 'It's not like you could call someone up and say: hey, this thing happened and I don't know how to process it. Oh, and I'm also bleeding really, really heavily and I have been for three weeks and I don't know if I'm dying. You really feel that fear.'

Then she ran into an acquaintance called Mary who was campaigning ahead of Repeal the Eighth. Mary was wearing a T-shirt with the Abortion Rights slogan: *Free, safe, legal.* So Anglin poured out her story. 'Just like that, it was like someone had given me a ticket to spill my heart out to a stranger. And I just told her everything . . . I started to feel normal again – and not like a criminal.'

Her own experience influenced the Everyday Stories project. She wanted to show the stress, the stigma and the silence of Ireland's abortion laws. She also wanted to show how hard it was for women's friends and partners to witness their distress. The men's stories often spoke of helplessness: 'I couldn't be there for my wife.' 'I couldn't fulfil the traditional male role of jumping in and saving the day. I had to sit in the waiting room and do nothing.' She found them hard to read; they reminded her of her own boyfriend's eyes as he tried to cheer her up with breakfast at the airport, 'and how he had to sit in the waiting room for six hours, not knowing what's going on behind the closed doors'.

*

Caoimhe Anglin ended our interview by speculating on what she would do if the Repeal campaign failed to win over enough of her fellow citizens. She would take a month off, maybe a little more, and then start fighting again. She was exhausted; but she wouldn't give up.

No one I spoke to before the referendum in May 2018 was complacent about the result. Brexit and the election of Donald Trump had convinced many activists that social liberalism was a spent force.

Diana King, canvassing in rural, conservative Donegal, emailed me a few weeks before the vote to say that she was very worried. Her door-knocking did not fill her with confidence.

I arrived in Dublin on Thursday, the day before voting began. It is every inch a cultural capital, but on a much more human scale than my home city, London: half a million residents, compared with 8 million. I kept bumping into well-known activists, journalists and public figures. The Repeal jumpers – slabby white letters on a black sweatshirt – were everywhere. The referendum question asked whether voters wanted to repeal the eighth amendment to the constitution 'so that provision may be made by law for the regulation of termination of pregnancies'. On the commuter train from Tara Street to Dun Laoghaire, I saw young men and women wearing badges saying 'Yes' – or its Irish equivalent, *'Tá'*. At 9.30 p.m., a few dozen activists gathered at the James Joyce bridge in Dublin. They wanted to see the sun set on the Eighth Amendment for the last time, they said. Cars, taxis and even lorries honked their horns at the sight of the huge knitted Repeal banner that led the procession.

Savita Halappanavar's face was everywhere, but the lamp posts were crowded with No posters too. Voters were urged to 'save lives', to 'love both'. Pictures of foetuses abounded, with messages about when their hearts start beating. 'I am 9 weeks old, I can yawn and kick. Don't repeal me,' read one. In a rhetorical flourish the Yes campaign said was imported from America, anti-abortion posters sometimes referred not to the 'unborn' but to the 'preborn'.

The involvement of the well-funded US pro-life movement was an open secret; both Google and Facebook, in the run-up to polling day, imposed restrictions on adverts related to the referendum. The campaign itself was occasionally bitter. 'I've been shouted at, spat at, called a baby murderer,' Lisa Wilkinson, director of the Elbowroom and organiser of the rally, told me on the way to the river. 'But we've tried to keep it positive.'

The next day, I walked down to the headquarters of the Repeal campaign, which were eerily quiet – everyone was helping to get out the vote. 'The last three months have lifted the lid on abortion in Ireland,' Orla O'Connor, the kind-voiced co-director of Together For Yes, told me. 'So the idea that abortion doesn't happen in Ireland, we don't have to think about it . . . It's the conversation that for so long, people have tried to avoid.'

The campaign achieved a fine balance between inclusivity and comprehensibility, which allowed it to build a coalition between younger, more radical activists and groups such as 'Grandfathers For Yes'. It reminded me of how proud Kitty was of the local Catholic girls' school in Derry, which had rebelled against a male teacher who tried to lecture them on the necessity to preserve the Eighth. 'They are enraged,' she told me. 'That's wonderful!'

The leaders of the main parties supported reform, which could have seen it characterised as an elite cause – but that would be to ignore the long history of the church in Ireland dictating moral issues. The Taoiseach, Leo Varadkar, had put forward his proposed legislation if the amendment was repealed: it was both more and less liberal than the English regime, with abortion on demand, but only up to twelve weeks. Crucially – unlike Brexit – people knew what a vote for change would mean.

Just as importantly, the Yes campaign's language was concrete, and focused on women: 'Your mother. Your daughter. Your sister. Her choice.'* The door-knocking group who kindly let me gatecrash their eve-of-voting celebration at the social club in Dun Laoghaire were a mixed bunch: retired men and women alongside young parents and students. 'What's been very different from previous campaigns is the number of women coming forward and talking

---

* There were grumbles afterwards that transgender men and non-binary people were not explicitly referenced; all I can say is that trying to explain to older swing voters in more rural areas why an abortion campaign was talking about men would have eaten up valuable campaigning time.

about their stories,' Orla O'Connor told me. 'It's been absolutely incredible . . . I think that for the first time Irish people really got to hear what the impact of the Eighth was.'

I found my visit to Dublin surprisingly emotional. I realise now that I *needed* the Eighth campaign. It followed two years when abortion rights came under attack across the world. One of Donald Trump's first acts as US president was to reinstate the 'global gag' rule, which bars charities and NGOs in the developing world from receiving government funding if they mention abortion. As president, Trump had four years to reshape the Supreme Court, giving conservatives a firm majority.* *Roe* v. *Wade*, the legislation which gave women 'existential freedom', was in jeopardy. In Britain, the grass-roots favourite for the next Conservative leader was Jacob Rees-Mogg, a Catholic father of six who said he was 'completely opposed' to abortion, even in cases of rape.

On Friday, as voting drew to a close, I went down to the memorial to Savita Halappanavar in south Dublin. It felt a little like a pilgrimage. Her face was painted on the wall in vivid pink, and people had left flowers and Repeal badges on the pavement. They had also left notes. One of them will always stay with me, because it showed how the abortion debate forged a connection between two women, neither of whom I will ever know. The message was addressed to Savita. 'I'm so sorry we let you down,' it read. 'It won't be in vain.'

*

You might know what happened next. I was back in my hotel room when *The Late, Late Show* broke into its programming with an exit poll. We'd been warned that its results might not be accurate because there was no baseline against which pollsters could measure change.

* This happened in July 2018 with the retirement of swing voter Anthony Kennedy, who was replaced by Brett Kavanaugh.

The last referendum on the Eighth had been in 1983, when every area in the whole country (except liberal south Dublin) was in favour of keeping it.

As it happened, the exit poll proved to be extremely accurate. It recorded a thumping victory for Yes: around seven in ten Irish voters wanted the Eighth to be repealed. Twitter went crazy. My WhatsApp was on fire. I was even getting text messages, like it was 2014 or something. In my political lifetime, I have not felt such an outpouring of relief, of pride, and of joy. The last was the most interesting, because the campaigners had worried that – unlike the referendum which legalised same-sex marriage in 2015 – they could not send out an upbeat message, in case they were accused of revelling in baby murder. But now the vote was won, there was real happiness. Women like Caoimhe Anglin would no longer have to make hurried, frightened journeys across the sea. Women like Orla O'Connor had removed the shame of speaking out. Women like Diana King had travelled across the border to canvass in the toughest spot of all – Donegal, the only region where a majority voted against repeal. Women would not have to stay pregnant in the knowledge there would be no baby to bring home. Men had rallied behind the cause, and in return, men like Caoimhe Anglin's partner would no longer have to watch their loved ones suffer, unable to help. It had been a difficult argument, but the campaigners had made it.

I stood in the courtyard of Dublin Castle the next day and watched a crowd cheer at the thought that the church and its ruling class of men no longer had control of women's bodies. The memory of this victory would nourish a generation of activists. And in the crowd, I saw a sign that promised the next fight was coming. It read: 'Now for the North.'

*

At the time of writing, I still don't know how the story of Kitty, Diana and Colette will end. Following the Irish vote, politicians at

Westminster began to organise to change the law in Northern Ireland too. They hoped to repeal the 1861 Act and let each of the devolved nations of the United Kingdom draw up their own framework for legalising abortion. Then they switched tack, trying to use the suspension of the assembly at Stormont to their advantage. In July 2019, Stella Creasy and others proposed that if Stormont did not reconvene by the autumn, abortion should be legalised. The idea neatly sidestepped the objections of the socially conservative Democratic Unionist Party (DUP), whose votes were propping up the Conservative government at Westminster. The law passed.

Some were uneasy about the decision being taken away from Stormont. To them, I would say that the DUP's views do not represent the majority of their constituents. A study using data from the 2016 Northern Ireland Life and Times survey found that 78 per cent of respondents supported legal abortion in cases of rape or incest, and 81 per cent for fatal foetal abnormalities. Nearly two-thirds – 63 per cent – agreed that 'it is a woman's right to choose whether or not to have an abortion'.

While waiting for the law to be enacted, the three women have savoured the smaller victories. In 2017, the police had raided the office of a well-known activist, Helen Crickard, on International Women's Day, but came away empty-handed. She was not prosecuted. A male activist's house had been raided a few days earlier, and around fifteen women were contacted by police to say that packages of pills had been intercepted. Despite this, no new prosecutions have been started, not even when activists took abortion pills outside the courts at a pro-choice rally in Belfast.

When I met them, Colette, Diana and Kitty were officially in 'legal limbo', but there seemed little appetite to take their case forward. They had returned to their normal lives, pausing only to visit a swanky hotel in Washington, DC to receive an award for their activism from an American magazine. 'They phoned me to say we'd been nominated for this, and it was such a shock,' said Kitty. 'I said, "No, we'd not be interested in this kind of thing," and he said, "It's gone to press." That was it.' The last time she had been in a Four Seasons hotel, Colette remembered, was to protest against a former head of Sinn Féin. 'We were there demanding women's rights. And we were thrown out.'

The police, they speculated, knew they were no longer dealing with isolated or marginalised women, who would be likely to confess quickly or accept a caution. 'You have to think of it like the anti-slavery movement,' Kitty told me. 'The gradualism. We're not going to get the dramatic revolution we all wanted. We won't get it except very, very steadily.'

*

I'm aware, writing this, of the temptation to focus on 'good' abortions – ones where the woman involved is blameless. She was raped, or the foetus couldn't survive anyway, or she needed medical attention to save her life. What about the woman who got drunk and forgot to insist on a condom, the woman who got food poisoning and her pill didn't work, the teenager – like me – who gambled it all on the withdrawal method, but lost?

Just like with divorce, you aren't entitled to human rights based on how blameless your behaviour has been. The 'good' divorce is because your partner cheated on you, or beat you up, or abandoned you. The 'bad' divorce is where you couldn't make it work, or you cheated on him, or you realised you never should have got married in the first place. Feminists must always resist any attempt to give the state the power to decide if they've been naughty or nice. Women deserve the vote, no matter what they do with it. They deserve to have sex without fearing pregnancy, even if society doesn't approve of their partners. They deserve refuges, even if they keep going back to him. They deserve to have maternity leave, even if it makes life harder for their employer. They deserve to be treated equally, even when their lives and bodies are different to those of men.

The abortion argument encapsulates the two types of difficulty that feminism must embrace. Even Difficult Women deserve human rights – and even difficult arguments must be made. It might be hard to defend a woman having her fifth abortion, but the alternative – that only the virtuous deserve control of their bodies – is worse. Not least because everyone's standards of virtue are different, and the morality of the age can shift quite abruptly. (When the pill was first introduced, it was limited to married women.) There is only one argument to make, and it's the one Kitty O'Kane made when knocking doors for Repeal the Eighth: 'Trust women . . . How far do you expect a woman to have to suffer so that you can decide on her behalf?'

Isn't that revolutionary? Trust women. Even when they've messed up, even when they were drunk, even when they should have taken more care, even when they're sleeping around, even when they are any one of the million other flavours of 'difficult'. Trust women.

POSTSCRIPT

On 22 October 2019, Stormont missed its deadline to reconvene: abortion was decriminalised in Northern Ireland (and gay marriages became legal). 'Your story just won't lie still,' said Diana, when I emailed her. She, Colette and Kitty would not be prosecuted; even better, the case which galvanised them – the mother arrested for buying abortion pills for her teenage daughter – had been dropped. Not everyone was happy, though. Diana had heard of a GP service that had put up a sign declaring, 'NOT IN OUR NAME'. She suspected the argument would continue 'for some time'.

Still, the activists in Derry savoured the moment. They celebrated with speeches in Guildhall Square, followed by a formal reception 'in council premises to make the point that we can't be ignored or treated as renegades any longer.' And then they headed to the pub.

11. THE RIGHT TO
BE DIFFICULT

I think that the past is all that makes the present coherent, and further, that the past will remain horrible for exactly as long as we refuse to assess it honestly.

James Baldwin

Feminism will always be difficult. It tries to represent half of humanity: 3.5 billion people (and counting) drawn from every race, class, country and religion. It is revolutionary, challenging the most fundamental structures of our society. It is deeply personal, illuminating our most intimate experiences and personal relationships. It rejects the division between the public and private spheres. It gets everywhere, from boardrooms to bedrooms. It leaves no part of our lives untouched. It is both theory and practice. And God, is it *complicated*. It resists simple categories and glib answers. Feminism always requires thought, and argument, and compromise within its ranks, before it can turn its artillery on the rest of the world. It needs clear goals, backed by a strong consensus, or it is liable to collapse into an ugly scrap over priorities. It needs leaders who don't become tyrants. It needs followers who spend more time fighting oppression than fighting each other. All that is extremely difficult.

And there is another problem, unique to feminism. It is a movement run by women, for women. And what do we expect from women? Perfection. Niceness. Selflessness. We worry whether women can 'have it all'. We dismiss female trailblazers as 'problematic' for holding typical attitudes for their age. And we pick apart feminism to see its failings, as if to reassure ourselves that women aren't getting above themselves. We describe women who challenge authority or seek power as unladylike, talkative, insistent, self-obsessed. We accuse them of 'putting themselves forward', of 'getting above themselves'. Feminists get a double dose of this: name any of the movement's pioneers and you will find people – including feminists – who hate her.

The critic Emily Nussbaum nailed the problem: 'When you're put on a pedestal, the whole world gets to upskirt you.'

Spending time with my own collection of Difficult Women has been instructive. It has helped me to shake off the habit of mixing love with admiration. I admire the achievements of Marie Stopes, but freely concede that she sounds like a *nightmare*. I admire the suffragettes, but I am deeply ambivalent about their use of violence. I admire Jayaben Desai, even though her protest failed. I admire Erin Pizzey, even though I wish she kept better company. All of these women belong in the history of feminism, not in spite of their flaws, but because we are *all* flawed. We have to resist the modern impulse to pick one of two settings: airbrush or discard. History is always more interesting when it is difficult. We can't tidy away all the loose ends and the uncomfortable truths without draining the story of its power. Everything is problematic. The battles are difficult, and we must be difficult too.

*

What can feminists learn from the Difficult Women of the past? First, that making progress means making enemies. There is no way to do feminism that will please everybody. But – but – aren't women supposed to be nice? Yes, they are, and it's bullshit. In 1854, Coventry Patmore wrote a poem idealising his wife, called 'The Angel in the House'. It is, to be frank, terrible: sickly in the worst tradition of Victorian sentimentality, and with a rhyme scheme about as subtle as a boot to the face. Brace yourself:

> *Her, the most excellent of all,*
> *The best half of creation's best,*
> *Its heart to feel, its eye to see,*
> *Its aim and its epitome.*

It was also influential, because two generations of female writers found it so vomitous that they were moved to respond to it. The problem with being an Angel, you see, is that angels know their place: *but darling, you're just better at changing nappies!* 'There was once a species of Angel inhabiting this planet,' wrote Charlotte Perkins Gilman in 1891:

> The advantages of possessing such a creature were untold . . .
> The human creature went out to his daily toil and comforted himself as he saw fit. He was apt to come home tired and cross and in this exigency it was the business of the angel to wear a smile for his benefit – a soft, perennial, heavenly smile. By an unfortunate limitation of humanity the angel was required, in addition to such celestial duties as smiling and soothing, to do kitchen service, cleaning, sewing, nursing, and other mundane tasks. But these things must be accomplished without the slightest diminution of the angelic virtues.

Every woman who has been told to 'cheer up, love' by a random bloke should empathise with this sentiment. It isn't enough to do our work, to be alive. We have to make everyone else feel good about themselves as we do it.

Want to see Coventry Patmore get duffed up some more? Of course you do. In 1931, Virginia Woolf gave a lecture to a society for professional women, in which she identified another problem with the Angel in the House – Angels were nice: writers can't be.

> I found, directly I put pen to paper, you cannot review even a novel without having a mind of your own, without expressing what you think to be the truth about human relations, morality, sex. And all these questions, according to the Angel of the House, cannot be dealt with freely and openly by women; they must charm, they must conciliate, they must – to put it bluntly – tell lies if they are to succeed . . . Killing the Angel in the House was part of the occupation of a woman writer.

You don't have to be a writer to feel this expectation. Today, we would call it 'female socialisation', and it starts early. The sociologist Barbara Rothman found that expectant mothers who did not know the sex of their offspring described the movement of (what turned out to be) girl or boy babies in broadly the same terms. But the mothers who knew their baby's sex used stereotypical language: male foetuses kicked in a 'strong' or 'vigorous' way; female ones were 'not terribly active'. As children, boys are 'boisterous', girls are 'bossy'. Try to imagine the adjectives swapped. It feels unnatural.

The experiences of transgender people show how much our lives are affected by the expectations projected on to us. In July 2006, the neuroscientist Ben Barres – born female, and raised as Barbara – responded in *Nature* magazine to a suggestion by Harvard University president Larry Summers 'that differences in innate aptitude rather than discrimination were more likely to be to blame for the failure of women to advance in scientific careers'. In other words: girls just suck at maths, OK? Barres provided evidence to the contrary, with his time living as a woman acting as his own experimental control group. After transitioning, he overheard an audience member say, 'Ben Barres gave a great seminar today, but then his work is much better than his sister's.' There was no sister. People just took Ben more seriously than Barbara.

Barres added that taking testosterone appeared to have increased his spatial abilities and made it harder for him to cry, but this was not the biggest change he experienced when he began to be perceived as male. 'By far, the main difference that I have noticed is that people who don't know I am transgendered treat me with much more respect,' he wrote. 'I can even complete a whole sentence without being interrupted by a man.' The travel writer Jan (formerly James) Morris had the opposite experience when she transitioned. 'The more I was treated as a woman, the more woman I became,' she wrote in her 1987 memoir *Conundrum*. 'If

I was assumed to be incompetent at reversing cars, or opening bottles, oddly incompetent I found myself becoming.'

These messages are beamed back at us – men are *this*, women are *that* – from the moment of birth. No wonder it feels obvious that there are striking, fundamental differences in temperament and interests between the sexes which no social movement can ever overcome. But it seems to me that if women are, on average, less assertive, less aggressive, less *difficult* than men, then it's not just down to chromosomes, or hormones. It's socialisation too. It's because the only refuge of the powerless is supplication. If you're in charge, you don't have to beg. You don't have to live your life on high alert for the responses of others. The world shapes itself around you. You don't have to ask nicely. You can *be* difficult without getting *called* difficult.

*

Feminism has to fight 'the tyranny of niceness'. It is, and has always been, one of the most potent forces holding women back. Feminism is not a self-help movement, dedicated to making everyone feel better about their lives. It is a radical demand to overturn the status quo. It sometimes has to cause upset. 'I cannot personally think of any widespread injustice that has been remedied by plodding worthily down the middle of the road, smiling and smiling,' wrote Jill Tweedie in 1971. 'If you are sure of the justice of your cause it must be better to have people thinking of it with initial anger than not thinking at all.' Millicent Fawcett saw her peaceful movement ignored while the violent suffragettes were condemned. Jayaben Desai and her fellow immigrants were ordered to be grateful they had a job at all. Marie Stopes was patronisingly informed that sex was a nasty business and women were better off ignorant. Today's feminists are still told to calm down, dear.

But there is no perfect way to make a demand on power. There is no way to do feminism which will protect you from being attacked.

You have to be honest with yourself: am I really being unreasonable? Or is the problem the rest of the world? If it is the latter, then don't be derailed.

When I interviewed an activist from Greenham Common, the 1980s protest against nuclear bases in Britain, she told me that at the start 'the *Guardian* was presenting us all as concerned mothers and grandmothers. the *Daily Mail* was representing us all as burly lesbians, and within about two months, one of the other tabloids was saying we were all fey Tinkerbells.' That contradictory set of criticisms is typical of how female activists are dismissed. The trick is to remember that there is no way to win, so don't even bother trying. I once did an event with my *New Statesman* colleague Laurie Penny, then in her twenties, and the classicist Mary Beard, who is a rare woman in public life with long, grey hair. Laurie said that she was constantly described as young, naive and stupid. Mary said that she was constantly described as old, clapped out and obsolete. Perhaps, Laurie suggested, there might be one single, beautiful day in a woman's life when she was neither too young nor too old, and everybody listened to her.*

Back in 1912, Constance Lytton – then forty-three – noticed the same tendency in newspaper reporting on the suffragettes. 'Con said one thing was very funny, to read the newspaper accounts of the hysterical girls of eighteen,' wrote Ethel Smyth to Lytton's sister Betty Balfour, 'and then look round Bow Street [police station] – the rows of rather grave, quite particularly quiet and sane women about my age!' If we try to make ourselves the perfect messengers for our movement, we will never get anywhere. There is no such thing as a flawless feminist.

The linguistics professor Deborah Cameron has studied how women are constantly told to change the way they speak and write. A woman's place is in the wrong, she concluded. We are told that we

---

* If it happens, I'll let you know.

say sorry too much, for example, and that this undermines our authority. No one asks if perhaps men don't say sorry *enough*.* Whatever men are doing must be right, because they have more power, money and influence. 'This endless policing of women's language – their voices, their intonation patterns, the words they use, their syntax – is uncomfortably similar to the way our culture polices women's bodily appearance,' wrote Cameron. Feminists will always be needled for our tone and our tactics, when what's really being criticised is our decision to speak up at all.

If a woman's place is in the wrong, a Difficult Woman's place is to point out why that's bullshit.

*

When I started researching this book, I felt wrung out. Too much noise, too many petty, endless arguments, too many personality clashes dressed up as great ideological battles. But then – isn't that politics? Isn't that people? There was something reassuring about finding out that the same arguments recurred over time. Can men be feminists? And is being sexy empowering or demeaning?

The suffragettes were divided over the question of 'sex war'. The writer Rebecca West worried that Christabel Pankhurst's obsession with chastity was puritan and alienating, and others were concerned that keeping the WSPU as an all-female organisation was 'anti-men'. In the 1970s, feminists argued over the emergence of mainstream pornography and its relationship with sexual violence. Lesbian separatists tried to convince women to give up their relationships with men. The same arguments have returned with the debate over prostitution – or sex work, as some would prefer it to be called. Is it inherently 'sex negative' – or puritan, as a woman of the 1910s might have put it – to criticise the sex industry? And when the Women's Equality Party was founded in 2015, there were

---

* Research suggests that women don't apologise more than men, anyway.

immediate arguments about whether men could be members. Sex and men. Men and sex. Both fun. Both endlessly debatable.

People are infinitely complex, and politics is the art of changing their minds. How angry is too angry? Which is best, militancy or legal reforms? What should be our priority right now? How far can you disagree with your allies before you have to break, decisively, with them? Who should be in charge?

We cannot expect a final, definitive ruling on the best tactics to use, because the problems we face keep evolving. The opposition shifts and slides, twisting into new forms, probing our arguments for weakness and our movement for divisions which can be exploited. Sometimes, radicalism is alienating to the persuadable centre ground, and we should accept a partial victory over total defeat. Think of truly universal suffrage following the first reforms of 1918, or birth control leading to abortion rights, or civil partnerships opening the door to gay marriage. Sometimes, we need to work with people whose views differ significantly from ours. In other cases, the gulf is too great. It is a mistake for 'gender critical' feminists, who question aspects of transgender ideology, to form alliances with right-wing Christian fundamentalists in the US who believe that changing your legal gender should not be permitted. A similar error was made by anti-porn feminists in the 1980s, whose efforts to point out the misogyny of the porn industry and its products were co-opted by religious conservatives into a broader reactionary agenda.* One shared goal does not cancel out such a fundamental divergence in world view.

Learning about these Difficult Women helped me to accept that backlash is inevitable. Every feminist action provokes an equal,

---

* 'In 1984 antiporn legislation devised by Andrea Dworkin and Catharine MacKinnon, defining pornography as a violation of women's civil rights, was introduced in the Indianapolis city council by an anti-ERA [equal rights amendment] activist, passed with the support of the right, and signed into law by the Republican mayor, William Hudnut,' reported the *Atlantic* in 1992.

opposite reaction. During the two world wars in Britain, women were needed to work outside the home, in the factories that supplied the conflict. Objections to a female workforce melted away. However, when the soldiers came back, the women were dismissed. Progress is not linear. Victorian women who struggled through housework in suffocating corsets would look with bewilderment at the strict gender division of modern toy shops.*

All this makes me feel pre-emptively exhausted, because the logical conclusion is that the fights of feminism will never be over. On our warming planet, it's easy to see the new ways women could get screwed. Where resources like water are scarce, women will be expected to put their needs last, as happened in Yemen and Sudan. Where there are wars and genocides, they will be raped and impregnated, left to carry their attackers' babies in a hostile society, as happened in Rwanda in the 1990s. Where there is tribal and religious violence, they will become trophies and pawns in male power games, as happened to the Chibok girls of Nigeria, and the Yazidi of Iraq. Strongmen leaders around the world already try to attack feminism, gay rights and religious tolerance as emblems of the 'decadent' West. That trend will surely intensify.

As birth rates in the developed world decline, expect to see a resurgence in natalism – policies to encourage women to have more children. This could be done with a carrot: better maternity-leave policies, more shared parental leave, less career penalties for carers. But it seems more likely that illiberal governments will prefer a stick, with women deprived of rights and opportunities to encourage them to fulfil their 'natural' motherly role. And if all this sounds like that nebulous category of bad things happening to other people a long way away, just think of Britain's ageing population and the

---

* Pink became a girls' colour only in the 1920s. Before then, blue was associated with the Virgin Mary, and therefore considered more feminine; pink was derived from strong, masculine red.

shortfall in funding for elderly care. Expect to hear paeans to 'loving families' as code for guilt-tripping women to do more unpaid labour.

Ultimately, though, the cure for feminist ennui is feminist campaigning. In the time I've been writing this book, the movement has achieved significant victories. We've seen just how wide the gender pay gap is (thank you, Harriet Harman). We've seen a judicial review of the parole of 'black-cab rapist' John Worboys and an agreement to wipe multiple soliciting convictions from the criminal records of women exploited into prostitution (thank you, Harriet Wistrich and her brave plaintiffs). Northern Irish women have gained the right to travel to England for abortions (thank you, Stella Creasy and others). Women from the Republic can now have safe, free, legal abortions in their home country (thank you, #RepealTheEighth). I've watched anti-FGM campaigners fight hard to get perpetrators brought to justice and to end the practice within a generation (thank you, Nimko Ali, Leyla Hussein and others).

Reading all that, I think – yeah, defenders of the sexist status quo *should* be worried.

*

A century and a half ago, women could not vote, own property or control their own fertility. Since then, we have taken a half-step towards equality, which brings its own difficulties. An unfinished revolution is messier than starting a fresh war. Feminism has won battle after battle, but it can be hard to keep going when howling injustices wither into stubborn inequalities.

To avoid the fate of Erin Pizzey – fighting one injustice and then leaving the movement – we need to remember that we are trying to overturn a system. I hope by now to have convinced you that the many strands of feminism are interwoven, and that one thread leads to another. There is, or should be, an underlying logic to everything we do.

It reminds me of the argument I keep having with a friend of mine. Does patriarchy exist? He says: *not here, not now*. I say: *bollocks*.

First, let's set our terms. To me, patriarchy is a system where men control most of the power and money, and use that control to their own advantage. It does not mean every individual man is consciously oppressing every individual woman. There are female billionaires (though relatively few) and destitute men on the streets. There are male rape victims and female CEOs. But if you gave anti-feminists a button which instantly switched the genders – so women were 70 per cent of MPs, men did far more unpaid care work, women ran 93 per cent of FTSE 100 companies, and men made up 90 per cent of domestic-homicide victims – I doubt they would press it. Yes, there are situations in which men are at a disadvantage. But step back and look at the overall picture. We are still nowhere near equal.

Yes, there are other countries where patriarchy is still far more visible. In less than 200 years, British feminists have dismantled most of the legal structures which ensured women's second-class status. According to the law, we *should* be paid the same, have the same voting rights, have the same access to schools and universities, have the right to get a divorce without it leaving us penniless. The state *should* ensure that we have enough money to live without a man to support us. Until October 2019, Northern Irish women are still expected to bear their rapists' children. We still have seats reserved in our Parliament for aristocrats whose titles pass through the male line. And enforcing our rights is another matter altogether. It is illegal to sack a woman for getting pregnant – but does every pregnant women have the resources to go to a tribunal? The benefits system is supposed to ensure that women fleeing abusers are protected. But refuge funding is fragile, and the housing shortage means families end up stuck for years in mouldy B&Bs. Women selling sex are more stigmatised than the men buying it, and they are easier to prosecute than punters.

I told my friend to imagine a ruined house. To me, that's what patriarchy is. We all built the house together, as a response to biological and economic pressures. Overall, it benefits men more to keep the current structure intact, but some women do fine out of it too. For all of us, male and female, dismantling the house is frightening, an encounter with the unknown. For some of us, any house is better than uncertainty. We don't know what taking out *that* brick will do. We don't know if the new roof will keep out the rain. We don't know what storm will come along, tempting us to prop up its walls with the same old bricks.

Still, over the last two centuries, feminists have started to dismantle the house of patriarchy, and rebuild it with better materials. We took the roof off and replaced it with one that sheltered everyone better. We're pulling the walls down, little by little. But here's something that anyone who's lived in an old house will tell you. You instinctively step over the squeaky floorboard in the night. You crouch reflexively when going through the doorway, built when most people were six inches shorter. You move through that space guarding yourself against the loose nails and rough floors without even knowing that you're doing it.

That's patriarchy, too – the unconscious assumptions that affect how we move through the world. A hundred years ago, 'wife-beating' was an accepted part of marriage. Today's domestic abusers no longer have the protection of the law, but they are shaped by a society which says that men are more violent, that men should control their wives, that men turning their anger on a partner is forgivable if they apologise later, that being cheated on is an injury to their pride and status which demands a violent response. These ready-made excuses are handed to them by the legacy of patriarchy. They are the old walls of the crumbling house. *She provoked me. It's only her word against his. He was a nice guy – he must have snapped.* We navigate through the ruined house without noticing its boundaries.

*

Feminism is difficult. What do we make of the female boss who pro-motes useless women, so she can stay as queen bee? Or those who treat feminism as a protection racket, revelling in the power of decreeing who is sexist and who isn't? Or those who care deeply about misogyny – when it is demonstrated by their political oppon-ents? When do demands for 'inclusivity' become a bad-faith tactic, suggesting that feminism must solve all the world's problems at the same time? How much do women want to be treated the same as men, when our biology and lives are different to theirs? When femi-nism is more popular with professionals than manual workers, how does it rebut charges that it is too middle class?* How much can any one woman claim to speak for the other 3.5 billion? And if none of us can, then can there be a feminist movement at all?

There is one simple fact, though: feminism is still needed. In Saudi Arabia, a guardianship system means that women still cannot travel abroad without the consent of a male relative. In India, women abort female foetuses because they worry about the cost of raising a girl. In Japan, women are still expected to give up work when they have children. In El Salvador, women are jailed for having miscar-riages. In rural Nepal, women die in freezing cold 'menstrual huts'. In Britain, our main opposition party has never had a woman leader. Across the world, women own less capital, earn lower wages and do more unpaid caring labour.

You will notice how many of these disadvantages relate to having a female body. That has become an unfashionable concept among younger feminists, who are wary of making arguments based on biol-ogy. They worry about being 'exclusionary' because not all women have a uterus or vagina, or about 'reducing women to genitals'. But

* 'Almost one in three people from the top social grade ABC1 - those in managerial, administrative and professional occupations - called themselves a feminist in a 2018 [YouGov] poll,' reported the BBC in February 2019. 'This compared with one in five from grades C2DE, which include manual workers, state pensioners, casual workers, and the unemployed.'

come on – feminists have fought hard to stop our bodies being unspeakable. We've tried to bust the taboos against talking about menstruation, the menopause, or the gorier bits of childbirth. Are we really going to tidy all that away again? We can welcome transgender people into feminism without junking the idea that biology matters. I don't believe I have a 'female brain' – good at sewing, bad at starting wars – but I do have a female body. And as a class, women are oppressed because it is presumed that they can bear children. That still applies even though many of us – like me – are childless. The principle of self-definition should be respected, but it does not cancel out material reality. An episiotomy doesn't care how you identify.

*

As I wrote this book, I could feel myself changing too. A few years ago, I felt trapped in a prison of other people's expectations. In trying to be 'nice', I spread myself too thinly. I said Yes when I should have said No. I worried that people would think I was lazy, or selfish, or . . . difficult.

This book starts with a divorce, because leaving my first husband was the first truly difficult decision I made. It was the moment I became properly independent: of my family (who were disappointed), of my friends (several of whom I lost), and of the expectations of society. Ending my marriage meant I couldn't be a 'good girl' any more. Such an obvious failure removed the possibility of perfection, which was itself liberating.

What else did I learn by spending time with my Difficult Women? That no wonder reactionaries hate feminism: it works. Throughout my research I kept saying, 'But that's within my mother's lifetime!' My mum was born into a world where women still promised to obey their husbands, where it was legal to pay women less for the same work, where there were no domestic-violence refuges, where it was illegal to have an abortion, where girls (like her) were told they didn't need to worry too much about an education because they would get married. My sisters and I were the first generation of women in our family to go to university. We were born when it was still legal for a man to rape his wife, and when Maureen Colquhoun was the only openly lesbian MP ever. To my three nieces, many of the struggles in this book will seem as distant as the fight of the suffragettes did to me. There has never been a better time to be a woman, but there is still a long fight ahead.

Finally, I have begun to understand why both the 1910s and the 1970s were such important periods for feminism, and why there is a temptation to depict them as 'waves'. Both saw huge, disruptive legal changes. The first women got the vote in 1918, and the first female MP was elected; a year later the Sex Disqualification (Removal) Act allowed women to enter the civil service, become vets and accountants, and act as lawyers, jurors and magistrates. The 1970s brought equal pay, the first maternity leave legislation, the right not to be sacked for getting pregnant, and the Sex Discrimination Act.

But those two decades were also moments when other factors collided with feminist campaigning. The entry of 1.5 million women into the workforce thanks to the First World War killed off the 'Downton Abbey Britain' of deference and domestic servitude, and gave women a taste of economic freedom. The Second Wave coincided with the creation of the pill, which became available to married women on the NHS from 1961, and to single women from 1974.

Independence and control: these are the keystones of feminism. Your own money and your own body. The first can help you achieve Virginia Woolf's dream of 'a room of one's own'. The second stops you being seen purely as a mother, or potential mother, to more interesting human beings: men.

*

Many feminist historians dispute the 'wave' model, saying that it imposes a simplified narrative arc on messy, complicated events. I don't disagree. But it is still useful. Imagine the tide coming in – every wave crashes a little further up the shore, before being pulled back to sea. We creep closer to equality, before something drags us back. Misogyny mutates. Sexism and feminism are like bacteria and antibiotics; the latter forces the former to evolve. As soon as one argument against women's rights becomes useless, another takes its place.

In the First Wave, the same two-year period gave women the right to vote and a law which attempted to kick them back out of the workforce. In the 1990s, the backlash took the form of nostalgia, suggesting that freedom was making women miserable. They had chosen careers over families, and lived blighted half-lives as a result. 'The "man shortage" and the "infertility epidemic" are not the price of liberation,' wrote Susan Faludi in 1992. 'In fact, they do not even exist. But these chimeras are the chisels of a society-wide backlash. They are part of the relentless whittling-down process – much of it amounting to outright propaganda – that has served to stir women's private anxieties and break their political wills.'

Faludi was right. There is still no man shortage or infertility epidemic. The institution of marriage endures – reinvigorated by its extension to gay couples. Four out of five women have children. The further we get from the 1950s, the easier it is to romanticise that time: the smell of home-cooked food, the mother in her apron, the father whistling as he comes home from work. Weren't we happier when life was simpler, and everyone knew their place? But women are being instructed to pine for a golden age which never existed. Ask the poor women who left their own children at home to clean that idealised house. Ask the bored housewife popping pills and pouring her heart out to Selma James or Betty Friedan. Ask the woman whose husband came home drunk and aggressive, having spent his whole pay packet already.

In any case, it is not the job of feminism to make us happy. It never promised that. It's the job of feminism to make us equal. Each wave gets us a little closer. Each advance prompts a backlash. We march onward.

*

In 1992, the American feminist Rebecca Walker wrote an essay for *Ms.* magazine entitled 'Becoming the Third Wave'. It was prompted by the Anita Hill case, where incoming Supreme Court Justice Clarence Thomas (a black conservative) was accused of sexual harassment by Hill (a black woman). He called the process 'a high-tech lynching for uppity blacks', suggesting it was driven by white liberals who were worried he would roll back abortion rights. The case became the biggest landmark in American discussions of sexual harassment until the #MeToo movement of 2017. Walker ended her essay with a rallying cry: 'Let this dismissal of a woman's experience move you to anger. Turn that outrage into political power . . . I am not a post-feminism feminist. I am the Third Wave.'

If Walker was the Third Wave, we might call the flowering of feminist activism enabled by the Internet (and particularly social media) the Fourth Wave. Running from Everyday Sexism to #MeToo, it awakened a new generation to the idea that, no, sexism hadn't been solved by their mothers and grandmothers. They were moved to anger. They were not post-feminism. They were the Fourth Wave.

Underneath all the energy, though, a generational split could be observed. Some young activists saw the older generation as conservatives, wedded to fixed ideas of what men and women could be, when they felt gender was much more fluid and playful. Their mothers' generation were equally bemused. They had tried to smash beauty standards and restrictive ideas about the nuclear family. They struggled to understand why their daughters were so desperate to have a big wedding, to wear high heels, to pore over Photoshopped selfies. Feminism can, and must, contain all these contradictions. But we should still try to turn our outrage into political power. If there is to be a Fifth Wave, what should our focus be?

Here is my own messy, imperfect, difficult answer: structures, structures, structures. Social progress is fast, captivating, enthralling. It is ferociously beautiful to see the world change at the speed of speaking out. But those advances won't survive unless we do the hard work of economic and legal reform to support them. We need to capture the lightning in a bottle. Look around the world, around Europe even: socially conservative governments want to restrict access to abortion, and are thwarted by courts and by laws. *Structures*. The founders of the United States spent a great deal of time drawing up a constitution, writing into existence a form of government which could resist the natural propensity of rulers towards tyranny. In the age of Donald Trump, we should thank them. Similarly, feminists should not rely on cultural assumptions to protect us, any more than we were content for wives to rely on the generosity of their husbands. We don't want chivalry – or its modern equivalent, pious lip service. Our rights must not depend on the court of public opinion: are we having the right kind of divorce, the right kind of abortion, the right kind of need for a domestic-violence shelter? We should insist on a legal framework, backed by government funding, which treats us as equals to men and enforces any breaches of that contract. Caring labour must be supported by the state, otherwise the 'second shift' will fall more heavily on women, particularly in countries with an ageing population and few plans for how to deal with it. The Fourth Wave was beautifully noisy and attention-grabbing, but now we need concrete victories that will last in a way hashtag campaigns cannot. The public pillorying of a scattershot crew of outright villains, low-level creeps and the occasional innocent man by the #MeToo movement is no substitute for ensuring full and free access to employment tribunals.

You might notice that I haven't said much about some of the hardy perennials of feminist commentary: leg-shaving, bra-burning, pube-waxing. It's not because I don't care about them or haven't thought about them. Personally, I don't wear high heels (can't walk in them, and object to the principle of a shoe that makes your feet *less* comfortable). I didn't take my husband's surname. I don't watch porn. I'm 100 per cent pro-bra as I have a cup size that requires serious cantilevering. I shave my legs because my socialised disgust with female body hair runs so deep that I couldn't concentrate on anything else if I had furry calves.

But all of these are ultimately personal decisions, rather than collective actions. And since we live in a deeply individualist society, debates over women's choices on these topics will never struggle to get airtime. (That said, it's noticeable that articles on leg-shaving often seem to come from young, white, fair-haired women who are otherwise gender-conforming. The decision not to depilate reads differently if you're dark-skinned and naturally hairy, if you are a butch lesbian, or if you're getting on a bit.*) My most hated headline format – 'Can you be a feminist and . . . ' – will never, ever die. In this climate, the most radical thing we can do is resist treating everything as a personal choice, and resist turning feminism into a referendum on those choices. Let's swim against the tide by talking instead about what we can do *together*.

I recently came across the list of demands from the Women's Liberation Conferences of the 1970s. These were discussed and debated over several years, and the original four became seven. Here they are:

1. Equal pay.
2. Equal educational and job opportunities.
3. Free contraception and abortion on demand.
4. Free twenty-four-hour nurseries.
5. Legal and financial independence for all women.
6. The right to a self-defined sexuality. An end to discrimination against lesbians.

---

* I am available to write pieces on why it's a cute feminist statement not to pluck your chin hair. Call me.

7. Freedom for all women from intimidation by the threat or use of violence or sexual coercion regardless of marital status; and an end to the laws, assumptions and institutions which perpetuate male dominance and aggression to women.

Fifty years later, these demands are both a reminder of progress made and arguments lost. (Free twenty-four-hour nurseries! How did that one work out?) They hold up pretty well. We can revisit them now, in light of everything we know about intersectionality, and the idea of overlapping oppressions. Take point 2: equal educational and job opportunities. Are migrant women being shuffled into particular types of low-paid jobs, such as cleaning and care work? How are older women faring in an ageist job market, where new technology is outpacing our capacity to retrain workers? Do jobs which are fine-tuned to deliver maximum, inhuman efficiency – delivery drivers, warehouse packers – discriminate against women because of their biology? Is there somewhere for them to breast pump? Do they get enough loo breaks? How about disabled women?

Those seven simple demands trigger a chain of difficult questions. Bring it on. Let's get free universal childcare back on the agenda. Let's pursue equal pay audits, continuing the work of Harriet Harman. Let's make it so no woman has to sell sex to survive. Let's call for abortion on demand, and end the figleaf of two doctors signing off the procedure. Let's demand more money for adult social care, so the burden of an ageing society isn't shouldered by women. Let's lock up fewer women, who are rarely violent offenders, and who are often victims of abuse themselves. Let's close the immigration detention centre at Yarl's Wood, since the traumatised women there are low flight risks. Let's ensure female-dominated occupations get a living wage. Let's find ways to prosecute rape which are fair to everyone involved.

Yes, it sounds like feminism has a very long To Do list. But come on – aren't you used to that?

*

Finally, there are many biases in writing history, but I want to acknowledge just one. A while ago, I joked on Twitter that history wasn't written by the victors, but by the people whose handwriting is legible on microfiche. Unfortunately, it's true. The handwriting of aristocratic Constance Lytton is better than that of Annie Kenney, who left school at eleven. This book also features many women – Maureen Colquhoun, Sophia Jex-Blake, Erin Pizzey and Jackie Forster – who wrote memoirs, published or not. One of Jayaben Desai's many talents was gaining publicity for the Grunwick strike; she also gave extensive evidence at a public inquiry. If we want to preserve women's history, we need both first-hand accounts by activists and journalism written as it happens. Then we need a concerted effort to keep the memories of pioneering women alive. All histories are imperfect, imprecise, subjective. Mine certainly is. The answer is to have more of them.

EPILOGUE: A MANIFESTO FOR THE DIFFICULT WOMAN

The Difficult Woman is not rude, petty or mean. She is simply willing to be awkward, if the situation demands it; demanding, if the occasion requires it; and obstinate, if someone tries to fob her off. She does not care if 'that's the way it's always been done'. She is unmoved by the suggestion that it's 'natural' for women to act a certain way or accept a lower status. It probably isn't, and even if it is – so is dying from preventable diseases. No one thinks we should succumb to cholera just because it's traditional.

The Difficult Woman has strong beliefs, but these are based on evidence. She is kind, but not compliant. She refuses to be guilt-tripped into picking up the slack left by someone else. She refuses to put her needs last, always, particularly if the men around her could stand to do a bit more. She asks for a pay rise. She doesn't make the tea when it's not her job. She expects her brothers to visit their elderly parents as much as she does. She doesn't care if you call her a hairy-legged lesbian, because perhaps she knows several hairy-legged lesbians, and they have pretty sweet lives. Perhaps she *is* a hairy-legged lesbian, and she's OK with that. She doesn't believe him when he says he'll never do it again, honest, and anyway she provoked him. She knows she will be called humourless for talking about feminism, but behind closed doors she and her friends roar with laughter, perhaps at his expense. She doesn't care if you think she looks too feminine, or not feminine enough. When a man sits straddle-legged on the Tube as if his testicles were delicate nuclear waste, she doesn't squeeze her knees together automatically to make room. She doesn't apologise for 'always fixating on women's issues'. She wears shoes she can walk in. She wears clothes she can eat lunch in. She wears make-up because it's bright and fun, not as camouflage or penance for having pores or wrinkles. She fights for joint custody of the armrest at the cinema. She laughs showing her teeth. She snacks in public without apology. She tries not to worry about her neck. She has a group of friends with whom she can exchange gory details of periods, childbirth, menopause and all the other panoply of unspeakable female experiences. Her friends make unbelievably gross jokes which would blow the minds of 'shocking' male comedians.

She feels an affinity with other women, the texture of their lives and experiences. She believes that whatever separates them is less important than what unites them. She listens to women who have been places she will never go – perhaps including that strange country called Motherhood – and knows that their choices are not a commentary on her choices. She doesn't believe him when he tells her she'll never find anyone else. She knows it wasn't the right time for her to have a baby, and she stands by her decision. She is a survivor, not a victim. She doesn't feel guilty if she can't breastfeed. She won't relax her afro because society tells her it's not 'professional': she *is* a professional, and whatever hair she wants is just fine, thanks. She doesn't think that saying no makes her 'frigid'. She doesn't doubt her own worth when a younger man gets promoted above her because he didn't take time out of the workforce. She's not ashamed to talk about her own body, because it's not dirty or disgusting. She enjoys the shocked look on people's faces when they see a disabled woman talking about sex, and she rolls her eyes when a man grabs her wheelchair, acting like he's a bloody hero for 'helping'. She knows she deserves a proper pension. She reports it to the police. She doesn't look like the women in magazines, and she doesn't want to.

She doesn't accept leaving a marriage poorer than her partner, because raising a family is work too. She and her girlfriend laugh when people ask 'Which one of you is the man?', because neither of them have to be. She doesn't feel a failure because she doesn't want children. She won't be talked down to because she's carrying a screaming toddler. She refuses to be dismissed just because she has grey hair. She doesn't feel guilty when she gets home from work and just watches television, or looks at clothes on eBay, or reads a book: she deserves some time that's just for her. She asks her male peers what they earn. She leaves him.

Above all, she knows that no woman can fight all these battles alone, no matter how difficult she is. Sometimes, she feels tired, and worn out. But one thing saves her, because a Difficult Woman should always find herself some other Difficult Women. They will help her remember that she – like hundreds of others before her, for hundreds of years before her – can use her difficulty to make a difference. Together, Difficult Women can change the world.

ACKNOWLEDGEMENTS

There are many things I did not know about writing a book before I started (good job, too). One of the discoveries has been that it wasn't a lonely process. I'm sure errors have crept in, and these are my fault alone, but there would be many more without the help I've received.

The thanks begin with my agent, Andrew Gordon, for firmly coaxing me into submitting my proposal; my editor at Jonathan Cape, Bea Hemming, for wonderful notes which helped me refine the manuscript; Liz Dexter, for the transcriptions (and encouragement); and Alice Robinson, for her research. I am grateful to all my interviewees, and to Stephen Bourne and Keith Howes for their memories of Jackie Forster; Harriet Harman and Clare Gosbee, for access to Harriet's (terrifying) archive of press clippings; and the staff at the LSE women's library, Wellcome Library, Glasgow Women's Library, Bodleian library, Warwick University Library and UEA library. Lyndsey Jenkins pointed me towards the friendship of Annie Kenney and Constance Lytton, subjects of her own fine biographies, and read the 'Vote' chapter before publication (bonus content: the anonymous letter slagging off the Pethick Lawrences was written by Jessie Kenney).

Debbie Cameron, Senia Peseta and the Women in the Humanities research group at Oxford supported me with an honorary writing fellowship, while Abigail Williams, Mark Damazer and the fellows of St Peter's College, Oxford, made me a visiting member of the college for a term. Both allowed me to spend time talking to students and holed up in the Bodleian reliving my (not very) misspent youth. On that note, thank you Mum and Dad for never following through on your threat not to pay my university tuition fees 'if you get one more piercing'.

Jason Cowley and the former and current staff of the *New Statesman* – particularly my podcast partner Stephen Bush, audio queen Caroline Crampton and features supremo Tom Gatti – were extremely understanding of my desire to go part-time, even though it made their lives trickier. A few small sections of this book appeared first in the *New Statesman*, and are reproduced with permission.

Any Difficult Woman needs comrades and inspirations, and I've been very lucky in mine. I can't recommend the work of Chimamanda Ngozi Adichie, Deborah Cameron and Caitlin Moran strongly enough. My life would be poorer without the energy of Caroline Criado Perez, the ferocity of Sarah Ditum, the wit of Hadley Freeman, the ingenuity of Tracy King, the creativity of Gia Milinovich, the intelligence of Rebecca Reilly-Cooper and the bravery of Janice Turner.

Some men are OK, too, I suppose: thank you to Alex Garland, for all his inspiration; Matt Gould, for his insight; Max Bolt for talking about leisure economies while a ten-week-old dozed in a sling on his chest; and Oli Franklin-Wallis, whose editing skills rescued a chapter which had swollen to twice its natural size. Robert Icke's careful notes sharpened my prose and his brutally insightful questions made this book better in a hundred ways. Thanks also to him for the title, the epigram and all the drama. (Sorry I didn't purge all the brackets.)

Emma Pritchard selflessly volunteered to read a draft from the perspective of The Youth; while Caroline 'Christabel' Criado Perez commented as someone who was *also* wrestling with a book and therefore had to put up with my whingeing. Sarah Ditum gave up her precious time to read the 'Time' chapter. Dr Frances Ryan and Fiona Rutherford made excellent suggestions for the Manifesto. My mother-in-law Gill Haynes kindly read the 'Vote' chapter, and I hope won't read any of the dirty bits now the whole book is out. Laura McInerney demonstrated exactly why we've been friends for fifteen years as she buoyed me with the confident assertion that I could 'knock it out in three months if I really tried'.

Last, and most: Jonathan, for the love, tea and feedback (not necessarily in that order).

SOURCES AND FURTHER READING

The following books provided key material for chapters:

Sundari Anitha and Ruth Pearson, *Striking Women* (Lawrence & Wishart, 2018)

Diane Atkinson, *The Criminal Conversation of Mrs Norton* (Arrow, 2013)

Diane Atkinson, *Rise Up Women!* (Bloomsbury, 2018)

Maureen Colquhoun, *A Woman in the House* (Scan Publishing, 1980)

Anna Coote and Tess Gill, *Women's Rights: A Practical Guide* (Penguin, 1974)

Anna Coote and Beatrix Campbell, *Sweet Freedom* (Picador, 1982)

Jack Dromey and Graham Taylor, *Grunwick: The Workers' Story* (Lawrence & Wishart, 2nd revised edition, 2016)

Millicent Fawcett, *What I Remember* (Putnam, 1924)

Ruth Hall, ed., *Dear Dr Stopes: Sex in the 1920s* (Penguin, new edition, 1981)

Elizabeth Homans, *Wages for Housework in the Decade of Women's Liberation* (Kindle edition)

Barbara Jacobs, *The Dick, Kerr Ladies* (Robinson, 2004)

Selma James, *Sex, Race and Class* (PM Press, 2012)

Lyndsey Jenkins, *Lady Constance Lytton: Aristocrat, Suffragette, Martyr* (Silvertail Books, 2018)

Lyndsey Jenkins, unpublished thesis on Annie Kenney (courtesy of the author, 2018)

Sophia Jex-Blake, *Medical Women: A Thesis and a History* (Hamilton, Adams & Co, 1886; accessed at https://archive.org/details/medicalwomenthes00jexb/page/n6)

Annie Kenney, *Memories of a Militant* (Edward Arnold & Co, 1924)

Anna Kessel, *Eat Sweat Play: How Sports Can Change Our Lives* (Macmillan, 2016)

Constance Lytton, *Prisons and Prisoners* (first published 1914; reprinted by Broadview Press, 2008)

Paulette Perhach, 'A Story of a Fuck-Off Fund', thebillfold.com, 20 January 2016

Erin Pizzey, *Prone to Violence* (Hamlyn, 1982)

Erin Pizzey, *This Way to the Revolution* (Peter Owen, 2013)

Katha Pollitt, *PRO: Reclaiming Abortion Rights* (Picador, 2014)

Jane Robinson, *Bluestockings: The Remarkable Story of the First Women to Fight for an Education* (Penguin, 2010)

Joe Rogaly, *Grunwick* (Penguin, 1977)

Mary Roach, *Bonk: The Curious Coupling of Science and Sex* (Canongate, 2009)

June Rose, *Marie Stopes and the Sexual Revolution* (Faber & Faber, 1992)

Arlie Russell Hochschild, *The Second Shift* (First published 1989, revised edition, Penguin, 2012)

Brigid Schulte, *Overwhelmed* (Bloomsbury, 2015)

Tim Tate, *Girls With Balls: The Secret History of Women's Football* (John Blake, 2013)

Margaret Georgina Todd, *The Life of Sophia Jex-Blake* (Macmillan, 1918)

Michelene Wandor, *Once A Feminist* (Vintage, 1990)

The following books and articles were generally useful in developing my thinking:

Rebecca Abrams, *The Playful Self* (Fourth Estate, 1997)

Chimamanda Ngozi Adichie, *We Should All Be Feminists* (4th Estate, 2014)

Anita Anand, *Sophia: Princess, Suffragette, Revolutionary* (Bloomsbury, 2015)

Margaret Atwood, *The Handmaid's Tale* (first published 1985, this edition, Vintage 2010)

Simone de Beauvoir, *The Second Sex* (first published 1949, this edition, Vintage Classics 1997)

Beverley Bryan, Stella Dadzie and Suzanne Scafe, *Heart of the Race: Black Women's Lives in Britain* (Virago, 1985)

Deborah Cameron, *On Language and Sexual Politics* (Routledge, 2006) – and everything else she's written!

Barbara Castle, *Fighting All the Way* (Macmillan, 1993)

Kira Cochrane, ed., *Women of the Revolution: Forty Years of Feminism* (Guardian Books, 2012)

Rose Collis, *Portraits to the Wall: Historic Lesbian Lives Unveiled* (first published 1994, this edition, Bloomsbury Academic, 2016)

Elizabeth Crawford, *The Women's Suffrage Movement* (Routledge, 2000)

Susan Faludi, *Backlash: The Undeclared War Against Women* (Vintage, 1993)

Susan Faludi, *In the Darkroom* (Metropolitan Books, 2016)

Cordelia Fine, *Delusions of Gender* (Icon Books, 2010)

Betty Friedan, *The Feminine Mystique* (first published 1963; this edition, Penguin, 2010)

Veronica Groocock, ed., *Changing Our Lives: Lesbian Passions, Politics, Priorities* (Cassell, 1995)

Lesley Hall, ed., *Outspoken Women: An Anthology of Women's Writing on Sex, 1870–1969* (Routledge, 2005)

Lesley Hall, 'Situating Stopes', archived at lesleyahall.net/stopes.htm

Cicely Hamilton, *Marriage as a Trade* (Moffatt, Yard and Company, 1909)

Gillian Hanscombe and Jackie Forster, *Rocking the Cradle: Lesbian Mothers* (Sheba Feminist Publishers, 1982)

Sandra Holton and June Purvis, eds., *Votes For Women* (Routledge, 1999)

bell hooks, Feminist Theory: From Margin to Center (Routledge, 1984)

Sandra Horley, *Power and Control* (Vermilion, 2002)

Jill Johnston, *Lesbian Nation* (Simon & Schuster, 1973)

Ariel Levy, *Female Chauvinist Pigs* (Simon & Schuster, 2005)

Ariel Levy, *The Rules Do Not Apply* (Fleet, 2018)

Audre Lorde, *Sister Outsider* (first published 1984; this edition Ten Speed Press, 2007)

Caitlin Moran, *How to Be a Woman* (Ebury Press, 2011)

Emily Nagoski, *Come As You Are* (Scribe, 2015)

Suzanne Neild and Rosalind Pearson, *Women Like Us* (The Women's Press, 1992)

Anne Perkins, *Red Queen: The Authorised Biography of Barbara Castle* (Pan, 2004)

Jess Phillips, *Everywoman* (Windmill, 2018)

The Radicalesbians, *The Woman-Identified Woman* (available at library.duke.edu, 1970)

David Spiegelhalter, *Sex By Numbers* (Wellcome Collection, 2015)

Amrit Wilson, *Finding A Voice: Asian Women in Britain* (first published 1988; this edition Daraja Press, 2018)

Naomi Wolf, *The Beauty Myth* (Chatto & Windus, 1990)

INDEX

abortion, 3, 5, 89, 91–2, 271, 279–302
  in Northern Ireland, 279–82,
    288–91, 299–302
  in the Republic of Ireland, 280,
    291–9
  in the United States, 279, 283–6,
    296, 298
Abortion Act (1967), 280–81, 284, 291
Active Birth Centre, London, 87
Adichie, Chimamanda Ngozi, 5, 118
adultery, 15–16, 19
Agbeze, Ama, 117–21, 126
ageism, 310
Ainsworth, Laura, 47
Alabama, United States, 285
Alden, Malcolm, 129, 133
Ali, Nimko, 314
American Quarterly, 86
anal sex, 81, 88
'Angel in the House, The'
    (Patmore), 306–7
Anglin, Caoimhe, 293–5, 299
Angry Brigade, 168
Anitha, Sundari, 130–31, 153–4
Anthony, Susan B., 104
anti-Semitism, 88, 205
Apex union, 139
Apple, 230

Arena Three magazine, 200
Arsenal F.C., 111
Arsenal Ladies F.C., 124
Arulkumaran, Sabaratnam, 292–3
Ashley, Jack, 160–61
Astor, David, 161
Atkinson, Diane, 15–16, 19, 46
Atkinson, Ti-Grace, 6
Atwood, Margaret, 3, 21
au pairs, 28
Austen, Jane, 3
Australia, 45, 118–19, 121

'bad sex', 81–2
Bajracharya, Chanira, 237
Balance of the Sexes Act (1975), 196, 201
Balding, Clare, 121
Baldwin, James, 304
Balfour, Arthur, 54–5
Balfour, Betty, 54, 63, 310
Barnard College, United States, 98
Barres, Ben, 308
Barrow-in-Furness, 245
Bartholin, Caspar, 78
Beard, Mary, 310
de Beauvoir, Simone, 4, 23, 70
'Becoming the Third Wave'
    (Walker), 321

Behind the Mask (gay rights
    group), 209
Belfast, Northern Ireland, 89, 280
Bell, John, 231
Bellevue Zoo, Belfast, 56
Benn, Tony, 61
Bennett, Theresa, 125
Bevan, Aneurin, 136
Bhudia, Devshi, 132
Biles, Simone, 114
Billfold, 34
Billinghurst, Rosa May, 54
Bindel, Julie, 185–7, 190
birth control, *see* contraception
birth rates, 313
BJOG journal, 83
'Black Friday' (18 November 1910), 54
Blackstone, William, 14
Blair, Tony, 145, 236, 288
Bloody Sunday Massacre (1972), 288
Bloomer, Amelia, 104
Bolsonaro, Jair, 5
Bomet, Kenya, 274
Bonaparte, Marie, 78–9, 83, 85
Bonk (Roach), 79
Boston Marathon, 102, 227
Bourne, Stephen, 198, 219
Boustead, Carrie, 103
Boy George, 161
bra-burning, 322–3
Brackenbury, Marie, 60
Brazil, 5
Brereton, Simon, 242, 244
Brexit, 152, 295, 297
British Broadcasting Corporation
    (BBC), 66, 114, 119, 141, 148, 155
    BBC Sports Personality of the
        Year, 121
British Council, 213
British Crime Survey (2018), 181

British Ladies' F.C., 102
British Pregnancy Advisory
    Service, 288
British Union of Fascists, 56
Brooks, Kim, 270–71
Brown, Gordon, 143, 147, 149–50
Brown, John, 228–9
Browne, Stella, 89
Bruce, Fiona, 284
Bullingdon Club, 24
Bulwer-Lytton, Elizabeth, 51, 59
Bulwer-Lytton, Emily, 51
Bulwer-Lytton, Lady Constance
    Georgina, *see* Lytton, Constance
Bulwer-Lytton, Victor, 50, 53
Bunsee, Bennie, 138
Burns, Robert, 224
BuzzFeed, 152

Callaghan, Jim, 142
Cambridge University, 233, 236
Cameron, David, 150
Cameron, Deborah, 228–9, 310–11
Campaign for Homosexual Equality,
    207, 214
Campbell, Beatrix, 71–2, 77, 162,
    187, 257
Campbell, Sir John, 16
Canada, 124, 274
'cancel culture', 6
Carneiro, Eva, 114
Cass Business School, 149
Cassidy, Jules, 199
Castle, Barbara, 33–4, 134–5, 141–2, 151
Cat and Mouse Act (1913), 47
Catholicism, 280, 282
Challen, David, 180–81, 183
Challen, Richard, 180–81, 183
Challen, Sally, 180–81, 183, 185
Chanel, Coco, 1–2

Chelsea F.C., 114
Cheltenham Ladies College, 233
child abuse, 180, 270, 285
child neglect, 269–71
child support, 59
childbirth, 86–7, 258, 283–4
   fertility, 206–7, 320
   miscarriage, 231, 281, 287
   parental leave, 145, 242, 247, 266,
      272, 301, 313, 319
   see also abortion; contraception
childcare, 5, 145, 241, 324
children *see* parenthood
China, 164, 167, 239, 285
Chiswick Aid Centre, 159, 161–2,
   169, 178–9
Christianity, 8, 280, 312
Church of England, 55
Churchill, Winston, 41, 53, 68, 108
civil partnerships, 32
civil rights movement,
   United States, 279
Clarke, Emma, 103
Clarke, Ken, 7
Clayton, Ashley, 241–2
Clegg, Nick, 150
Clinton, Bill, 15, 72
Clinton, Hillary, 146
clitoris, 77–80, 83
Clue (period tracker), 231
'cohabitation rule', 27
Collabra, 270
Colquhoun, Keith, 194, 204
Colquhoun, Mary, 212–13
Colquhoun, Maureen, 193–6,
   200–206, 208, 211–14, 219–20,
   246, 319
Commonwealth Games, 121
Commonwealth Immigrants Act
   (1968), 130

Conservative Party, 143, 150, 255,
   298, 300
contraception, 27–8, 87–9, 91–2, 319
Conundrum (Morris), 308
Cooper, Brittney, 171
Coote, Anna, 25, 27–9, 71–2, 77, 162, 187
Corbyn, Jeremy, 151, 205, 208
Covent Garden Market Authority, 202
Craig, Keita, 166
Craigie, Jill, 67
Creasy, Stella, 67, 288, 300, 314
Creighton, Sarah M., 83
Crenshaw, Kimberlé Williams, 137, 169
Crickard, Helen, 300
Criminal Conversation of Mrs Norton,
   The (Atkinson), 15
Criminal Law Amendment Act
   (1885), 211
Crouch, Naomi S., 83
Cumberbatch, Benedict, 24
custody laws, 17–19, 36, 207, 251
Custody of Infants Act (1839), 19, 36
cycling, 84, 104

Dagenham women's strike (1968),
   77, 134–6
Dahl, Roald, 242
Daily Express, 26
Daily Mail, 67, 145, 162, 204, 310
Daily News, 107
Dalla Costa, Mariarosa, 255
Daltrey, Roger, 161
Dambusters (film), 196
Das Kapital (Marx), 254
Davidson, Ruth, 219
Davison, Emily, 47, 55–6, 61, 64,
   68, 233
Dederer, Claire, 110
DeGeneres, Ellen, 219
DeGraffenreid, Emma, 137

Democratic Unionist Party (DUP), 300

Dempster, Nigel, 204

Derry/Londonderry, 288, 290, 302

Desai, Jayaben, 130–34, 137, 140–43, 151, 153–5, 159, 306, 309, 325

Desai, Sunil, 129–30, 132–4, 139, 155

Devlin, Colette, 279–81, 289–92, 299–302

Dick, Kerr Ladies F.C., 101, 104–8, 110, 112, 124

Dick, Kerr Ladies, The (Jacobs), 104

Dick, W. B., 105

Difficult Women (Gay), 7

Difficult Women (Plante), 7

Dimmock, Charlie, 120

Diva magazine, 219

divorce, 13–23, 30–38, 72, 301
  no-fault divorce, 31–2, 37
  right to, 36–7

Dixie, Lady Florence, 102–3

domestic violence, 159–63, 165–6, 173–84, 187–90, 316
  against men, 163–4, 179–84, 188–90
  coercive control, 175–8, 181
  intimate-partner violence (IPV), 174, 180

Domestic Violence Act (1976), 187

Donegal, Republic of Ireland, 299

Douglas, James, 78

Douglass, Frederick, 3–4

Dromey, Jack, 130, 139–41, 143–5, 155

Drummond, Flora, 61

Dublin, Republic of Ireland, 296–9

Dugdale, Una, 55

Duncan Smith, Iain, 24, 33

Dundee, Scotland, 56

Durbar Square, Nepal, 236

Durham University, 234

Dworkin, Andrea, 3, 186, 266, 312

East London Federation, 43

Eat Sweat Play: How Sports Can Change Our Lives (Kessel), 113

Edinburgh, Scotland, 223–5, 227–31

'Edinburgh Seven', 223–5, 227–8, 232, 234–5

education, 223–48
  in Britain, 240–41, 247
  equal opportunities, 245–8
  female education restrictions, 238–40
  gender quotas, 239, 246
  male-dominated subjects, 239–40
  medicine, 223–36, 239–40
  teachers, 241–2, 247
  underachievement of boys, 242–5

Eighth Amendment (Republic of Ireland), 291–4, 296, 299

El Salvador, 287, 317

El Vino, London, 23–7

Elam, Paul, 163, 184–5

Elbowroom, The, 296

Elizabeth I, Queen of England, 233

Elizabeth II, Queen of the United Kingdom, 55, 200

Ellis, Havelock, 89

Emma (comic artist), 265

employment, 109, 112, 129–55, 251–2, 273–4
  equal opportunities, 194–6, 201–3, 245–8
  equal pay, 112, 135
  gender inequality, 243, 247, 308
  gender pay gap, 148–50, 259–60, 268, 314
  gender quotas, 246
  industrial disputes, 77, 107, 110, 129–43, 153–4
  and parenthood, 267–9

trade unions, 129–30, 133–4,
 136–43, 145, 151–4
tribunals, 152
workers' rights, 77, 131–2, 135, 152–3
workplace sexual harassment, 4, 152
see also housework; unemployment;
 unpaid work
Engels, Friedrich, 252, 254
England Roses netball team, 121
English Collective of Prostitutes
 (ECP), 256
English Defence League (EDL), 169
Equal Opportunities Commission, 195
Equal Pay Act (1970), 135, 203
Equalities Office, 144–5, 147–8
Equality Act (2010), 149–50
erectile dysfunction, 82
eugenics, 90–92
European Union, 152, 288
Eve Was Framed (Kennedy), 158
Everyday Stories project, 293, 295

Facebook, 296
faked orgasm, 80–82
Falloppio, Gabriele, 78
'false consciousness', 255
Faludi, Susan, 320
Family Allowance, 255–6
Family Planning Association, 91
Fawcett, Millicent, 58–9, 61–2, 68, 93,
 148, 202, 228, 233, 309
Fawcett Society, 148
female genital mutilation (FGM),
 79, 314
'female socialisation', 308–9
Feminine Mystique, The (Friedan),
 166, 253–4
feminism
 definition of, 5, 186

First Wave, 320
Second Wave, 6, 28–9, 33, 35, 159,
 194, 319
Third Wave, 321
Fourth Wave, 5, 321, 321–2
fertility, 206–7, 320
Fey, Tina, 282
Fighting All the Way (Castle), 135
Fihlani, Pumza, 209
Financial Times, 243
Finer Report (1974), 59
Fleet Street, London, 23–7, 134
Fleshlight, 97
football, 101–12, 114–16, 123–6
Football Association, 101, 106, 108,
 111–12, 124–5
force-feeding, 46–9, 51–4, 60
Ford Motors, 77, 134–6
foreplay, 80
Forster, Jackie, 196–201, 206–8, 211,
 214, 217–19
Forster, Peter, 196, 198
Frankland, Alfred, 106, 112, 124
Freeman, Jo, 169–70, 172
Freemasons, 24–5
Freud, Sigmund, 4, 77–9
Friedan, Betty, 166, 217–18, 253–4
'fuck-off fund', 35–7
Furlong, Julie, 216

'G spot', 78
Gadsby, Hannah, 216
Galloway, George, 144
Gandhi, Indira, 140
Gandhi, Mahatma, 68, 131, 140
Garrett Anderson, Elizabeth,
 226–7, 232–4
Garrick Club, London, 24
Gate Gourmet strike (2005), 154

Gates, Reginald Ruggles, 73–4, 90
Gateways club, 200
gay marriage, *see* same-sex marriage
gay rights *see* LGBT rights
Gay News, 198
Gay, Roxane, 7
'gender critical' feminists, 312
gender pay gap, 148–50, 259–60,
    268, 314
gender stereotypes, 305–9
General Medical Council, 235
General Motors, 137
General Strike (1926), 134
genitalia, 78–9, 83
Geymonat, Melania, 210
Gill, Tess, 23–9, 165, 173, 207,
    228, 251
Gilman, Charlotte Perkins, 251, 307
Girls With Balls (Tate), 102
Glasgow Women's Library, 196–7, 218
Goldberg, Michelle, 169, 171
Good Friday Agreement (1998), 282
Goodison Park, 108
Goodnight Stories for Rebel Girls
    (Favilli), 1
Google, 296
Gracie, Carrie, 148
Gräfenberg, Ernst, 78
Grayling, Chris, 152
Green Lady Hostel, Littlehampton, 45
Greenham Common protests, 310
Greer, Germaine, 3, 7, 92–3
Griffith Joyner, Florence (Flo-Jo), 114
Groocock, Veronica, 198
Ground Force (TV series), 120
Grunwick (Taylor), 155
Grunwick dispute (1976–8), 129–34,
    137, 139–43, 151, 153–5
Guardian, 57, 150, 162, 166, 184, 219,
    240, 252, 257, 293

Guardiola, Pep, 123–4
Gunter, Jen, 82–4

Halappanavar, Savita, 292–3, 296, 298
Hale, Brenda, Baroness Hale of
    Richmond, 30–32
Hall, Lesley, 84–5, 89–93
Hall, Radclyffe, 194
Halperin-Kaddari, Ruth, 281
Handmaid's Tale, The (Atwood), 21–2
Hanscombe, Gill, 219
Hardie, Keir, 40, 43
Harlequin Ladies rugby team, 119
Harman, Harriet, 144–5, 147–51, 314
Harrell, Debra, 270
Harry, Duke of Sussex, 55
Hart, Luke, 176–8, 184
Hart, Ryan, 176–7, 184
Harvard University, 308
Hazarika, Ayesha, 143–4, 147–51
Heart of Midlothian F.C., 104, 107
Hewitt, Patricia, 144
Hewlett, Maurice, 73
Hicks, Bill, 278
Hill, Anita, 321
Hill, Octavia, 225
Hillsborough disaster (1989), 142
Hinduism, 236–7
Hitler, Adolf, 88
Hochschild, Adam, 273
Hochschild, Arlie Russell, 128, 262–7,
    272–3, 275
Hollywood Reporter, 7
homosexuality, 193–220
    homophobia, 209–11, 213
    lesbian separatism, 217
    lesbianism, 86, 88, 168, 193–4,
        197–200, 204–20
    LGBT rights, 135, 152, 197, 203, 210,
        214, 214–15, 217

and parenthood, 206–7, 272
police attitude to, 210
same-sex marriage, 14, 32, 36, 62, 299, 312
Honest Ribbon website, 180
Horgan, Goretti, 289–90
'horizontal hostility', 255
Housby, Helen, 121
House of Lords, 67, 196
housework, 252–8, 265, 272, 275
see also unpaid work
How to Be a Woman (Moran), 115, 168–9, 186
Howes, Keith, 198
Humphreys, Emma, 185
Humphrys, John, 148
Hussein, Leyla, 314

Ignatieff, Michael, 205
immigration, 28, 130–31, 136–7, 188, 205
Imperial College, London, 240
Imperial Typewriters, 138–9
in vitro fertilisation (IVF), 206–8
Income of Nations, The (Studenski), 275
Independent, 162, 287
Independent Labour Party, 43
India, 5, 130, 140, 284, 317
Indiana University, 268
industrial disputes, 77, 107, 110, 130–43, 153–4
Dagenham (1968), 77, 134–6
Gate Gourmet (2005), 154
General Strike (1926), 134
Grunwick (1976–8), 129–34, 137, 139–43, 151, 153–5
police attitude to, 142–3
International Jewish Anti-Zionist Network, 256
International Labour Organisation, 195
'intersectionality', 43, 137, 170–73

Inverdale, John, 123
Invisible Women (Criado Perez), 230, 257
Iran, 280
Iraq, 313
Ireland, Republic of, 3, 37, 314
abortion rights, 280, 291–9
see also Northern Ireland
Irish abortion referendum (May 2018), 295–9
Irish Home Rule, 44, 136
Irish Times, 291
Islam, 280
Israel, 47–8, 256, 289

Jacobs, Barbara, 101, 104, 107
Jacobs, Emma, 243, 245
James, C. L. R., 253
James, Selma, 252–8, 275
Jameson, Jenna, 15
Janner, Greville, 195
Japan, 239, 317
Jenkins, Lyndsey, 47
Jenkins, Roy, 201
Jex-Blake, Sophia, 223–30, 232–6, 245, 247–8, 251
Johannesburg, South Africa, 209
Johnson, Virginia E., 85
Johnston, Jill, 217
Jones, Kenney, 161
Jones, Marshae, 285–6
Joseph, Keith, 143
judicial system, 30–31
Justice for Women, 185

kamlari, 237
Kathmandu, Nepal, 236–8
Kavanaugh, Brett, 3, 298
Kelly, Grace, 196
Kennedy, Anthony, 298

Kennedy, Florynce, 254–5
Kennedy, Helena, 158
Kenney Taylor, Warwick, 63, 66
Kenney, Annie, 42–6, 49–51, 54–5,
    57–60, 62–8, 105, 325
Kenney, Jessie, 49, 56, 59, 63, 65–6
Kenny, Louise, 291
Ker, Alice, 53–4
Kerr, John, 105
Kessel, Anna, 113–17, 125
Keynes, John Maynard, 274
King, Billie Jean, 114, 121
King, Diana, 279–81, 289–91, 296,
    299–302
Kinsey, Alfred, 85–6
Knighton, A. L., 111
Knock golf club, 56
Koedt, Anne, 77, 80–81, 93
kumari, 236–8
Kuper, Simon, 243, 245

labia, 83–4
Labour Party, 43, 107, 143–5, 147,
    150–51, 193, 205–6, 219–20, 274
Ladies of Llangollen, 193
Lamb, William, 2nd Viscount
    Melbourne, 14–17
language, 228–9, 311
Lansbury, George, 43
Larkin, Philip, 96
Late, Late Show, The (TV
    programme), 298
Lawrence, Jennifer, 7
Leeds Revolutionary Feminist
    Group, 217
leg-shaving, 322–3
leisure time, 251, 260–64, 267
Lenin, Vladimir, 256
Lenton, Lilian, 48
Lesbian Nation (Johnston), 217

lesbianism see homosexuality
Letts, Quentin, 145
Lewinsky, Monica, 15
LGBT rights, 135, 152, 197, 203, 210,
    214, 214–15, 217
Liberal Democrats, 150
Liberal Party, 41
Lih-Mei Liao, 83
Lindsay, Lilian, 230
Linehan, Graham, 293
Linehan, Helen, 293
Lister, Anne, 193–4, 215–16
Lloyd George, David, 51, 55
Lloyd, Jillian, 83
Lloyds Bank, 109
London Evening News, 207–8
London Fashion Week, 115
London Marathon, 113
London Pulse, 118
Loofbourow, Lili, 81–2
Lozano, Luis, 244
Lutyens, Emily, 54
Lytton, Constance, 46–7, 49–55, 57,
    59–60, 63–4, 87, 310, 325

MacKinnon, Catharine, 312
Macrander, Hester, 250
Mahfouz, Sabrina, 103
Major, John, 288
Makin, Bathsua, 232
Making of the Black Working Class in
    Britain, The (Ramdin), 138
Malcolm X, 21
male chauvinism, 81
Manchester City F.C., 123
Mansfield, 137
marathons, 102, 113, 227
Marie Stopes clinics, 288
    see also Stopes, Marie
Marion, Kitty, 49

Markle, Meghan, 55
marriage, 37–8, 55, 251–4
  annulment, 37, 74
  marriage rights, 13–14, 18,
    20–22, 27–9
  married names, 21–3
  prenuptial agreements, 29
  separation, 31–2
  see also divorce
Married Love (Stopes), 75–7, 85, 87–9
Married Woman (Maintenance) Act
  (1920), 59
Married Women's Property Act
  (1870), 14, 36
Marx, Karl, 254
Marxism, 254–5, 266
Mary Poppins (Travers), 44
Masood, Khalid, 177
Masters, William H., 86
masturbation, 71, 78–9, 85
maternity leave, 145, 242, 247, 301, 319
  see also parental leave
Matrimonial Causes Act (1857), 19
Matrimonial Causes Act (1923), 19
Matters, Muriel, 60–61
Matthews, Helen, 102–3
Maude, Aylmer, 74–5, 86
Mauresmo, Amélie, 123
May, Theresa, 7, 67
#MeToo movement, 5, 97–8, 152,
  321–2
Mean Girls (film), 282
Medical Act (1858), 226
Medical Act (1876), 235
Medical Women: A Thesis and A
  History (Jex-Blake), 223
Melbourne, Lord, see Lamb, William,
  2nd Viscount Melbourne
Meltiv, Danielle and Sasha, 270
Memories of a Militant (Kenney), 45

Men Explain Things to Me (Solnit), 4
men's rights movement, 163–4,
  179–80, 183, 188
menstruation, 75, 230–31, 238–9
Metallurgical Company,
  Newcastle, 105
Metamorphosis (Forster), 208
Michaels, Sheila, 21
Middlesex Hospital, 226
migrant workers, 130–34, 136–8,
  142–3, 153–5
Miller, Arthur, 81
Miller, Claire Cain, 269
Miller, Millie, 204
Minto, Catherine L., 83
miscarriage, 231, 281, 287
Miss World pageant (1970), 168
Mitchell, Hannah, 44, 251
Modi, Narendra, 5
Moore, Anna, 184
Moran, Caitlin, 82, 115, 168–9,
  172, 186
Morantz, Regina Markell, 86
Morris, Jan, 308–9
mortgage applications, 28
Mother Jones magazine, 270
motherhood see parenthood
'Mouse Castle', 60
'Mrs Graham's XI', 102
Ms magazine, 21, 169, 321
Muholi, Zanele, 209
Muirfield golf club, 24
Mullaly, Claire, 153
Mumsnet, 259
munitionettes, 104, 136
Murdoch, Rupert, 134
Murray, Andy, 121–3
Murray, Judy, 122
Murray, Len, 143
My Story (Parks), 279

Nanette (TV show), 216
natalism, 313
Nation, 169
National Association for the
    Advancement of Colored
    People, 279
National Children's Bureau, 207
National Council for Civil
    Liberties, 24
National Farmers' Union, 202
National Women's Conference, 162
Nature magazine, 308
Navratilova, Martina, 114
Nazism, 2, 90
Neild, Suzanne, 197, 208–9
Nepal, 236–9, 247, 317
Nepalganj, Nepal, 237–8
netball, 117–19, 121
Netherlands, 116, 274
Network Rail, 202
Neville, Phil, 116
New England Hospital for Women
    and Children, 226
New Statesman, 168, 310
New York Times, 83, 268, 269, 271
Newcastle United F.C., 111
Nia (charity), 181
Nigeria, 313
non-binary people, 216, 297
Northern Ireland, 5, 314, 315
    abortion rights, 279–82, 288–91,
    299–302
Northern Ireland Life and Times
    survey (2016), 300
Norton, Brinsley, 17, 19
Norton, Caroline, 14–20, 36–7, 251
Norton, Fletcher, 17, 19
Norton, George, 14–19, 37
Norton, William Charles, 17, 19

'Notes on the Anatomical Causes of
    Frigidity in Women'
    (Bonaparte), 79
NSPCC (National Society for the
    Prevention of Cruelty to
    Children), 269
Nussbaum, Emily, 306

O'Connor, Orla, 297–9
O'Kane, Kitty, 279–81, 289–91, 297,
    299–302
Observer, 161
Offences Against the Person Act
    (1828), 160
Offences Against the Person Act
    (1861), 281, 290, 300
Olympic Games, 102, 113, 123, 227
On Language and Sexual Politics
    (Cameron), 229
online feminism, 169–71
Onlywomen Press, 217
Operation Lighthouse (Luke & Ryan
    Hart), 184
oral sex, 72
Organisation for Economic
    Co-operation and
    Development, 242–3
orgasm, 71–2, 75, 77–80, 85–6
Orgreave, Battle of (1984), 142
Orwell, Sonia, 7
Osborne, George, 150
Our Ostriches (Stopes), 75
Overwhelmed (Schulte), 260, 262, 273
Oxford University, 228–9

Paisley, Ian, 280
Pakistan, 239
Palestine, 47, 256
Pall Mall Gazette, 102

Pankhurst family, 3, 57–8, 62, 93
Pankhurst, Adela, 42
Pankhurst, Christabel, 41–3, 45, 55, 57–8, 62, 64–6, 311
Pankhurst, Emmeline, 42–3, 55, 57–8, 61–2, 202
Pankhurst, Sylvia, 42–3, 47, 64–5
parental leave, 145, 242, 247, 266, 272, 301, 313, 319
Paris, Jasmin, 113
Paris Review, 110
Parks, Rosa, 279–80
Parliament, 67–8, 194–6, 315
Parr, Lily, 101, 105–7, 111–12, 124–6, 251
Parris, Matthew, 193
Pasteur, Louis ,223
Patel, Lakshmi, 131
Patmore, Coventry, 306–7
patriarchy, 163, 187, 315–16
Patyna, Joanna, 207
Pearson, Rosalind, 197, 208–9
Pearson, Ruth, 154
Pechey, Edith, 232
penetration, 71, 72–3, 78–80, 82, 84–5, 211
Penny, Laurie, 310
Perez, Caroline Criado, 230, 257
Perhach, Paulette, 34–5
period trackers, 75, 230–31
Pethick Lawrence, Emmeline, 42, 49–50, 63–7
Pethick Lawrence, Frederick, 42, 63, 65–7
Philip, Duke of Edinburgh, 55, 205
Philippines, 37
Phillips, Jess, 145
pill, the 319
Pizzey, Erin, 159, 161–70, 173–5, 178–81, 183–90, 256, 306, 314

Planned Parenthood organization, 286
Plante, David, 7
Pollitt, Katha, 145, 283
populism, 5
Pornhub, 96
pornography, 93–7, 218, 311–12
Potter, Jenny, 196
Powell, Enoch, 151, 205, 212
'Power of Women and the Subversion of the Community, The' (James & Dalla Costa), 255
Pratt's gentlemen's club, London, 24
pregnancy, 271–2, 282–4, 308
   see also childbirth
prenuptial agreements, 29
Prescott, John, 144
Press Association, 205
Preston Ladies F.C., 124–5
primogeniture, 67
Pringle, Mia Kellmer, 207
Prisons and Prisoners (Lytton), 52, 57, 59–60
PRO (Pollitt), 283
pro-life movement, 296
Prone to Violence (Pizzey), 173, 175
prostitution, *see* sex work
PubMed, 82
pubs, 23–4
Putin, Vladimir, 5

Queen's College, London, 225

Rabinovitch, Dina, 162
racism, 205
radical feminism, 164–5, 167–8, 312
'Radmacher' case, 29
Ramdin, Ron, 138
rape, 28, 72–3, 163, 182–3, 209, 211, 281, 319

Rapinoe, Megan, 101
Rathbone, Eleanor, 58
Rational Dress Society, 103–4
Raytheon, 289–90
Redford, Florrie, 108
Redouane, Rachid, 177
Rees-Mogg, Jacob, 298
Refuge (charity), 159, 173, 187, 190
refuge movement, 159–62, 165–6, 187–8
Registration of Marriage Bill, 22
Relf, Mary Alice and Minnie, 286
Repeal the Eighth Amendment
    campaign, 293, 295–9
respectability politics, 20
Restoration of Pre-War Practices Act
    (1919), 112
Rhys, Jean, 7
Rich, Adrienne, 218
Richards, Cecile, 286
Richardson, Jo, 187
Richardson, Mary, 56
Riddell, Fern, 56
Rise Up Women (Atkinson), 46
Rivera, Maria Theresa, 287
Roach, Mary, 79
Robinson, John, 261
Roe v. Wade case, 283, 285, 298
Roe, Grace, 62
Roe, Humphrey, 76, 86
Rogaly, Joe, 129, 133
Rokeby Venus, 56
Rook, Jean, 26–7
Room to Read (charity), 238
Rose, June, 73, 76, 87, 90
Ross, Deborah, 162
Rossetti, Dante Gabriel, 223
Rothman, Barbara, 308
Rowling, J. K., 172, 242
rugby, 116–17, 119
Rugby World Cup, 117

'running-away money', 34–5
Russel, Alexander, 234
Russia, 5, 256
Rwanda, 313

St Andrews University, 234
St Helens Ladies F.C., 108
same-sex marriage, 14, 32, 36, 62,
    299, 312
Sanger, Margaret, 92
Sappho magazine, 199–200, 207, 212,
    218–19
Saudi Arabia, 36, 239, 280, 317
Scargill, Arthur, 141
Scarman, Leslie, Baron Scarman,
    133, 142
Schulte, Brigid, 260–62, 268, 273
Scotsman, 227, 228, 234
Scott, Alexander, 48
Scream Quietly or the Neighbours Will
    Hear (Pizzey), 161
Scruton, Roger, 78
Second Congress to Unite Women
    (1970), 218
Second Sex, The (de Beauvoir), 70
Second Shift, The (Hochschild), 263–4,
    267, 273, 275
'Section 28', 213
Serano, Julia, 214–15
Serious Crime Act (2015), 175
Sewall, Lucy Ellen, 226
Sex Discrimination Act (1975), 23–6,
    28, 194–5, 201–3, 319
Sex Disqualification (Removal) Act
    (1919), 147, 319
sex, 71–98, 311–12
    anal sex, 81, 88
    'bad sex', 81–2
    clitoris, 77–80, 83
    faked orgasm, 80–82

foreplay, 80
'G spot', 78
masturbation, 71, 78–9, 85
oral sex, 72
orgasm, 71–2, 75, 77–80, 85–6
penetration, 71, 72–3, 78–80, 82,
   84–5, 211
pornography, 93–7, 218, 311–12
sex education, 71–2, 235, 282
sex industry, 93–7
'sex positive' feminism, 94
sex work, 94, 185, 204, 256, 311
sexism, 7, 67, 82–3, 114–15, 123, 126,
   136–7, 203–4, 227–8, 240
sexology, 85
sexual assault, 3, 5, 7, 54, 97–8, 152, 183
   see also #MeToo movement; rape
Sexual Behaviour in the Human Male
   (Kinsey), 85
Shakya, Trishna, 237
Shaw, George Bernard, ix, 75, 201
Sheffield Evening Telegraph and
   Star, 102
Shelley, Mary, 17
shooting, 227
Siaya, Kenya, 274
Sibiya, Thando, 209
Siddal, Elizabeth, 223
Simelane, Eudy, 209
Singh, Sophia Duleep, 50
Sinn Féin, 301
'Situating Stopes' (Hall), 90
Skeel, Alex, 178
Skelton, Helen, 7
Skidelsky, Robert, 274
Skinner, Dennis, 194
Sky, 119
slavery, 3, 21
Slut's Cookbook, The (Pizzey), 188
Smith, Chris, 193, 208

Smith, Karen Ingala, 181
'Smurfette syndrome', 145
Smyth, Ethel, 310
social media, 5, 115, 168–73, 251
Solnit, Rebecca, 4
Sopher, David, 207–8
Sorrows of Rosalie, The (Norton), 17
South Africa, 209
South Wales Daily News, 103
Spanish flu, 62
Spare Rib, 138
sperm donation, 207
Spine Race, 113
sport, 102–126, 227
   cycling, 84, 104
   darts, 113
   football, 101–12, 114–16, 123–6
   male domination, 112–16
   marathons, 102, 113, 227
   netball, 117–19, 121
   rugby, 116–17, 119
   shooting, 227
   snooker, 113
   tennis, 102, 117, 121–3
   and trans women, 135–6
Stagecoach, 202
Stalin, Joseph, 167
Stewart-Park, Angela, 199
Stewart, Patrick, 184
Stock, Kathleen, 215
Stone, Emma, 7
Stopes-Roe, Harry, 88, 90–91
Stopes, Marie, 63, 73–7, 84–93, 211,
   306, 309
Stormont parliament, 300, 302
Stoya, 95–8
strikes see industrial disputes
Striking Women (Anitha &
   Pearson), 154
Studenski, Paul, 275

Sturgeon, Nicola, 67
Sudan, 313
Suffragette Fellowship, 56
suffragettes/suffragists, *see* women's
    suffrage
Summerskill, Shirley, 203
Sunday Chronicle, 89
Sunday Graphic, 65
Sunday Times, 118
Surgeons' Hall, Edinburgh, 229–31
Surgeons' Hall riot, 223–5
Sweet Freedom (Coote & Campbell),
    71–2, 77, 162
Switzer, Kathrine, 227
Switzerland, 68, 235

Taliban, 239
Tate, Tim, 102, 109, 124
tax returns, 27
Taylor, Graham, 155
Taylor, James, 62–3
Taylor, Shanesha, 270
Telegraph, 114
tennis, 102, 117, 121–3
terrorism/terrorists, 177, 182
Tharu, Sangita, 237–8
Thatcher, Denis, 146–7
Thatcher, Margaret, 139, 146–7, 154,
    166, 200, 206, 213, 233
This Way to the Revolution (Pizzey),
    164, 167
Thomas, Clarence, 321
Thoreau, Henry David, 52
Thoughts on the Education of
    Daughters (Wollstonecraft), 232
'Three Guineas' (Woolf), 225
Times, The, 49, 53, 56, 193, 234
Tlhwale, Lesego, 209
Today (radio programme), 115

Todd, Barbara, 199–200, 204, 206,
    208, 212–14, 219
Todd, Mairi, 204
Todd, Margaret, 225
Together For Yes campaign, 297
toilets, 131–2
Tokyo Medical University, Japan, 239
Tottenham Hotspur F.C., 118
Tower of London, 56
Toynbee, Polly, 150
trade unions, 129–30, 133–4, 136–43,
    145, 151–4
transgender people, 185–6, 214–16,
    297, 308–9, 312, 318
    and sport, 135–6
Trump, Donald, 2, 5, 295, 29, 3228
TUC (Trades Union Congress),
    145, 153
Tweedie, Jill, 252, 257–8, 266, 309
Twitter, 168–72, 325

Undying One, The (Norton), 17
unemployment, 273–4
United States, 5, 35, 45, 124, 218, 239,
    267, 269–70, 322
    abortion rights in, 279, 283–6,
    296, 298
universal basic income (UBI), 274–5
Universal Credit, 33–4
universal suffrage, 61–2
University Hospital Galway, 292
University of East Anglia, 54, 66
University of Edinburgh, 223–5,
    227–31, 234–5
University of London, 224
unpaid work, 251, 252–69, 272–5

vagina, 77–9
Varadkar, Leo, 297

Vatican City, 68
Vice (media company), 152
Victoria, Queen of the United
    Kingdom, 211, 223, 232–3
Vindication of the Rights of Women, A
    (Wollstonecraft), 7–8
Virgin Trains, 202
Voice for Men, A (website), 163, 180, 184
Votes For Women newspaper, 57

Wages for Housework campaign,
    252–8, 275
Walker, Ann, 216
Walker, Rebecca, 321
Wallis, Mary, 91
Watt, Frank, 111
Walton Prison, 60
Walton, Liverpool, 52
Wandor, Michelene, 256
Ward, George, 132, 139, 142–3, 151, 154–5
Warton, Jane, *see* Lytton, Constance
Washington Post, 137
*We're Here: Conversations with
    Lesbian Women* (Stewart-Park &
    Cassidy), 199, 206, 214
Weldon, Fay, 161
welfare state, 35–6
Well of Loneliness, The (Hall), 194
Wellcome, Henry, 84
West, Rebecca, 7, 311
Whalley, Joan, 101, 105
What I Remember (Fawcett), 58
Whipple, Beverly, 78
White Ribbon movement, 180
White's gentlemen's club, London, 24
Who's Who, 162, 204
Wilkinson, Sophie, 197, 209–10
Williams, Serena, 113, 117, 123
Williams, Venus, 123

Wilson, Amrit, 131
Wimbledon Lawn Tennis
    Championships, 102
Wistrich, Harriet, 185, 314
'woke-washing', 203, 205
Wollaston, Sarah, 284
Wollstonecraft, Mary, 1, 7–8, 17, 232
Woman in the House, A (Colquhoun),
    194, 200, 204
Woman's Hour (radio programme), 155
Woman's Own, 206
'Woman's Place, A' (James), 253
Women and Economics (Gilman), 252
Women Like Us (Neild & Pearson),
    208–9
Women on Waves, 288–9
Women's Aid, 159, 187
Women's Equality Party, 311–12
Women's Football World Cup, 101,
    114, 119
Women's Freedom League, 59
Women's Institute, 25
Women's Leisure, What Leisure?
    (Green), 262
Women's Liberation Movement, 161–2,
    165, 167–8, 187, 254–5, 257
Women's Rebellion, The (radio
    play), 65–6
Women's Rights: A Practical Guide
    (Coote & Gill), 27–9
Women's Social and Political Union
    (WSPU), 42–4, 47, 49, 56, 61,
    64, 311
women's suffrage, 41–68, 136, 147, 201,
    251, 306
    force-feeding, 46–9, 51–4, 60
    militancy, 51–9
Women's Super League, 116, 119
Woods, Alice, 107

Woolf, Virginia, 225, 307, 319
Worboys, John, 185, 314
work, *see* employment
World Health Organisation, 284
World War I (1914–18), 42, 58, 61, 75, 77, 108–9
   and women, 77, 104, 106, 109, 112
World War II (1939–45), 43
Worshipful Society of Apothecaries, 226–7

Worth, Jordan, 178
Wycombe Abbey School, 197

Yemen, 313
Young, Janet, 146
Youngjoo Cha, 268
Yousafzai, Malala, 222, 239, 247

Zhang Shan, 227
Zwicky, Fritz, 16